Understanding New Religious Movements

Second Edition

John A. Saliba

ALTAMIRA
PRESS

A Division of Rowman & Littlefield Publishers, Inc.
Walnut Creek • Lanham • New York • Oxford

AltaMira Press
A Division of Rowman & Littlefield Publishers, Inc.
1630 North Main Street, #367
Walnut Creek, CA 94596
www.altamirapress.com

Rowman & Littlefield Publishers, Inc.
A Member of the Rowman & Littlefield Publishing Group
4501 Forbes Boulevard, Suite 200
Lanham, MD 20706

PO Box 317
Oxford
OX2 9RU, UK

British Library Cataloguing in Publication Information Available

Library of Congress Cataloging-in-Publication Data

Saliba, John A.
    Understanding new religious movements / John A. Saliba. – 2nd ed.
        p. cm.
    Includes bibliographical references and index.
    ISBN 0-7591-0355-0 (alk. paper) – ISBN 0-7591-0356-9 (pbk. : alk.
paper)
    1. Cults. 2. Sects. I. Title.

BP603.S25 2003
200'.9'04—dc21   2003007342

Printed in the United States of America

∞™ The paper used in this publication meets the minimum requirements of American
National Standard for Information Sciences—Permanence of Paper for Printed Library
Materials, ANSI/NISO Z39.48–1992.

Understanding New Religious Movements

CONTENTS

PREFACE

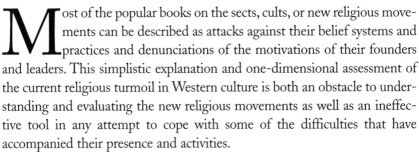

Most of the popular books on the sects, cults, or new religious movements can be described as attacks against their belief systems and practices and denunciations of the motivations of their founders and leaders. This simplistic explanation and one-dimensional assessment of the current religious turmoil in Western culture is both an obstacle to understanding and evaluating the new religious movements as well as an ineffective tool in any attempt to cope with some of the difficulties that have accompanied their presence and activities.

The rise of religious and spiritual movements is a complex phenomenon that involves many different facets of Western cultural and religious life. The reasons why they have been successful are not obvious. The teachings they propound are frequently not only obscure and confusing but also challenging. Their practices do not always conform to the ethical standards of the Judeo-Christian tradition or to the legal norms of Western culture, and the lifestyles of their followers diverge radically from what the majority of people are accustomed to.

Because they are nontraditional and marginal, new religious groups can easily appear to be a threatening force that lies beyond comprehension and control. Precisely because they are perceived as dangerous incursions into the established way of life, the question of how one interprets and responds to them ceases to be solely a matter of academic interest. It becomes a practical problem that demands immediate consideration, if for no other reason than because it has repercussions on the lives of many people.

This book is based on the assumption that examining the new religions from different academic perspectives is a necessary preliminary step for understanding their presence in our age and for drafting an effective response to their influence. Rather than limiting the observations to the boundaries of one discipline, this study has taken the admittedly more perilous path of considering various approaches, even though these differ in their assumptions, methods, theories, and goals. Thus, historical and sociological approaches are more likely to adopt a position that is religiously neutral. Psychology and psychiatry, however, make a definite evaluation of the mental and emotional health of cult members and the effects membership in new religions might have on their lives. In like manner the legal issues brought about by their presence require that some assessment be made of their activities. Theological reflections are always made from a particular faith perspective and aimed at evaluating religions from well-defined doctrinal and/or moral standpoints.

This book begins with a broad overview in which various definitions and generalized features of a new religion are critically examined and adopts an inclusive typology that has received scholarly recognition. It then moves to present the historical, psychological, sociological, legal, and theological reflections on and debates about the significance of the new religious movements in our times.

Chapter 2 gives a brief survey of a few select religious movements that have appeared in the history of Western culture. Specific examples, such as the Cathars of the Middle Ages and the Mormons of the nineteenth century, are cited to show that knowledge of the beliefs and practices of past religious movements and of the environments in which they flourished can enhance our understanding of new religions in the twentieth century.

Chapter 3 discusses, in the context of specific studies, the issue of whether there is a "cult personality" that can help identify those young adults who are most likely to join a new religion. It summarizes and evaluates the main psychological theories of conversion to, and involvement in, a new religion. It also shows that the popular theory of brainwashing is only one of several options that have been proposed to explain conversions to the new religious movements.

Western sociologists are playing a leading role in the study and interpretation of the new movements. Chapter 4 provides a critical summary of how sociologists are studying the new religions and of what they are saying about their origin and nature. Models used by social scientists for understanding the new movements are also briefly presented.

Chapter 5 looks at the legal aspects of the new religious movements. The main legal issues that have come to the fore in court trials are surveyed, with special references to a number of particular court cases involving such groups as the Hare Krishna movement, Transcendental Meditation, Scientology, and the Unification Church.

No book on the new religions will be complete without a theological inquiry, which is attempted in chapter 6. New religious movements challenge the theological systems of established religions and question those revealed doctrines that are assumed to be absolutely true. Several theological approaches and responses to the new movements will be critically analyzed. Particular emphasis will be placed on the need to develop a theology of religion in the context of the current efforts to establish a relationship of dialogue among people of different faiths.

Finally, chapter 7 will reflect on the major difficulties that confront counselors and therapists when they are called to advise or treat those individuals who have been affected by the activities of cults. Some practical suggestions will be made to guide counselors and ministers of religion who are called to help cult and ex-cult members and their parents.

It would be a mistake to assume that this book will offer, once and for all, a final, all-encompassing picture of the phenomenon of new religious movements and/or a solution to all the problems their presence has raised. The discussions conducted in diverse academic settings testify to the variety of irreconcilable opinions among those who have been studying the new religions for the past few decades. They also show that the quest for simple, unequivocal answers is unrealistic.

An attempt has been made to update the previous edition and to include recent materials on the debate regarding the new religious movements. The major issues surrounding "cults" have not been solved. Scholars still disagree about the reasons why new religions come into being and about the best way to understand and respond to them. Legal battles are still being fought in several countries. Many changes have occurred in the way some of the new movements operate and relate to the public. The aims of this new edition remain the same as the previous edition. It hopes to expose its readers to the diversity of viewpoints and perspectives on the new religious movements. It endeavors to encourage readers to make broader and more balanced reflections on the major religious phenomena that have come into being in the second half of the second millennium and are still part of the contemporary religious landscape. By discussing in a public forum certain aspects that are frequently ignored in popular literature, the following pages aspire to engage more people in the debates on the meaning of the cultural and religious changes that are currently taking place in Western society. By bringing in various scholarly and academic reflections on the controversy, this book attempts to raise the general level of the debate that has, to the detriment of all concerned, so often degenerated into an unrelenting diatribe. And, lastly, by seeing the new religions from various perspectives, readers increase the possibility not only of understanding them but also of developing a response to new religions and coming to terms with their presence in our midst.

The new religious movements seem to be here to stay. They are reflections on what might be happening in society at large. Even if most of them do not survive or remain on the fringes of both society and traditional religion, they might be pointing to religious trends that will eventually become part of the mainstream. Studying them may help us understand ourselves as well as social and religious change better. The importance of the presence of the new religions may be much greater than the relatively small number of people who have joined their ranks might indicate.

In a period of human history when cultures meet and interact on a daily basis and when the Earth is becoming a kind of global village, the rise of new religions and spiritual movements acquires a special significance. Irvin Hexham and Karla Poewe clearly express the importance of the study of new religions when they conclude their book with the following statement:

> New Religions open their members to highly creative lifestyles that enable them to envision themselves as citizens of the global city that our world has become. Like Christian missions, they are global movements that energize their followers with a new vision of the world. . . . By uprooting traditions from their social and historical contexts, new religions propose new ways of life that give members a reason for living and hope for the future. Whether any of today's religions will become a world religion that embraces a large proportion of humanity is, as Rudyard Kipling would say, "another story."[1]

Note

1. Irvin Hexah and Karla Poewe, *New Religions as Global Cultures: Making the Human Sacred* (Boulder, CO: Westview Press, 1997), p. 167.

NEW RELIGIOUS MOVEMENTS

A s the twenty-first century begins, scholars no longer question the appropriateness of devoting time to the study of what are variously termed cults, new religions, or new religious movements. What had once been thought of as a passing phenomenon of the 1960s counterculture has proven to be a significant long-lasting and dynamic force in Western culture. New religious movements have not only commanded the attention of millions of people, especially young adults, but their growth has been punctuated by several dramatic violent incidents that have called their legitimacy into question.

In the text that follows, John Saliba, a professor of religious studies and a Jesuit priest, will explore the broad range of questions about new religious movements. Drawing upon more than three decades of observations and a broad knowledge of the body of scholarly literature, he will provide an overview from the various scholarly disciplines most concerned with understanding and responding to this relatively new factor in the continually evolving culture of North America and Europe. The task of this introduction will be much more limited, to answer a simple question—What's *new* about the new religions?

The term new religions or new religious movements (NRMs) came into general usage in the 1970s as a substitute for the older term "cult." In the 1960s, Japanese scholars called attention to the "new religions" of Japan, which had flourished in the decades following the imposition of religious freedom on that country following World War II. American religious scholars were searching for an alternative to the term "cult," which was being corrupted by groups opposed to the growing religious pluralism in the West. Simultaneously, academics from various fields were trying to comprehend the disruption of social stability attributed to the baby boomers (the original hippies) who were coming of age as the 1960s drew to a close. In the late 1960s, a spectrum of religions never before seen in the West suddenly began to appear. Through the 1970s, they continued to increase in number.

Now, a generation later, we can begin to put some perspective on the 1960s. We are aware that in 1965, a new immigration bill allowed massive movement of Asians to America in a way not seen since the 1920s (when immigration from Asia had been cut off). We also are aware that the disruption caused by the coming of age of the baby boomers, and a society unprepared to receive them into the labor force, happened to coincide with the pressure put on the job market by the arrival of so many new immigrants. However, we now also understand that the new religious movements, made visible by the social disruption at the time the counterculture blossomed, were part of a much more persistent trend in the West that could be traced to at least the late nineteenth century.

Throughout the mid-nineteenth century, Christianity dominated Western culture, and of course, to this day it remains the religion of the majority. Previously, its primary challenge had come from the world of Esotericism. In the seventh century Rosicrucianism arose, followed by Freemasonry, ceremonial magic, and Theosophy. These movements were hardly visible, however, as in Europe they were largely defined as "nonreligious," a tactic that allowed them not only to survive but even to thrive in countries where state churches dominated religious expression. However, by the late nineteenth century, not only had Western Esotericism expanded, but a variety of religious alternatives had appeared. Mormonism, Spiritualism, Christian Science, and New Thought emerged in America and quickly established initial centers in Europe. Of equal importance, in the decades immediately preceding World War I, initial centers of Buddhism, Hinduism, Islam, and a variety of other Eastern and Middle Eastern religions (from Taoism to the Baha'i Faith) began their spread into the West.

By the 1960s, numerous alternatives to Christianity had established worshiping communities in North America and Europe, while at the same time, Christianity had split into hundreds if not thousands of new denominations. In a religiously free society, disagreements and controversy were decided by the minority parties breaking fellowship and establishing new religious communities. Throughout the twentieth century in the West, decade by decade and country by country, the number of different religious groups grew, the only spurts in growth being noted as different countries relaxed state control on religious organizations. That growth in the number of new religious organizations has continued to the present and shows no sign of slowing. Certainly since World War I, each decade has seen the emergence of several hundred new religions in both North America and Europe, the number increasing each decade as the population grows and urbanization increases.

Understanding long-term trends is the first clue to answering the question—What's so new about the new religions? They are one important *symbol of the real increase in freedom accorded to individuals in the West.* While given the choice, most Westerners have remained attached to the dominant Catholic and Protestant Christian churches, an increasing number have chosen other spiritual paths—some old traditions brought from other parts of the world, some newly created alternatives developed in the West.

The long-term trend toward greater religious pluralism also suggests the second insight—most new religions are old religions. It is a difficult task to create a new religion; the human community has done a fairly thorough job of exploring spiritual options and discovering what works religiously. Thus, when we look at what we have termed the new religions we generally find expressions of the world's old religions such as the International Society for Krishna Consciousness (Bengali Hinduism), the San Francisco Zen Center (Japanese Zen Buddhism), the Ahmadiyya Muslim Movement (Islam), Tenrikyo (Shintoism), the Kabbalah Centre (Judaism), Subud (Indonesian Sufism), ECKANKAR (Punjabi Sant Mat), or the Healing Tao Centers (Taoism). Of course, among the new religions are numerous representatives of Christianity (Children of God, The Way International), and Western Esotericism (Church of Scientology, Church Universal and Triumphant). Most new religions are old religions that are arising in a new context (such as an Eastern religion being transplanted to the West) or a new organizational expression of the more familiar Western Jewish, Christian, or Esoteric tradition. (A few new religions look new because they are conscious syntheses of two or more of the older traditions, most notably the Unification Church.)

But simply being a "new" religious organization does not earn a group designation as a new religion (or more pejoratively a "cult"). After all, many of the largest denominations in America are also relatively new expressions of their older denominational tradition, the United Methodist Church having been formed in 1968, the Presbyterian Church (USA) in 1983, and the Evangelical Lutheran Church in America in 1988. Even bodies of Eastern and Middle Eastern religions that primarily serve transplanted non-Western ethnic communities are not treated under the rubric of "new religion," even though many are newly arrived, since World War II. Neither the Buddhists Churches of America, the Islamic Society of New America, nor the many temples erected by Indian Americans to perpetuate their Hindu faith in America would be included in any list of new religions.

New religions are not just new, they are innovative. And most often, they are not just new sectarian expressions of an older religious tradition, but a distinctly different expression that adds to or takes away from the tradition in ways that challenge the tradition in what the great majority feel to be an unacceptable manner. For example, the Sikh Dharma community led by Yogi Bhajan not only teaches an orthodox form of the Sikh Faith, but also teaches kundalini yoga, teachings derived from tantric Hinduism. The Apostolic or "Jesus Only" Pentecostal churches (one of which became the subject of a landmark new religions' case in 1995 after one of their members was unsuccessfully deprogrammed), deny the Trinity, a key Christian doctrine.

More often than not, groups that have become known as new religions have adopted behavior patterns that have placed them at odds with both the dominant religious community in the place where they are operating and with secular authorities. Some of the new religions, for example, have adopted new sexual mores. The Children of God developed an innovative evangelism technique known as flirty fishing that on occasion involved the evangelist/missionary (usually a female) engaging in sex with a potential convert (usually a male). Though discontinued, the Children of God's successor group still allows and even promotes sexual contact among its adult members. Some of the ceremonial magic groups teach the form of esoteric sexuality advocated by British magician Aleister Crowley.

The single attribute shared by the most controversial of the new religions in the 1970s was high-pressure proselytization followed by the members being invited into life as a full-time worker/evangelist for the movement they had joined. The seeming separation of new recruits into a religious life angered many of their family members who not only disagreed with their choice but were hurt by the seeming rejection it implied. They became the original core of the present cult awareness movement. It would be this attribute of groups such as the Unification Church and the Hare Krishna movement that would make them the early targets of anti-cult rhetoric and action.

Most egregious of all, on rare occasions, new religions have become the subject of violence and death. Jonestown, Waco, the Solar Temple, Aum

Shinrikyo, and Heaven's Gate have become well-known designations of violent religious incidents and the communities associated with them. In the face of these cases, even the most staid objective social scientist may feel ready to revive the older rejected "cult" label. Yet, after the first wave of horror at the dramatic loss of human life that occurred in such groups, the observer of new religions must draw back and carefully examine those groups for what they teach us about religion in general, including the violence that simultaneously had invaded older religions in places such as Israel and Ireland.

With this brief overview of the new religious movements of the late twentieth century and the long-term trend in religious pluralism in which they participate, we can begin to answer our starting question—What makes a new religion and what makes it new? What are the new religions whose life is to be examined in the text below? New religions are those innovative and dissenting groups on the fringe of the larger religious community. They are the groups that challenge the beliefs and practices of the majority party while attempting at the same time to challenge the secularity of modern life. We group the different "new" religions together not for attributes they share—they believe and practice a bewildering array of ideas and rituals—so much as for the attributes they lack. They dissent in a serious way from commonly accepted beliefs and practice.

And the more controversial new religions—the one you are already likely to know something about and the ones whose names will appear most often in the pages that follow—not only dissent, but do so in a manner that arouses the religious community (by denying cherished beliefs), concerns the secular community (by disturbing the social order or committing illegal acts), or both (by advocating what the majority see as immoral ideas—be it cloning or sex outside of marriage).

That having been said, the new religions still have much to teach us. While many of the new religions date to the nineteenth or early twentieth century, many more are quite new and still in their first generation. Hence, they are living laboratories for examining the origin and development of religious community, the problems they must solve, and the obstacles they must overcome if they are to become a mature viable religious option for the public. What we see in today's new religions may inform the way we understand the first generation Christians in Palestine or the original Buddhists in India. While most new religions will remain small and locally confined, a few will be successful. Among the many new groups founded in the nineteenth century, a few groups like the New Apostolic Church, the Latter-day Saints, and Baha'is stand out, each having become large influential international bodies. Among new entries into the field, the Scientologists, the Unificationists, and several of the Hindu guru-oriented groups have shown signs of breaking out of their original settings and now, with their second generation of leadership, of opening viable communities in a significant number of countries around the globe.

The new religions also remain a challenge. Their very presence in our communities challenges the old familiar structures by which we guide our life and from which we draw security. Many of us look upon our religion as something that should offer a haven from the fast-paced world of the twenty-first century. New religions, however, seem to participate heartily in the change that is all around us. Their future is in a remade society in which they may have a larger role than the one they play in the present. It behooves us, the citizens of the new century, to carefully consider these different religions and come to some thoughtful conclusions as to how we will live with them as our neighbors. There is no sign of their disappearing.

In the pages that follow, Saliba will offer a variety of standing places from which to view the new religions. Psychology, sociology, history, anthropology, religious studies, the law—each offer insight into the life of the new religions. In the process of moving from one perspective to the other, the reader will gather the most important building blocks from which he or she can then construct a meaningful picture of the world of the new religions.

Studying new religions is a most interesting process. Along the way one encounters the bizarre, the appealing, the discomforting, the horrific, and the sinister—the depths of silliness and the heights of idealism. In looking at different groups, one often wonders at the appeal of shallow religiosity, is occasionally surprised by the sophistication of philosophical inquiry, is disappointed at callous leadership, and is amazed at the loving care shown by some anonymous believers. New religions are a lot like life.

J. Gordon Melton
2003

THE NEW RELIGIOUS MOVEMENTS IN CONTEMPORARY WESTERN CULTURE: AN OVERVIEW

The word "cult," commonly used to refer to many new religious groups, is so laden with diverse meanings and replete with emotional content that it might have lost one of the major functions of linguistic designation, that is, to convey accurate and useful information.[1] The word "cult" comes from the Latin *colere*,[2] which means "to tend" or "to till," and is the root word for "culture," "cultivate," and "respect." By derivation it also means to care for a god or goddess by ritual and acts of devotion and thus to honor, revere, and worship the deities. It is only in relatively recent times that the word has acquired a largely negative connotation.[3] In Western theological discourse, the word "cult" (*cultus* in Latin) traditionally refers to a specific and structured form of worship or ritual within a religious tradition, for example, the cult of Christian saints in the Middle Ages or the cult of the Mother Goddess in the Ancient Near East.[4]

Some professional writers, especially psychiatrists and lawyers and the majority of news media reporters, prefer the negative significance currently attached to the word "cult." They have made it a habit to employ it consistently to refer to all those groups they have judged to be deviant, dangerous, corrupt, and pseudo-religious. The result is that the very mention of cults tends to arouse fear and panic with the ensuing endeavors to mobilize social, legal, and religious resources to offset their success and to initiate legal actions to curtail or prohibit their activities.

The truth of the matter, however, is that cults or new religions represent diverse and complex organizations whose significance cannot be gauged without reference to the changing sociocultural and religious situation of the second half of the twentieth century. Consequently, their nature, characteristics, significance, and implications cannot be summarized, much less encapsulated in, a single narrow definition. Ideally, it would be better to abandon the use of the word "cult" altogether. However, the term has become a household word and has acquired a permanent foothold in academic literature.[5] In this book an effort has been made to employ it sparingly. When used, it is applied in a broad and neutral sense to refer to the relatively new religious (or quasi-religious) and spiritual groups that have sprung up in the West especially since the 1960s. Such a usage, in spite of its shortcomings, points to two undeniable facts, namely, that the new religions stand apart from society and traditional religion and require special attention.

The professional and popular literature on new religions is not only voluminous, but also varied in its understanding and evaluation of, and response to, the phenomenon. Interpretations of, and reactions to, the new religious movements go hand in hand with preconceived notions of what a cult is. Three major, distinct (though sometimes related) definitions of a cult emerge from a survey of the literature on the subject.

Three Definitions of a New Religion

Theological Definitions

The theological slant on the meaning of the word "cult" is most evident in Christian Evangelical literature. The late Walter Ralston Martin (1928–1989), who founded and, until his death, directed, the Christian Research Institute,[6] now located in Rancho Santa Margarita, California, dedicated his life's work to the refutation of sects and cults. In one of his major works on the subject, which has become one of the most influential resources in evangelical circles, Martin defines a cult as "a group, religious in nature, which surrounds a leader or a group of teachings which either denies or misinterprets essential Biblical doctrine."[7] In his seminal work on the cults that deals with traditional sects and other religious groups prior to 1970, Martin starts with Charles Braden's vague definition of a cult. Braden considers as cults all "those religious groups that differ significantly from those religious groups that are regarded as the normative expression of religion in our total culture."[8] He then adds: "a cult might also be defined as a group of people gathered about a specific person or person's misinterpretation of the Bible."[9]

Slightly broader, but still consistent with Martin's position, is that adopted by James Sire who, more specifically, defines a cult as:

Any religious movement that is organizationally distinct and has doctrines and/or practices that contradict those of the Scriptures as interpreted by traditional Christianity as represented by the major Catholic and Protestant denominations, and as expressed in such statements as the Apostles' Creed.[10]

Martin's and Sire's views are representative of many Christians who are concerned with the presence and activities of the new movements.

Most of the features of the new religions that Martin lists are theological or religious in nature. Thus, for example, he points out that a cult possesses a new Scripture that is either added to or replaces the Bible as the sole revealed Word of God. Cults believe in ongoing revelation and stress experience rather than theological reasoning. They imbue common theological parlance with connotations that are quite different from what most Christians accept. While Martin assigns some sociological and psychological features to a cult, his definition is essentially a theological one. New religious movements are lumped together and seen as unorthodox or heretical groups. They are unchristian, unbiblical, or pseudo-Christian organizations. The response to them must, therefore, be one of theological refutation or rebuttal. Cults have to be denounced as religious paths that falsely claim to preach the truth and lead humankind to salvation. Since they are conceived as spiritually corrupt, the response to them has been dominated by apologetic debates and by a crusading spirit reminiscent of the religious controversies and conflicts of the post-Reformation era.

This theological definition of a cult has persisted in evangelical literature. Ron Rhodes,[11] for example, maintains that cults are "religious groups" or "new religious movements" that deviate from their doctrinal beliefs of their respective traditional religious background. Thus the Church of Jesus Christ of Latter-day Saints and Jehovah's Witnesses would be cults of Christianity and the International Society for Krishna Consciousness (ISKCON) and Transcendental Meditation cults of Hinduism. Like Martin and Sire, Rhodes uses doctrinal integrity as the principle for evaluating cults. Hence, those groups that propose a new revelation, deny the sole authority of the Bible, the Trinity, or the divinity of Christ, refuse to accept that human beings are saved by God's grace, and redefine basic

Christian terms are all cults. Rhodes selects several of "the most significant cults and new religious movements" and schematically compares their major beliefs with those of Evangelical Christianity.

Another extensive attempt to define cult has been made by the London-based Cult Information Centre (CIC); an organization aimed at counteracting the influence of cults. The CIC examines the definitions found in the dictionary together with current secular, psychological, and religious definitions and concludes that they are all deficient. Secular (and, by implication, academic) definitions are especially criticized for being "of no use to Christians seeking to minister to cult members." A cult is described as

> a group which exhibits the characteristics of cults outlined elsewhere on this site, and exhibits one or more of the following: It derives its identity from a major religion but differs markedly from the religion in its beliefs and practices; It does not have a codified system of beliefs all its followers are required to accept; It was founded by someone using fraudulent claims to gain credibility and acceptance.[12]

In spite of its theological slant, this definition incorporates both sociological and psychological features that have been ascribed to the new cults. Thus among their nine major characteristics are "false prophecy" and "use of mind-numbing techniques," and among their over thirty "other" features are the understanding of Scripture out of context, vagueness of doctrine, deceptive recruitment techniques, and manipulation of fear and guilt to control members.

This conventional theological analysis of the word "cult" has attractive features. It is simple, direct, and intelligible to the average person who is committed to a traditional Christian church. It concentrates on the fundamental issues of religious truth and correct moral behavior, clearly pointing out the errors of all innovative groups. It also proposes a reaction to the cults consistent with the definition. It encourages Christians to engage in a stronger and more direct evangelization and missionary endeavor and to preach the true biblical message more effectively. It further makes an attempt to win back those who have abandoned their traditional faith and to condemn more emphatically the doctrines of the new religions. Rhodes, for instance, makes it a point not only to describe the beliefs of the new religious groups and compare them with orthodox Christianity.

He challenges these beliefs and provides theological tools for refuting them.

But a closer look at this attractive definition shows that it has too many flaws either to reflect the correct nature of the phenomenon of religious movements or to elicit a proper theological response. The first problem with the definition of a cult as an unorthodox religious group is that it leaves unsolved the question of Christian orthodoxy. Sire's definition seems to include all traditional Christianity (Catholic and Protestant) under the standard of orthodoxy, thereby bypassing the many debates that have split the Christian Church throughout the ages. Martin seems to propose a narrower standard, namely, that of Evangelical Christianity. His approach excludes several well-established Christian churches and sects that are judged to be unorthodox and hence liable to be called cults. In fact, some evangelicals and fundamentalists,[13] Martin not included, have at times referred to the Catholic Church as a cult, together with the Church of Jesus Christ of Latter-day Saints (Mormons), the Way International, the Unification Church, and the Hare Krishna movement. The CIC starts with a "yardstick" approach to truth. It rejects the Roman Catholic and the Evangelical Christian standpoints and omits reference to the Greek Orthodox position. Its perspective is that of mainline Protestantism (maybe Anglican), though without any apparent awareness of the variety within Protestantism itself.

Second, the definition fails to acknowledge the variety of beliefs and practices that one encounters among the new religions themselves. Even if one approaches them from a specific and narrow theological perspective, it would be impossible to label them all "unorthodox" in the same way and to the same degree.

Third, calling cults unorthodox Christian groups does not help us understand them. The designation of, for instance, a self-styled Pagan group as an "unorthodox" Christian sect makes a self-evident proposition that reveals little about the nature of Paganism. Contemporary Paganism is certainly not based on heretical Christian doctrines since Paganism predates Christianity. Members of Pagan groups readily admit that they are not Christians and that their religion did not come into being as a negative reaction to, or confrontation with, Christian doctrine.

Fourth, this theological definition of a cult doesn't address itself to, much less answer in a satisfactory manner, questions regarding religious pluralism.[14] The contemporary flourishing of non-Christian religions in the Western world, whose tradition has been overwhelmingly Judeo-Christian, leads one to ask several theological questions. Why are there different religions at all? Does genuine religiousness or spirituality exist in all religions? Why do novel religious groups come into being? Why do some people brought up in one particular religious tradition abandon their faith? And how should people of different faith persuasions relate to one another? Although the theological definition of a cult as an unorthodox group might be religiously satisfying, it lacks theological depth and specification and fails to answer many of the fundamental issues related to the emergence of these new religious groups.

Fifth, theological definitions are often mixed in with, or buttressed by, negative psychological and/or sociological features. This procedure complicates and obscures the issues. Martin's book includes a chapter on the "Psychological Structure of Cultism," a structure that includes close-mindedness, antagonism, and institutional dogmatism.[15] Geisler and Rhodes direct the attention of their readers also to the "Sociological Characteristics of a Cult," which include authoritarianism, exclusivism, dogmatism, and so forth.[16] All these negative features, however, can be found in several traditional churches. The CIC adds "Racial Superiority," for example, to its nine leading features of a cult. But racism has been rampant centuries before the emergence of the new cults and has also been a long-standing problem within the major traditional Christian churches.[17] Besides, the majority of new religious movements do not recruit members from only one particular race or ethnic group. The CIC also claims that mental illnesses are more common among cult members than among the general population—a statement that has still to be documented by hard evidence.

These reflections should not lead one to conclude that there are no conditions under which the differences between major traditions (such as Judaism and Christianity) and the newer religious expressions should not be spelled out in detail. The presence of new religious movements could indirectly urge believers of different traditions to foster a deeper understanding of their respective faiths and to strive for a clearer exposition and defense of their beliefs and practices. The criticism of a theological definition of the cult simply points to the urgent need for a more thorough assessment not only of what the new religions teach, but also of the many factors that contribute to their rise and success. Only then can a theological appraisal be safely made.

Psychological Definitions

While the theological definition of a cult has relied on normative principles that distinguish orthodox from unorthodox Christianity, the psychological definition has focused on the way the new religious movements recruit and maintain their members and how they affect those who join them.[18] Two distinct and opposed ideas of what a cult is have emerged in psychological and psychiatric literature.

The first, and more prevalent, definition is that cults are dangerous institutions that cause severe mental and emotional harm to those who commit themselves to their creeds and lifestyles. A cult is considered a spurious group, headed by a powerful leader who dominates the life of his or her followers and offers them false solutions to all their problems. It recruits members by deceitful means, then indoctrinates them and controls them by methods of mind control. Cults are, therefore, destructive groups or organizations.[19] Almost two decades ago Philip Cushman defined a cult as a group that:

> is controlled by a charismatic leader who is thought to be God or some one who carries an exclusive message from God that elevates him or her above others; fosters the idea that there is only one correct belief and only one correct practice of that belief; demands unquestionable loyalty and complete obedience to its restrictive ideas, rules, and totalistic methods; uses methods of mind control; uses deception and deceit when recruiting and interacting with the outside world; systematically exploits a member's labor and finances; attacks and abandons members who disagree with or leave the group.[20]

This negative view of a cult that stresses manipulation, mind control, and deception as constitutive elements of a cult has persisted in psychological literature.[21] It has been adopted and expanded, with a few modifications, by the American Family Foundation (AFF) whose journal, *Cultic Studies Review*,[22] provides "Information on cult, psychological manipulation, psychological abuse, spiritual abuse, brainwashing, mind control, thought reform, abuse churches, extremism, totalistic groups, new religious movements, exit counseling, recovery, and practical suggestions."[23] Although the AFF seems to distinguish between cults and new religious movements, the tendency to include all new groups under the negative label of "cult" dominates its literature.[24]

Many of the elements of this definition have influenced writings not only on religious movements but also on political and corporate institutions. Dennis Tourish and Tim Wohlforth,[25] writing on political cults, hold that these are mind-controlling groups. And Dave Arnott[26] states that there are many corporate organizations ruled by leaders who use mind-control methods to manipulate their members.

Those psychologists and psychiatrists who propound this view contend that they have arrived at this negative definition of a cult through their counseling of ex-cult members, whose behavioral patterns suggest that their intellectual and emotional lives have been literally impaired by the teachings and lifestyles of the new religions. They further imply that membership in a new religion cannot be looked upon as a result of a free act of commitment given after careful consideration.

The appeal of this definition has been phenomenal. As has been pointed out above, it has been incorporated by many Christians into their theological definition of a cult and employed as a weapon to denounce cults in general. And it has been used in many court cases in attempts to justify legal actions directed against the new religions.[27] Part of the reason why so many people have accepted this approach is that it does offer very comforting news both to parents and ex-cult members. Parents can look at their offspring's involvement in a new religious movement as a rash and hasty action taken under duress or pressure, with little knowledge of the cult itself and even less awareness of what full commitment entails. They can explain the changes in the behavior of their sons and daughters by having recourse to the theory that membership in a new religion has rendered them so sick that they are in need of traditional psychiatric help. Ex-members, on the other hand, may find this explanation comforting since it assumes that, when they adopted and clung to their new religious lifestyles, they were not acting as free, responsible persons.

This approach to marginal religious groups has encountered great opposition not only from sociologists,[28] but also from some psychologists and psychiatrists who have interviewed and given tests to many cult members and looked more carefully at their family and social backgrounds. A second psychiatric viewpoint has emerged that sees the new religions in quite a different light. New religious movements are judged to be helpful organizations that provide an alternative therapy to many young adults as they are faced with making momentous decisions at important junctures in their lives. Cult membership, it is claimed, has led many people to give up their addictions to drugs and alcohol and to introduce into their lives a measure of intellectual security, emotional stability, and organized behavioral patterns that contrast sharply with their previously confused and chaotic existences.

The definition given to a new religious movement is, therefore, broader and less negative. Marc Galanter, for instance, relates cults to charismatic groups and describes their members as follows:

> Members of charismatic large groups typically (1) adhere to a consensual belief system, (2) sustain a high level of social cohesiveness, (3) are strongly influenced by group behavioral norms, and (4) impute charismatic (or divine) power to the group or its leadership. The concept of *cult* adds the issue of religious deviancy and rejection of participation in majority culture.[29]

Galanter reflects on the possibility that involvement in new religions can both relieve and exacerbate psychopathology and suggests various ways in which psychiatrists can intervene. In certain cases, he thinks, "zealous group modalities may come to serve as useful adjuncts to psychiatric care."[30]

This interpretation of novel religious movements is not usually accepted outside professional circles, yet it has several advantages. It explains why many converts appear to be relatively healthy and content, even though their lifestyles are certainly out of the ordinary. Further, it directs attention to those problems that young adults faced before they ever thought of joining a marginal religious group. And finally, it leaves open the possibility that involvement in a new religion might have diverse effects on different people and that, consequently, negative generalizations on the individual psychological states of members are unwarranted.

It must be added, however, that this view does not quite explain why people seek a solution to their problems by joining a fringe religious group. Experiences of crises are part and parcel of life and are open to various solutions. Many people, faced with a life crisis, find help within the religion of their upbringing or seek traditional psychological counseling. Although some psychiatrists have pointed out that cults could be "dangerous detours for growing up,"[31] they have not explained clearly why joining a new religion is a risky procedure and why some individuals need to mature through membership in an alternative religion.

Psychiatric definitions of a cult are, as a rule, wanting because they take only one narrow viewpoint of religious involvement, namely, that of individual psychology. They consequently tend to neglect both the obvious social aspects and the spiritual dimensions of involvement in a new religious movement. They fail to relate the presence of such movements to contemporary sociocultural developments and religious change. They differ from the theological definition in that they are not concerned with religious truth, and their main thrust is to relate involvement in intense religious groups to specific forms of human psychopathology or psychological weakness.

Sociological Definitions

Unlike the theological and psychological writings on new religious movements, sociological literature provides us with such a great variety of reflections that it is practically impossible to come up with a short, clear-cut, universally acceptable definition.[32]

Four major ideal concepts of religious institutions or groups are discussed in sociological literature—church, denomination, sect, and cult. The way these disparate organizations are related both to one another and to society at large, their evolution over the course of time, and the factors that influence their development have been the subject of debate among sociologists well before the debate over the new religions.

While the words "church" and "denomination" are used to refer to mainline religious organizations, "sect" and "cult" are applied to those relatively small groups that are sociologically marginal and deviant. These latter groups are relatively small religions that are on the fringes of both society and the mainline religious traditions. Just like "church" and "denomination," "sect" and "cult" are overlapping concepts. Several sociologists, such as Rodney Stark and William Bainbridge,[33] maintain that sects denote those religious communities that have split from one of the major churches or denominations. Cults or new religions, on the other hand, are composed of converts from different traditional backgrounds who gather around a charismatic leader.

Sociological definitions of a new religion have been, however, the least popular. This is probably because sociologists make no judgment on the truth or falsehood of the cults' beliefs (as in the theological approach) or on the good or bad effects of cult involvement on individual members (as in the psychological approach). Besides, many sociological studies of specific cults do not support the prevalent contentions that the new religions are evil institutions that are recruiting new members by deceitful means and maintaining them by forceful indoctrination programs. Nor do they subscribe to the view that cult members become psychologically weak and intellectually inferior people dominated by tyrannical leaders. Even if one disagrees with the nonjudgmental approach of sociologists, one has to admit that they have provided the most complete descriptions of many of the new lifestyles as well as penetrating insights into the phenomenon of new religions as a whole.

Cults as New Religious Movements

Because of the ambiguous and derogatory meaning that the word "cult" connotes, attempts have been made, largely by sociologists and religionists, to find a better phrase to designate those religious phenomena popularly known as cults. Phrases like "new religions," "unconventional," "fringe," "alternative," or "nontraditional" religions, "intense religious groups," and "new religious movements" are common. The last phrase (NRMs for short) is often used in professional literature, even though it has serious deficiencies.

One of the more frequent objections to the latter centers on the word "new." Calling the cults "new" can be rather misleading. "Despite the apparent novelty and recent proliferation of cults," writes Willa Appel, "there is no evidence to suggest that they represent anything radically new. In size, origin, and evolution, the present cults tend to conform generally to those of the past."[34] The emergence of new religious groups is certainly not unprecedented in the history of the West or in the history of the human race as a whole. The variety of religions (with their many branches) testifies to the constant flourishing of "new" religious groups in different historical eras and cultures. Further, it is doubtful whether the "new" cults have actually given birth to novel and unusual ideas, doctrines, or practices. The current wave of interest in astrology, for instance, is certainly not new in Western culture,[35] nor does it seem to have produced any great insights in the field of astrology, the use of computers notwithstanding.[36] Even if some of the leaders of the new religions have combined theological ideas in an original way, their achievement is hardly unique. The history of religions gives evidence to the fact that theological insights have appeared throughout the course of human history. Moreover, the late Jeffrey K. Hadden found the phrase "new religious movements" weak as an "analytical tool."[37] He argued that (1) it does not communicate "profoundly important information that is carried by the separate concepts" of cult and sect; (2) it is not a clear concept; and (3) it presents problems when used in public discourse.

There are, however, several reasons why the new religious movements of the second half of the twentieth century could be called "new." The first is that they have occurred in a period of Western history when several indicators, such as the drop in church attendance, show institutionalized religion to be on the decline. Society is becoming more secularized and the repercussions are being felt in the traditional churches. The trend to "demythologization" (i.e., the removal or reinterpretation of mythological and/or miraculous accounts in the Scriptures) has been in full swing for a while. Thus, for example, Christian beliefs in the Virgin birth and in the Incarnation are being rejected or rethought and recast in less mythological language.[38] The secularization process has been interpreted by many scholars as a sign that religion is having less influence on people's lives. The apparent revival of religion, seen both in the growth of evangelical and fundamentalist churches and in the success of new religions, seems to go against the current trend. The development of different mythological themes, for instance, among those who believe in flying saucers, and the reemphasis on divine intervention in daily life, for example, among Charismatics, have been moves in unexpected directions. The new religions are perceived as a novelty because their emergence has surprised many observers of the religious scene.

The contemporary marginal religious groups are also new in the sense that they seem to accompany the changing sociocultural conditions of the

West, where geographic boundaries are becoming less rigid and intercultural communication more prevalent. People are becoming aware of the religious diversity that surrounds them and of the possible options now available to them. The fairly large number of new religions adds to this wide spectrum of beliefs and practices that are being marketed in the public forum.

The new religions might also be considered new in that, until very recently, those who joined them were first-generation converts. This means that the majority of their members were first brought up and educated in a traditional church and then took the important step of abandoning the faith of their parents. Becoming a member of an alternative religion is not merely a relatively minor change from one Christian denomination to another. It means that the convert is embarking on a venture that implies the acceptance of a radically different lifestyle and belief system. The convert is charting for him- or herself a new religious map. Some cult antagonists have argued that the new movements are pseudo-religious because of the erratic and unpredictable behavior of some gurus and charismatic leaders whose lifestyles have not been representative of either Eastern or Western spirituality and morality. But if one looks at the major constituents of religion, namely, belief in a sacred, transcendent power and concern for ultimate and spiritual matters in human life, then the cults have to be called "religious."[39]

The new religions can also be appropriately called "movements" in the sense that they reflect important transitions in people's lives. They are small currents in society that may be pointing to greater upheavals and changes in religious life. They cause a shift not only in the converts' previous religious allegiance, but also in the behavior of people who are affected by the change. Because the cults have become an issue discussed in the public forum and in law courts, they may also trigger modifications in social norms that could have undesirable repercussions on the relationship between church and state. New religions may be indicative of social and psychological turmoil. To call the cults "new religious movements" is certainly fitting, in spite of the qualifications that must be carefully made to this label.

One must note, however, that the expression "new religious movements" may not have lasting and universal value. Some groups are already developing their own traditions in which their children are being brought up and educated. Many of the adherents of these traditions will not be converts and their beliefs and practices not newly acquired. Whether, like their parents, they will abandon the religion of their upbringing to seek spiritual nourishment elsewhere remains to be seen.

Some Major Features of the New Religions

Besides the debate on the definition of a new religion, one encounters an even more acrimonious controversy about those characteristics that distinguish the new groups from traditional ones. Both scholarly and popular literature is replete with descriptions of the main qualities that enable one to discriminate between cults and the mainline religious organizations. Many of these characteristics are related to the definition of a cult. Two diverse schools of thought can be found in contemporary literature. Both need to be considered, since their respective views have been debated in society at large and in the law courts. One tends to take a rather negative approach and lists the pejorative qualities of cult ideology and lifestyle. Another adopts a somewhat neutral or cautionary optimistic perspective that concedes that there are good features in the new religious movements, features that may outweigh, in the long run, the defective elements in their beliefs and practices and offer an explanation of why people get involved in them. The major problem with these attempts to depict a cult is that new religions do not form one amorphous or homogenous group with exactly the same characteristics. They do, however, share some traits and can thus be grouped together under one name.

Negative Features

A widely accepted representative model that lists schematically the unfavorable qualities of the cults has been provided by James and Marcia Rudin,[40] who have taken a leading role in denouncing the new religions. Their view is that practically all cults are dangerous institutions that threaten the individual's mental and physical health, the family's well-being, and the established cultural traditions as a whole. The Rudins list fourteen attributes of the new cults that can be summarized as follows:

1. The swearing of total allegiance to an all-powerful leader, believed to be the Messiah

2. The discouragement of rational thought

3. Often-deceptive recruitment techniques

4. A weakening of the members' psychological makeup

5. The manipulation of guilt

6. Isolation from the outside world

7. Complete power of the leader who decides whatever the members do

8. Dedication of all energy and finances to the cult, or sometimes, to the benefit of the leader

9. Full-time employment of cult members without adequate pay

10. Encouragement of attitudes that are anti-woman, anti-child, or even anti-family

11. Belief that the end of the world is near at hand

12. An ethical system that adopts the principle that the end justifies the means

13. An aura of secrecy and mystery

14. Frequently, an aura of violence or potential violence.[41]

This rather overwhelming and frightening image of a cult has persisted to some degree in both religious and secular literature.[42] Writing some twenty years after the Rubins, Rabbi Marc Gellman and Monsignor Thomas Hartman, in a popularized introduction to religion, define cults as "false religions" and then categorically declare that "Cults are not religions."[43] They list eleven negative cultic features and assert that a cult turns one's relative or friend "into a zombie, cuts them off from reality, deprives them of sleep and freedom, and keeps them brainwashed."[44] Though the Rudins are careful to inform their readers that their comprehensive list of characteristics is a generalization, the overall impression one gets is that they are typical and that many of them are found in most of the new religions. It would be difficult, if not impossible, however, to find a single new religious movement to which even a few of the mentioned

15

characteristics are applicable. Some of the listed traits (such as the discouragement of rational thought) can be easily misunderstood or taken out of context. Others (such as the requirement that members work full time without pay) could also be ascribed to some of the mainline religions, more particularly to monastic institutions in both the Christian and Buddhist traditions. Some practices, such as the use of members to beg to raise funds, are applicable only to a handful of groups or have largely been discontinued. The following reflections on three of the more commonly mentioned negative characteristics are intended to show that the prevalent image of a new religion is somewhat imprecise, misleading, and often incorrect.

The All-Powerful Tyrannical Leader

The first feature listed by the Rudins, which seems to allude to a ritual act in which total allegiance is sworn to a leader, can be misunderstood if considered without reference to the ideology that demands total obedience to religious founders. That some cult leaders have final authority over their disciples in both spiritual and material matters is certainly the case. These leaders sometimes claim that they receive special revelations and instructions directly from God or some divine, unearthly source. Or again, as in the case with many sectarian gurus of Indian origin, they are accepted as representatives of God and are obeyed accordingly. Benjamin Walker, in his encyclopedia of Hinduism, writes that

> the Living Guru is believed to be the embodiment of the founder-deity and he is thus the last in line of succession starting from the god. As he is the deity incarnate, salvation is possible through him alone. . . . Frequently the living guru himself is actually worshiped.[45]

The sacred literature of several new religions includes, besides the Bible, an additional book written by a founder and given the same divine authority as the Bible itself. The *Divine Principle*[46] of the Unification Church is an excellent example. Other new religions rely on the writings and lectures of their leaders for providing the best guidance for reaching the goals proposed by the movement. The writings of L. Ron Hubbard, the (now deceased) founder of the Church of Scientology, are a case in point. Still others, like the Church Universal and Triumphant[47] and the

Aetherius Society[48] rely, respectively, on the revelations from the Ascended Masters to Elizabeth Clare Prophet, or the transmissions from extraterrestrial beings to George King. Not many of the new movements maintain that their leaders and/or prophets are the Messiah in the Christian meaning of the term. It is a common feature among all religions to locate a supernatural basis for religious authority on which believers base their beliefs and practices. Reliance on this authority ultimately depends on a faith commitment and not on indisputable, logical deduction or empirical evidence.

There are definitely gurus who have misused their authority, cult leaders who are pompous, self-righteous individuals, and spiritual leaders who have overinflated egos.[49] The abuse of power, however, is a problem one finds in all religious traditions and is certainly not just a "cult" problem.[50] Being a great charismatic personality does not automatically imply holiness or even good ethical conduct, as disclosures about television evangelists in the 1980s demonstrated.[51] But it would be unrealistic to make the blanket statement that all the leaders of new religious movements are corrupt, pseudo-religious prophets who are mainly interested in financial gain and power, just as it would be unfair to call all politicians crooks and all evangelical preachers hypocrites.

Cults as Proselytizing Religious Groups

Another of those features that are constantly mentioned in the context of new religious movements is their high-handed evangelism or proselytization. Cult members appear to be overly enthusiastic followers of a particular charismatic leader or as fanatical preachers of a particular belief, like the imminent coming of the end of the world. To many members of the mainline (nonevangelical) churches they appear too zealous in sharing their spiritual experiences, too intent on advertising their religious beliefs, and a little too forceful in their efforts to recruit people to their worldviews, lifestyles, and/or plans for a better society.

Images of such missionary endeavors are plentiful and tend to persist even when the cults change or abandon them. Members of the Hare Krishna movement are remembered for their dancing at major street corners, for talking to people about the joys and benefits of chanting their mantra, and for accosting travelers at airports to hand out their colorful literature for a donation. Again, one can mention the evangelizing techniques of the Unification Church on college campuses where students are accosted and invited to a dinner at the house shared by several members. In the early 1970s the Jesus People frequently stole the headlines by their bold street ministry that included accosting people and asking them whether they had been saved. Some will also vividly recall those occasions when they were targets of evangelical activities of older and more established religious groups. The Mormons still have their young adults embark on missionary programs that include visiting people in their homes, talking to them about religious matters pertinent to Mormonism, and distributing their literature. Many churchgoers, returning to their parked cars after Sunday worship, have found propaganda literature of the Seventh-Day Adventists attached to the windshields of their cars. Members of new religions seem very active in disseminating their spiritual knowledge and recounting their experiences that led them to their new commitments or confirmed them in their religious beliefs.

When one reflects, however, on the number and variety of new religious organizations in the West, the vision of a cult as, essentially, a forceful evangelistic endeavor begins to fade. In the Western world there are probably several hundred religious groups that have been labeled "cults." Of these, the number of controversial ones, those that have stirred up public concern and antagonistic reactions, number around fifty. When one tries to enumerate those groups that employ vigorous proselytization methods, one is apt to come up with a very short list. The majority of new religions do not advertise in public but keep a rather low profile; neither do they have their members at street corners selling flowers or on college and university campuses discussing philosophical and theological issues; nor do they send missionaries from door to door. Those that make active recruiting a major portion of their daily activities are the exceptions, not the rule. There are, for instance, many Buddhist groups that do not engage in heavy propaganda. It is thus possible that many people have become members of new religions because they discovered on their own the group they joined, rather than because they were actually sought after and successfully recruited by pushy devotees.

Linked to the idea that members of all cults are heavy proselytizers is the assertion that they consciously employ deceptive techniques to lure people to join them. This is probably one of the more serious attacks against the cults. But, once again, it would be difficult to substantiate this charge against the new religious movements in general and, thus, unrealistic to enumerate deception as one of the main features. In fact the two most-quoted examples of deceptive evangelization methods are the recruitment practices of the Unification Church[52] and of the now defunct Peoples Temple.[53]

Deceptive recruiting practices, when and if they occur, might present societal problems. Ways should certainly be devised to cope with them. But the customary accusation that members of new religions intentionally use deception could stem from misunderstanding and/or overgeneralization. In many cases involving groups who recruit openly, deception is hardly possible. The devotees of the Hare Krishna movement, dancing and singing their mantra at a street corner or in front of a large department store, couldn't possibly be intentionally disguising their identity. Their literature could hardly be mistaken for gospel tracts and their temple worship could not mislead anybody. Similarly, a visit to a Zen temple cannot lead even the casual visitor to conclude that he or she has just been given a tour of a Christian monastery.

Cults as a Rigid, All-Embracing Institution

A third image of a cult is that of an organization that has tight control of its members who live in communes or close-knit communities. Several cults certainly fit into this pattern. Those members of the Hare Krishna who do not marry, the "sannyasin," live a monastic lifestyle. In New Vrindaban, a Hare Krishna center in West Virginia,[54] the devotees, some married, others not, live in a commune-style environment with many daily activities, like meals, shared in common. The Unification Church and several Yoga groups have community dwellings or ashrams, even though the number of individuals living communally may represent only a small percentage of the membership.

Not all new religions, however, have communal living as a requirement for membership. Most of the members of, for example, Scientology, Transcendental Meditation, several Christian fundamentalist groups, and occult organizations do not live in communal settings. Even among those who encourage community living, varieties of lifestyles are allowed. Not all members of the Hare Krishna movement are expected to live a monastic life and not all members of the Church Universal and Triumphant share commune-style ranches. Once again, the popular image of the cult as a tight monastic institution does not always conform to the facts.

Another reason why the cults have been accused of applying a rigid socialization process to maintain their members is that they seem so dogmatic in their teachings. Members of new religious movements claim that they have found answers to all their religious questions and mundane problems. In a changing complex world where religious pluralism is rampant, one wonders how people can be so absolute in their views and so intolerant of diverse opinions. Individuals are drawn to particular alternative religions because their members appear happy in their living arrangements, satisfied with their involvement, and able to speak about their commitment with certainty. One must further bear in mind that committed members do not usually find a disciplined religious doctrine and lifestyle restrictive. To them, they are rather conducive to the spiritual goals they hope to attain.

New religions have also been criticized for demanding their members to dedicate a lot of time to the spread of the movement's ideology. Further, they appear to regulate and control the daily lives of the devotees and, in some cases, to dictate how members should relate to one another and to the outside world. The arranged marriages of the Unification Church are a typical example.[55] Such customs appear to be directly opposed to the Western stress on individual freedom.

It is possible, however, that the control that leaders of new religions have over their members could be better understood as a manifestation of intense commitment and dedication. Some new religions seem to fit into the sociological concept of "total institution." Samuel Wallace writes:

> When any type of social institution—religious, educational, legal or medical—begins to exercise total control over its population, that institution begins to display certain characteristics: communication between insider and outsider is rigidly controlled or prohibited altogether; those inside the institution are frequently referred to as inmates—subjects whose every movement is controlled by the institution's staff; an entirely separate social world comes into existence within the institution, which defines the inmate's social status, his relationship to all others, his very identity as a person.[56]

Erving Goffman, who has written at length about the restrictions of total institutions, lists five types of such groups, the last being "those establishments designed as retreats from the world even while often serving as training centers for the religious; examples are abbeys, monasteries, convents, and other cloisters."[57]

Attractive Features

One must, consequently, be weary of writers who draw up elaborate lists of unfavorable characteristics that are indiscriminately applied to all new religions. Several of the features listed above, like proselytization and dogmatism, can be found also in traditional religions or churches. One should be even more suspicious of those who seem to detect nothing else in the new religions but negative elements and nefarious intentions on the part of leaders and recruiters.

One of the main problems with the listing of negative features of cults is that it makes it extremely difficult to explain why young adults would even consider joining them. There must be appealing qualities that draw people to the fringe religions. It is precisely these qualities that one must know if one is to understand the reasons for their success and to respond appropriately. The selected characteristics[58] listed below are general and refer to those qualities that are both sought by would-be members and promised by the new religions themselves. The fact that a large percentage of those who join new religions leave after a year or two suggests that these religions do not always deliver what they promote and leave many of their members disappointed. It should also be emphatically stated that even obviously attractive features are not necessarily an unmixed blessing.

Great Enthusiasm

Probably one of the more obvious features in most, if not all, members of new religious movements is their enthusiasm for the new faith they have discovered and the lifestyle they have embraced. Enthusiasm may not always translate itself into great missionary fervor and proselytizing activities, but its presence is strongly felt. Gatherings of members at which guests are invited may include testimonies that relate the great benefits of membership. Stories of personal conversion and testimonies, typical also of Evangelical and Pentecostal Christians, have an appealing and almost irresistible quality. They tend to leave a strong impression that members are passionately involved in a worthwhile cause and have found the peace and security that so many people desire.

Underlying this enthusiasm is the dedication and commitment that members so openly exhibit. To people, especially relatives and friends of cult members, no matter what their own religious commitment might be, the intense and unqualified dedication of young adults to marginal religious groups can be both bewildering and threatening. To those dissatisfied with their current religious orientation, the beliefs and practices of new religious movements might appear both challenging and promising. And to those who are concerned about the lack of religiousness in contemporary Western culture, life in a new religion may seem to offer a haven from a society that stresses utilitarian, materialistic, and self-gratifying values and downgrades those higher aspirations normally linked with religion.

Religious enthusiasm[59] is not a characteristic found only among members of new religious movements. Despite its appeal, enthusiasm could, if unchecked, degenerate into fanaticism and lead to tensions and conflicts between religious groups. In their enthusiastic campaigns to enlist new members, some of the new movements have been rightly accused of making themselves public nuisances, failing to respect the sensitivities of others, and unjustly criticizing the works and achievements of traditional churches. When condemning the recruitment techniques used by new religions, it would be wise to bear in mind that many of their methods are hardly original and have, at times, been deployed by Christian evangelists and missionaries.

Stress on Experience

Another notable, though by no means unique, characteristic of the new movements is their stress on experience. They offer not just different creeds, moralities, and lifestyles, but also spiritual experiences. Members of new religions, such as Pentecostal and born-again Christians, talk about the "unique" religious feeling they have come in touch with since their conversion. Whether it is speaking in tongues, or the practice of meditation, or the recitation of a mantra, or contact with the guru, the message is the same. The individual claims that he or she has been transformed by the experience. This explains, in part, why it is difficult to convince members of new religions that they have chosen a wrong path.

Central to religious life in all traditions is the experience of the holy.[60] Such an experience, however, can be deceptive or hallucinatory. Some drugs can, apparently, create spiritual and mystical experiences, especially the feeling of being one with God and/or of having achieved cosmic consciousness.[61] Scholars have explored the possible similarity between the "mystical" experiences of Christian saints and the altered states of consciousness or peak experiences of those who have experimented with mind-altering drugs. Many conversion experiences reported by members of new religious movements have been likened to the effects of the drug LSD. In the earlier years of the Jesus movement young adults were encouraged to abandon their counterculture lifestyle and to accept and experience Jesus. They claimed they were "high" on Jesus, an obvious reference to the drug experiences they had before their conversions.[62]

It is understandable that the promise of a deep, lasting religious or spiritual experience is alluring. The evaluation of such experiences is, however, far from easy. There are no universally accepted criteria for determining the validity and authenticity of a spiritual experience. The suggestion that spiritual experiences require critical reflection and need to be balanced by reason tends to be rejected by many converts both to new and more traditional religions. Even if one adopts a definite theological opinion on the nature of religious experience, conversions to the new religions cannot be simply dismissed as spurious. The new religions tend to idealize, channel, and control specific experiences, but they do not, as a rule, discourage or stifle self-reflection, as is so commonly thought.

The Practice of Spiritual Disciplines

New religions do not necessarily succeed in attracting members because they present overwhelming theological systems and irresistible philosophical arguments or because they have achieved their goals of creating ideal communal-living arrangements. Converts talk about the personal benefits of membership. The cure of personal ills, the resolution of individual problems, and the improvement in their mental and psychological health are at times advertised as the advantages of becoming a member of a new religion. The practice of meditation or contemplation is a good example of a remedy offered by some of the new religions. Practitioners of Transcendental Meditation, for instance, have dedicated a lot of effort to convince people that the daily, structured recitation of the personal mantra, given individually to each initiated member, leads to physical, emotional, intellectual, and spiritual improvement and promotes a better social existence.[63] Meditation, it is argued, has a calming, beneficial effect on the human body and mind and on the personality as a whole. In an industrialized society that is characterized by a fast-moving pace that allows little time for solitary self-reflection, which tends to increase anxiety, and that often leads to alienation and depersonalization, the recitation of mantras, or a period of quiet reflection in a yoga posture, could certainly be appealing.

In many of the new religions spiritual practices become part of the daily routine of each member. They may provide a much-desired escape from the hectic lifestyle of Western culture. In this respect it is easy to compare them to the prayerful and meditative lifestyles found in more traditional, religious institutions, such as Christian and Buddhist monasteries. Once again, however, religious practices and lifestyles require careful scrutiny. Long hours of meditation, ascetical practices, and monastic regimes are not automatically beneficial to everybody. When members of new religious movements ignore medical care and replace it with meditation, faith-sharing sessions, and mantra recital, the concern about their mental and physical health is certainly justifiable.

The Varieties of New Religions

Many attempts have been made to draw up a descriptive classification or typology of cults and/or sects. Because of the divergences that exist in their doctrines, goals, ritual practices, and lifestyles, the new religions are not amenable to a simple classification that elicits universal approval. Particularly because of the influx of Eastern religious systems, the traditional distinction between church, denomination, sect, and cult is not fully adequate to express the current pluralistic religious scene. One of the more useful comprehensive typologies of religions, including new ones, is that proposed by J. Gordon Melton in his monumental work, the *Encyclopedia of American Religions*.[64] Melton's approach is to divide the religions of the world into twenty-four different family groups, about half of which belong to the Christian tradition.

Within each family, the member bodies share a common heritage, a theology, and lifestyle. One of the main advantages of his typology is that it is mainly descriptive and aims at situating the individual groups into one of the main religious and/or philosophical traditions. By so doing it (1) stresses the continuity that the new religions have with other alternative religious groups in the history of the West and/or with the major religions of humankind, and (2) provides an intellectual framework for understanding the beliefs and practices of the new religions.

Several of the families that Melton identifies are particularly applicable to the new religious movements. These are: (1) the Pentecostal family (which includes the Charismatic movement); (2) the Communal family; (3) the Christian Science–Metaphysical family; (4) the Spiritualist, Psychic, and New Age family; (5) the Ancient Wisdom family; (6) the "Magic" family; and (7) the Eastern and Middle Eastern families (two distinct groups). In his directory of listings Melton adds two groups, namely, "Unclassified Christian Churches" and "Unclassified Religious Groups," which are not easy to place within the framework of the twenty-four families. In the brief descriptions that follow some of the major identifying marks of each of these families are summarized.

The Pentecostal Family

Pentecostal Christians are those whose religious lives revolve around the experience of seeking and receiving the gift of speaking in tongues (glossolalia) as a sign of baptism in the Holy Spirit. Other gifts, like healing, prophecy, wisdom, and the discernment of spirits, are said to flow from the presence of the Spirit. Modern classical Pentecostalism is a revival movement that began in 1901. The emergence of the Charismatic (or neo-Pentecostal) groups, in the late 1960s, within the mainline Christian Churches can be included within this family, even though there are significant differences, both in theology and ritual practice, between the two spiritual movements.

The Communal Family

The central distinguishing mark of this family is the sharing of a communal lifestyle, a custom that, as reported in the Acts of the Apostles (4:32–35), was adopted by some Christians in the early history of the

Church. The founding of such communities, including monastic institutions, has occurred throughout the history of the Christian Church. Many attempts to create Christian communes took place in the nineteenth century. A strong leader, an equally strong system of social control and behavior, economic self-sufficiency, and separation from the outside world are the main elements of such experiments in community living. The Society of Brothers, the Shakers, and the Amana Community are all examples of communities founded in the nineteenth century. The Farm (led by Stephen Gaskin), the Church of Armageddon (founded by Paul Erdmann), and Findhorm (founded by Peter and Eileen Caddy and Dorothy Maclean) are examples of more recent communes. Communes, like the Ananda Cooperative Village of Swami Kriyananda, belong more to Eastern religions in their beliefs and ritual practices.

The Christian Science–Metaphysical Family

This family, known also as "New Thought" in academic literature, stresses the need to understand the functioning of the human mind in order to achieve the healing of all human ailments. Essentially a religious philosophy that stresses individualism, New Thought developed its own creed in which attunement with God is the primary goal of the individual's life. Meditations and affirmations are its main religious practices.

Metaphysics/New Thought is a nineteenth-century movement and is best exemplified by such groups as the Unity School of Christianity, the United Church of Religious Science, Divine Science Federation International, and Christian Science. More recently founded movements in this family include the following: the Institute of Esoteric Transcendentalism (headed by Dr. Robert W. C. Burke); the Church of Inner Wisdom (founded by Dr. Joan Gibson); the School of Pragmatic Mysticism (formed by Mildred Mann); and some splinter groups from Christian Science, like the International Metaphysical Association.

The Spiritualist, Psychic, and New Age Family

The interest in the powers of the human mind and spirit, powers known as ESP (extrasensory perception), has been part of recorded human history. Parapsychologists who investigate paranormal phenomena have made efforts to place their investigations on par with the work of physical scientists. Spearheaded by the work of Dr. J. B. Rhine (1895–1980) of Duke University and his colleagues, the study of ESP includes experiments on telepathy, clairvoyance, psychokinesis, spiritual healing, and precognition. With this group is included the area known as the occult, which nowadays refers to "hidden wisdom" and embraces various forms of divination like astrology, the tarot, palmistry, and the I Ching. The lifestyles of those interested in ESP and occult matters are based on paranormal experiences to which a spiritual or religious significance is attributed. Occult wisdom is also seen as a link to divine knowledge and power, and occult practices take place in a ritual atmosphere similar to the rites of traditional churches.

Going a step further than parapsychology and the occult is spiritualism, a religious philosophy that is based on the belief in personal survival after death. Its distinctive feature is the belief that there can be direct contact between the living and the dead, a contact achieved through a medium. Mediums can also function as "channels," that is, contacts with evolved spirit entities that communicate their higher wisdom to humankind. Many New Age groups and individuals (that include such well-known figures as the actress Shirley MacLaine) rely on teachings that have been received through "channeling."

The New Age, which began to be announced in the early 1970s, has its historical roots in those movements that, like Spiritualism, Theosophy, and New Thought, have stressed mystical experiences and relied to some degree on the teachings of Eastern religions. It is a rather complex amalgamation of thought and practice that unites Western and Eastern religious beliefs and practices. Organic farming, unorthodox healing techniques, meditation and yoga, the development of higher consciousness, various occult practices, and belief in reincarnation all appear as part of the New Age movement, which has no central organization and no commonly accepted creed.

The beliefs and practices of the spiritualist, psychic, and New Age family are varied and, at times, confusing, since they tend to be syncretistic. They combine traditional Christian doctrines, like the acceptance of the Bible as revealed authority, and the belief in an afterlife with occult beliefs and practices, like the conviction that unidentified flying saucers will soon come to save the human race from disaster, and the consultation of one's horoscopes. In ritual practices they could blend a reading and exposition of scripture with an exercise in psychokinesis. Melton includes within this family various Swedenborgian organizations, the Association for Research and Enlightenment (Edgar Cayce), the Society for the Teaching of the Inner Christ, UFO religions like the Aetherius Society, and various spiritualist churches and New Age communities.

The Ancient Wisdom Family

The Ancient Wisdom family came into being when a group of occultists split from Spiritualism in the late nineteenth century. Basic to this religious group is the belief in a body of hidden wisdom that has been passed from ancient times throughout the ages by special teachers who had mastered it. The Rosicrucians, the Theosophists, Occult Orders, and several I AM groups are among the most representative of this family.

The distinguishing mark of this religious family is the stress on the need to make contact with those people who are currently the bearers of ancient wisdom. These teachers are thought to live in remote areas of the world, like the mountainous regions of Asia. The rediscovery of ancient texts, often in magical and mysterious fashion, is an important aspect of the quest for the hidden knowledge. Special individuals, who are revered for their knowledge of, and close connection with, the occult realm, emerge as leaders of new religious movements.

A concept common to both the Ancient Wisdom family and some other new religious groups is that of the Great White Brotherhood. This brotherhood is made up of superhuman adepts or spiritual masters who are said to guide the human race in its development. Members of this group are evolved human beings who have reached a certain level of proficiency in occult matters and in the practice of good (hence "white") magic.

The "Magic" Family

Another cluster of new movements are united by their belief in magic, which refers to the principle that human beings can, through ritual actions, control and manipulate the occult and mysterious forces of nature.[65] This family has roots in the pre-Christian world. Its features include the acquisition of the secret wisdom of the ancients and the use of esoteric rituals.

Following Melton, one can distinguish four strands of the magical family: "Ritual Magic," "Witchcraft," "Neo-Paganism," and "Satanism." Ritual magic originated in nineteenth-century England under the influence of Theosophy, Spiritualism, and secret societies like the Rosicrucians and Freemasons. Several societies, largely secret, came out of these groups that made the practice of magical rites a central feature of their organization. Different traditions of magic have developed both in Europe and in North America. Examples of these groups would be the Builders of the Adytum and various branches of the Ordo Templi Orientalis.

There is a debate within the occult community about the origins of modern Witchcraft. Many practitioners of Witchcraft believe that their religious beliefs and practices date back to the ancient, pre-Christian religion of Europe that, in spite of continuous persecution, survived in an unbroken chain in small, hidden groups (or covens) throughout Europe. Scholars have found no evidence that modern Witchcraft is a survival of a pre-Christian European religion. Those who practice Witchcraft call their religion "Wicca." They worship many goddesses and gods, including a mother goddess who is at the center of their ritual. They also value living in harmony with nature.

Although the designations "neo-Paganism" and "Witchcraft" are habitually used interchangeably, the former is somewhat broader and includes those who follow the ancient religions of Greece, Egypt, and Scandinavia. In popular literature, both terms have negative connotations. Witchcraft has been associated with Satanism for centuries. Practitioners of Witchcraft, however, use it to describe a religious system that focuses on nature, a use that is being adopted by historians of religion and social scientists.

Satanism proposes a religious philosophy and practice that is antithetical to Christianity. It arose as a rebellion to Christian teachings, and its tenets are directly opposed to Christian doctrines. One of its main rituals, the Black Mass, is a parody of the Roman Catholic Eucharistic liturgy. In spite of the tendency to lump Witches and Satanists together, the adherents of Wicca insist that they are not Satanists, even though both accept the principle of magic. Contemporary Satanists have been accused of all sorts of illegal and pathological behavior, such as sadomasochism, sexual perversity, grave robbing, and animal sacrifice. In current literature there is an acrimonious debate on whether these accusations are justifiable or not.[66] Anti-cult literature, often reinforced by psychiatric evaluations and police reports, focuses attention on the incidence of Satanic-related crime. Others, sociologists in particular, see little solid evidence to confirm such claims. It is difficult to assess the number and size of satanic groups and to prove or disprove the charges against their members, because, among other reasons, they usually form secret societies. Claims that Satanism is actually on the rise still have to be substantiated by some hard data.

The Eastern and Middle Eastern Families

Until recently, Western society has been largely made up of Christians with a small minority of Jews and adherents of Eastern religions. The influx of immigrants both to Europe and the United States has led to the establishment of Muslims, Hindus, and Buddhists communities, all of which have become noticeable minorities in many countries.[67] Many of the new religious movements either stem directly from one of these major religions or borrow heavily from their philosophies and lifestyles. In Melton's classification the Middle Eastern family includes Judaism and Islam, while the Eastern family comprises Hinduism, Buddhism, and other relatively minor religions of East Asia. None of these groups are new religions. Their missionary endeavors in the West society began in the late nineteenth century, though they have certainly increased dramatically since the late 1960s. In Western societies there are several Hindu and Buddhist organizations whose membership consists largely of Christian and Jewish converts, and these are treated in academic literature as new religious movements.

The Havurah communities, founded in the 1960s, are among the more recent additions to Jewish religious movements. They are a product of dissent within the Jewish synagogues and are attempts to recapture and to incorporate in one's lifestyle the more traditional Jewish elements. Havurah communities have borrowed from Hasidic Judaism and occultism and stress fellowship and mysticism. The House of Love and Prayer, founded in San Francisco by the late Rabbi Carlebach (1925–1994), is one of the better known of these new Jewish groups. There are also several black Jewish congregations that were established in the early twentieth century.

Also stemming from the Middle East are many Islamic groups. Besides Sunni and Shi'ite Muslims, the main two branches in Islam, there are a few Black Muslim organizations, Baha'ism, Sufism, and the Gurdji-eff Foundation. Not all these groups are new religious movements. Many Muslims in the West are either immigrants or converts to one of the branches of Islam. Baha'ism originated over a century ago. Sufism, which represents the mystical tradition in Islam, came to the West in the early twentieth century and experienced a major expansion in the late 1960s and early 1970s. The Sufi Order in the West consists of a loose federation of small groups who follow the mystical tradition of Islam. Groups like Sufism Reoriented (founded by Meher Baba) and the Guru Bawa Fellowship are examples of contemporary Sufi movements in the West. Eastern religions, mainly Hinduism and Buddhism, have been the most conspicuous religious movements in the West since the late 1960s. Hindu groups, such as the Hare Krishna movement, Transcendental Meditation, and various Yoga ashrams and societies, Buddhist associations and meditation centers, especially Zen, and a few newer Japanese religions, such as Nichiren Shoshu (Soka Gakkai) and Mahikari, have at times figured prominently in the news. Other Eastern religions, like Sikhism and Jainism, are also represented, though in much smaller numbers. Eastern religions have contributed to the increasing religious pluralism in a traditionally Christian, Western world.

It should be stressed that the Eastern and Middle Eastern religious groups in the West must be understood in the framework of the major religions from which they originate and take their vitality. In one important sense these religious movements are not "new"; their belief systems, ritual practices, and lifestyles have a long tradition. Their expansion to the West and success in gaining converts is, however, a relatively recent phenomenon.

New Unclassifiable Christian and Religious Groups

The last group in Melton's classification consists of religious bodies that cannot be easily classified. Included in this are churches with a largely homosexual membership, mail-order denominations, and eccentric organizations, which do not fit comfortably in any of the divisions outlined above. Religious syncretism is a major feature of these groups, some of which are also interested in occult beliefs and experiences.

This family group draws attention to the fact that the typology of the new religious movements is not governed by absolute, incontestable rules.

Some groups could fit comfortably in more than one of the families described above. While there is general agreement about the majority of Melton's family clusters, scholars disagree with regard to the placement of a number of individual new religions. The Unification Church is a typical example of such disagreement. Gordon Melton includes it with the Spiritualist, Psychic, and New Age family,[68] Robert Ellwood and Harry Partin[69] with the oriental movements, and Eileen Barker[70] with Christianity.

New Religions as a Problem in Modern Society

The negative view of new religions has found public expression in three major charges that have repeatedly appeared in psychological and popular literature, in the media, and in debates in the law courts. The new movements are condemned for being anti-self, anti-family, and anti-society. They are judged to be dangerous institutions that have to be suppressed or eradicated.

Are the New Religions Anti-Self?

The first general reaction to the cults has been that those who join them are bound to experience psychologically harmful effects. Converts to a new religious movement make commitments that are manifest in the intense dedication to their newly acquired religious beliefs and practices and/or to their charismatic leaders or gurus. Entry into these movements entails a radical change both in ideology and lifestyle. Although such an alteration in one's personality does not necessarily occur suddenly (as is so widely held), when it happens it can be visibly detected by the manner in which converts talk and act. That parents and health professionals should express concern over such drastic changes is understandable. But whether this transformation is self-destructive behavior is a question not easily answered. The nature of religious commitment is such that ardent and zealous conduct of the converted person is a normal consequence. Extreme ascetical practices that sometimes follow commitment might have harmful physical and psychological effects. But the precise conditions under which asceticism can be detrimental to one's health are debatable. Structured activities that demand self-sacrifice have been part and parcel of all religions throughout the history of the human race. Judging by the number of cult members who have defected, one could conclude that many have found life in the new religions too strenuous. The majority of those who remain, however, do not seem to have been badly affected by the strict monastic living conditions or by the harsh spiritual disciplines and exercises. A few, no doubt, might have been hurt by the experience. That a communal, disciplined lifestyle could create psychological and intellectual problems for some people is possible. But accusations that membership in any of the new religions is detrimental to every member's health cannot be sustained by the data at our disposal.

Are the New Religions Anti-Family?

A second accusation against the cults is that they have divided families. There is ample proof to show that family conflicts can be either aggravated or stirred up when young adults leave the religion or church of their upbringing to join another one (whether this be a new one or not). The individual who joins a new religion leaves his or her natural family with its traditional way of life to become part of a broader family that espouses a different lifestyle and a conflicting belief system. The particular leader of the new religious movement and his followers are chosen as substitutes to one's parents and siblings. One recalls, in this context, the demands Jesus made on those who were faced with the option of responding to his call. In both the Gospels of Matthew and Luke, the sayings of Jesus can easily be interpreted as divisive of the family. "He who loves father and mother more than me is not worthy of me; and he who loves his son or daughter more than me is not worthy of me" (Matthew 10:37). "If anyone comes to me and does not hate his own father and mother and wife and children and brothers and sisters, and even his own life, he cannot be my disciple" (Luke 14:26).

The accusation that new religious movements put strains upon family life and relationships is well-founded. But the statement that they are destroying the family in Western society is unrealistic, because it does not take into account all the factors that have been affecting the well-being of the family since the second half of the twentieth century. The rising divorce rate and the changing moral norms have probably influenced the family more than any other factor. There are numerous problematic family situations that have nothing to do with the new religions at all. Divorce, child abuse, the misuse of drugs and alcohol, teenage runaways, and familial quarrels (including violence between married couples) make the family problems created by involvement in new religions seem rather small. In some instances, unwholesome family conditions might have driven young adults to seek better "family" relationships elsewhere. Truly enough, the new religious movements have added to family difficulties that have to be addressed, but these difficulties have to be placed in perspective.

Are the New Religions Anti-Society?

The final accusation against the cults is that they are against current social norms and hence destructive of society. This suggests either that they are gnawing at the traditional cultural values and/or that they have grandiose plans to take over the government. This former is highly dubious, the latter rather implausible.

There is no doubt that many new religious movements do exist in tension with society that is seen as unconcerned with ultimate religious goals. While it is true, however, that some marginal religions stress nontraditional values, others simply do not. The followers of late Bhagwan Shree Rajneesh followed for a while a style of interpersonal relationship that has aroused the furor of several nations. And the Children of God (now called simply "The Family") at one point adopted sexual practices that differed radically from both the civil and religious mores of Western and Eastern cultures. On the other hand, those who joined a branch of the Jesus movement gave up the practice of using illegal drugs and accepted more traditional sexual behavior. Some contemporary groups espouse at the same time nontraditional and traditional beliefs and practices. The Unification Church, for instance, endorses a rather unusual marriage custom in which the partners are randomly chosen by the leader, thus de-emphasizing, if not abolishing, the romantic element. Yet on the other hand it places great importance on traditional sexual mores and on conjugal fidelity. It is more than likely that the new religions are expressing, rather than causing, the changes that society has been going through in the second half of the twentieth century.

Most of the new religions have not taken an active role in political matters.[71] In this respect the Unification Church is an exception. Several observers of the new religious movements are concerned about its religious and political goals that are not quite distinguished. The anti-communist stand of the Unificationists, popularly known as the "Moonies," and the public impression that they are overtly involved in political matters may appear to question the tendency in Western countries not to mix politics with religion.[72] The Reverend Sun Myung Moon is portrayed in the public media as a forceful leader who has the goal of instituting a religious theocracy that would change the very structure of Western society. One is left with the impression that the Unification Church proclaims one faith, one leader, one nation, and that its main goal is to fight the godless archenemy, namely, communism.

There is, however, another side to the political teachings and activities of this church. First, the Unification Church has never talked of, much less hinted at, overthrowing any Western government. Second, its political activities have always taken place within the traditional boundaries of Western democracy. Further, though the official teachings of the church are very anti-communistic, they do not present a new trend in Western society. Anti-communistic rhetoric has been part of the political scene since the Bolshevik Revolution. Unificationists look on democracy as part of their religious ideology, and hence it is unlikely that they will plan any actions that run counter to the democratic principles prevalent in the West. Finally, in the Western world, membership in the church is relatively small and both its influence and presence appear to be declining. Consequently, the Unification Church is unlikely to make an impact on the political scene. One would probably have more reason to fear the rise of Christian Evangelicals and their involvement in politics.

Cults are often accused of fomenting the anti-social attitudes because they are perceived as prone to violence. While, as pointed out above, several cults have definitely shown signs of violent behavior toward themselves and others, it must be stressed that they represent a very small minority of the many hundreds of cults that have emerged in the past forty years.[73] Besides, cultic violence must be seen in the context of the rise of religious violence worldwide and not in isolation.[74]

Can Cults Be Dangerous?

Because of the many negative accusations leveled at the new religions, the question has been raised as to whether they are actually dangerous and should therefore be suppressed or their activities curtailed. There is little doubt that new religions and spiritualities need to be evaluated. How can one discern whether one particular group contains features that are dangerous or at least risky? The phrase "killer cults"[75] is based on the documented existence of groups that were suicidal and/or homicidal. Since the mid-1970s, the following cults, namely, the Peoples Temple (U.S.A.), the Branch Davidians (U.S.A.), the Order of the Solar Temple (Canada), Aum Shinrikyo (Japan), Heaven's Gate (U.S.A.), and the Movement for the Restoration of the Ten Commandments of God (Uganda), have dominated the public's perception of what a cult is like. These cult tragedies are exceptions, but they leave a lasting impression. It is easy to forget that by far the majority of the new religious movements have no criminal tendencies.

One of the most precise ways of determining whether a cult (or any religious organization) is safe has been developed by James Lewis. Lewis maintains that the question to ask is "whether or not the social dynamics within a particular religion are potentially dangerous to its members and/or to the larger society." He argues that charismatic leadership and the claim of divine authority are not "meaningful dangerous signs." It is the use, or rather misuse, of the leader's authority that dictates, rather than advises, and that considers the leader unbound by the ethical and legal standards that apply to all his or her followers, that calls for scrutiny. Good examples of these are the sexual practices of some gurus, who nonetheless insist that their followers remain celibate, and child abuse. Those groups that belief that the end of world is close at hand need not be considered dangerous unless they are stockpiling weapons to participate in some final battle. Lewis summarizes the dangerous traits as follows:

1. The organization is willing to place itself above the law. With the exceptions noted earlier, this is probably the most important characteristic.

2. The leadership dictates (rather than suggests) important personal (as opposed to spiritual) details of the followers' lives, such as whom to marry, what to study in college, and so forth.

3. The leader sets forth ethical guidelines members must follow but from which the leader is exempt.

4. The group is preparing to fight a literal, physical Armageddon against other human beings.

5. The leader regularly makes public assertions that he or she knows are false and/or the group has a policy of routinely deceiving outsiders.[76]

Michael Langone[77] has also attempted to draw up guidelines for evaluating new religions. He outlines some major psychological, ethical, social, and theological concerns. Though the theory of brainwashing seems to underline his analysis, he brings to attention some useful criteria. Thus he maintains that theological beliefs must be considered when assessing how dangerous a group might be. He mentions tax evasion and deceptive fund-raising with social concerns, though these could hardly be labeled as "dangerous"; they are social, rather than cult, issues. He encourages tolerance in matters such as unconventional dress and different religious beliefs. Julia Mitchell Corbett has grouped together ten "warning signals" that are usually mentioned when the dangerous or harmful elements of cults are stressed. While admitting that there is the potential for harm, she writes:

> I would emphasize again that these features are not restricted to religious groups, and that such considerations should be kept in mind when dealing with secular groups as well. It should also be emphasized that specific groups will probably not display all these characteristics, nor will all groups display them to a high degree. Many can be found to some extent in conventional religions and secular groups.[78]

David Barrett suggests that one should avoid generalizing from the few cults that have committed murders, homicides, and other crimes and points out that these are common problems in all societies and may have nothing to do with religion. He insists that the way to prevent these kinds of tragedies is "not by banning movements, not by demonizing them as dangerous cults, but by seeking to understand their world view, by observing them carefully but not intrusively, and by seeking to diffuse situations that might otherwise get horrendously out of control."[79]

Conclusion

The new religious movements have certainly raised many heated debates in our society. They have probably unearthed more problems than they have caused. An appraisal of their ideology and practices and a look at their emergence across cultures do not justify a fearful or belligerent reaction to their persistent presence. Neither, however, should their existence and their activities be ignored or taken lightly. New religions certainly address themselves to the eternal question of religious truth; they invoke our emotional and intellectual response; they stimulate us to self-reflection and self-critique; they often foment conflict between individuals and their families and society at large; and they leave many people confused and hurt in their wake. They are, however, more of a challenge than a threat. They present an opportunity rather than a menace. A better way of understanding them and coping with the difficulties they have created or brought into focus is to look on them as both partners and rivals in the religious quest. To panic and react by engaging in verbal or physical attacks, lengthy legal suits, religious crusades, or social reprisals to eradicate them or curtail their activities may lead to more serious problems.

The following chapters will delve into the various dimensions of the new religious options, hoping to increase our understanding of their presence in, and impact on, Western culture. Then we will be equipped to reach some conclusions as to what direction our response should take.

Notes

1. Robert Ellwood, "The Several Meanings of *Cult*," *Thought* 61 (1986): 212–24.

2. Confer Charleton T. Lewis and Charles Short, *A Latin Dictionary* (Oxford: Clarendon Press, 1958), pp. 369–70.

3. See *The Oxford English Dictionary* (Oxford: Clarendon Press, 1989), vol. 4, p. 119; and *Webster's English Dictionary* (Cambridge, MA: G. & C. Merriam and Company, 1959), pp. 642–43. Confer also Stephen J. Stein, *Alternative American Religions* (New York: Oxford University Press, 2000), p. 14.

4. See, for instance, the definition of "cult" given by Lewis R. Rambo in his essay "Cult," in *The Westminster Dictionary of Theology*, ed. Alan Richardson and John Bowden (Philadelphia: Westminster Press, 1983), p. 137. For a purely theological definition, without any reference to the new religious movements, confer Karl Rahner and Herbert Vorgrimler, *Theological Dictionary* (New York: Harder and Herder, 1965), p. 112. Good examples of the use of the word "cult" in the context of devotion to Christian saints are

Barbara Abou-el-Haj, *The Medieval Cult of Saints: Formations and Transformations* (Cambridge, UK: Cambridge University Press, 1994); and Graham Jones, *The Saints of Wales: An Inventory of Their Cults and Dedications* ([S.I.]Oakville, CT: Celtic Studies, 2001). E. O. James, in his book, *The Cult of the Mother Goddess: An Archeological and Documentary Study* (New York: Praeger, 1959), provides an example of the use of the word "cult" in the context of prehistoric religions.

    5. Confer Jeffrey K. Hadden, "Cult Group Controversies: Conceptualizing 'Cult' and 'Sect'," http://religiousmovements.lib.Virginia.edu/cultsect/concult.htm (accessed June 6, 2002).

    6. The Christian Research Institute (CRI), formerly located in Santa Ana, California, and one of the oldest apologetical and counter-cult organizations, is now under the leadership of Hank Hanegraaff. The CRI has been involved in internal conflicts and controversies for the past decade. See http://www.gospelcom.net/apologeticsindex/h13.html (accessed July 12, 2002).

    7. Walter Ralston Martin, *The New Cults* (Santa Ana, CA: Vision House, 1980), p. 16. This definition is repeated in a slightly different form in other works of Martin. See, for example, *The Kingdom of the Cults: An Analysis of the Major Cults Systems in the Present Christian Era* (Minneapolis, MN: Bethany Fellowship, 1968), p. 11; and *The Rise of the Cults* (Santa Ana, CA: Vision House, rev. ed., 1980), p. 12.

    8. Charles Braden, *These Also Believe* (New York: Macmillan, 1951), preface.

    9. Martin, *The Kingdom of the Cults* (1968), p. 11. See also the most recent, posthumously published edition of this work (Minneapolis, MN: Bethany House Publishers, 30th anniversary edition, 1997), p. 17.

    10. James Sire, *Scripture Twisting: 20 Ways Cults Misread the Bible* (Downers Grove, IL: InterVarsity Press, 1980), p. 20.

    11. Ron Rhodes, *The Challenge of the Cults and New Religions: The Essential Guide to Their History, Their Doctrine, and Our Response* (Grand Rapids, MI: Zondervan, 2001), p. 22ff.

    12. See CIC's Web page http://www.geocities.com/iaim_scott/identifying.htm (accessed July 1, 2002).

    13. Good examples of this are Russell P. Spittler, *Cults and Isms: Twenty Alternatives to Evangelical Christianity* (Grand Rapids, MI: Baker Book House, 1977). The Apologetic Research Coalition (ARC), a Christian Evangelical organization, dedicated to the rebuttal of new religious movements and now apparently no longer active, routinely included the Catholic Church with "cults." Confer Keith Edward Tolbert, *The CRC Cult Resource Guide, 1990–91* (Trenton, MI: Apologetic Research Coalition, 1990). More recently, Norman L. Geisler and Ron Rhodes, in their work, *When Cultists Ask: A Popular Handbook of Cult Misinterpretations* (Grand Rapids, MI: Baker Book House, 1997), include Roman Catholicism with non-Christian religions, together with the Jehovah's Witnesses, Christian Science, The Family (Children of God), Transcendental Meditation, Occultism, and the New Age.

    14. Pluralism is a major topic discussed in contemporary religious and theological writings. See, for example, Harold Coward, *Pluralism in World Religions: A Short Introduction*

(Oxford: OneWorld, 2000); Paul J. Griffiths, *Problems of Religious Diversity* (Malden, MA: Blackwell Publishers, 2001); and James L. Fredricks, *Faith Among Faiths: Christian Theology and Non-Christian Religions* (New York: Paulist Press, 1999). For a survey of current theologies of religion see Paul F. Knitter, *Introducing Theologies of Religion* (Maryknoll, NY: Orbis, 2002).

15. Martin, *The Kingdom of the Cults* (1968), pp. 23–33, and (1997 edition) pp. 35–48. Confer James J. Lebar, *Cults, Sects, and the New Age* (Huntington, IN: Our Sunday Visitor, 1989), especially pp. 14–18.

16. Geisler and Rhodes, *When Cultists Ask*, pp. 11–12.

17. See, for example, C. Douglas McConnell, "Confronting Racism and Prejudice in Our Kind of People," *Missiology* 25 (1997): 387–404; and Jeffrey Gros, "Eradicating Racism: A Central Agenda for the Faith and Order Movement," *Ecumenical Review* 47 (January 1995): 42–51.

18. Confer Louis J. West and Margaret Thaler Singer, "Cults, Quacks, and Nonprofessional Therapies," in *Comprehensive Textbook of Psychiatry*, ed. H. Kaplan, A. Freedman, and B. Sadock (Baltimore: Williams and Wilkins, 1980), pp. 3245–58; and Margaret Thaler Singer and Janja Lalich, *Cults in Our Midst* (San Francisco: Jossey-Bass Publishers, 1995).

19. The designation "Destructive Cultism" dates from the 1970s. See, for instance, by Eli Shapiro, "Destructive Cultism," *American Family Physician* 15, no. 2 (1977): 80–83.

20. Philip Cushman, "The Politics of Vulnerability: Youth in Religious Cults," *Psychohistory Review* 12 (1984): 6.

21. Confer, for example, Jean-Marie Abgrall, *Soul Snatchers: The Mechanics of Cults*, translated by Alice Seberry (New York: Agora Publishing, 2000).

22. The American Family Foundation used to issue two publications, the *Cultic Studies Journal*, which contained articles on various cults and cult issues, and *The Cultic Advisor*, which reported news about various new religious movements. Since 2002 these two publications have merged under the title *Cultic Studies Review*, which incorporates both reports from around the world and articles.

23. See AFF's Web page http://www.culticstudiesreview.org (accessed July 23, 2002).

24. American Family Foundation, "Cult-101: Checklist of Cult Characteristics," http://www.csj.org/infoserv_cult101/checklits.htm. See also Michael D. Langone, "The Definitional Ambiguities of 'Cult' and the AFF Mission," http://www.csj.org/infoserv_cult101/aff_termdefambiguity.htm; and Herbert L. Rosedale and Michael D. Langone, "On Using the Term 'Cult'," http://www.cjj.org/infoserv_cult101/essay_cult .htm. (All Internet references accessed July 13, 2002).

25. Dennis Tourish and Tim Wohlforth, *On the Edge: Political Cults Right and Left* (Armonk, NY: M. E. Sharp, 2000), pp. 119–20.

26 Dave Arnott, *Corporate Cults: The Insidious Lure of the All-Consuming Organizations* (New York: American Management Association, 2000), pp. 124–25.

27. Consult Herbert Richardson, ed., *New Religions and Mental Health: Understanding the Issues* (New York: Edwin Mellon Press, 1980). This collection of essays contains proposed legislation on new religions in the United States and Canada. For a more recent assessment of some of the legal issues see Anthony Bradney, "New Religious Movements:

The Legal Dimension," in *New Religious Movements: Challenge and Response*, ed. Bryan R. Wilson and Jamie Cresswell (New York: Routledge, 1999), pp. 81–100.

28. A typical example of this is David G. Bromley and Anson D. Shupe's book, *Strange Gods: The Great American Cult Scare* (Boston: Beacon Press, 1981). Sociological views on new religions are discussed in chapter 4.

29. Marc Galanter, "Charismatic Religious Sects and Psychiatry: An Overview," *American Journal of Psychiatry* 139 (1982): 1539.

30. Marc Galanter, "Cults and Zealous Self-Help Movements: A Psychiatric Perspective," *American Journal of Psychiatry* 147 (1990): 543–51, quote on p. 550.

31. See, for example, Saul Levine, *Radical Departures: Dangerous Detours to Growing Up* (New York: Harcourt, Brace, Javanovich, 1984).

32. For a comprehensive overview of the sociology of cults see Thomas Robbins, *Cults, Converts, and Charisma* (Newbury Park, CA: Sage Publications, 1988). Confer also Lorne L. Dawson, *Comprehending Cults: The Sociology of New Religious Movements* (New York: Oxford University Press, 1998).

33. See, for instance, Rodney Stark and William Bainbridge's essay "Concepts for a Theory of Religious Movements," in *Alternatives to American Mainline Churches*, ed. Joseph H. Fichter (New York: Rose of Sharon Press, 1983), pp. 3–27. For a thorough elaboration of Bainbridge and Stark's theory of religion and cults see their book, *A Theory of Religion* (New Brunswick, NJ: Rutgers University Press, 1996).

34. Willa Appel, *Cults in America: Programmed for Paradise* (New York: Holt, Rinehart and Winston, 1983), p. 10.

35. One should add that interest in astrology is not restricted to Western culture. See, for example, Suzanne White, *Chinese Astrology: Plain and Simple* (Boston: Charles E. Tuttle, 1998); and David Frawley, *Astrology of the Seers: A Guide to Vedic/Hindu Astrology* (Twin Lakes, WI: Lotus, 2000).

36. Confer James R. Lewis, *The Astrology Encyclopedia* (Detroit: Gale Research, 1994); and S. Jim Tester, *A History of Western Astrology* (Woodbridge, Suffolk: Boydell Press, 1987). For popular accounts consult Grant Lewis, *Astrology for the Millions* (St. Paul, MN: Llewellyn Publications, 6th rev. ed., 1990); and Rae Orion, *Astrology for Dummies* (Foster City, CA: IDG Books Worldwide, 1999).

37. See Jeffrey K. Hadden, "Cult Groups Controversies: Conceptualizing 'Cults' and 'Sect'," in Hadden's Web page on new religious movements, http://religiousmovements.lib.virginia.edu/cultsect/concult.htm (accessed July 19, 2002).

38. See, for example, Andrew M. Greeley, *The Mary Myth: On the Femininity of God* (New York: Seabury Press, 1977); John Hick, ed., *The Myth of God Incarnate* (Philadelphia: Westminster Press, 1977); Michael Green, ed., *The Truth of God Incarnate* (Grand Rapids, MI: Eerdmans, 1977); and Michael Goulder, ed., *Incarnation and Myth: The Debate Continues* (Grand Rapids, MI: Eerdmans, 1979).

39. For a discussion on the meaning of religion see James C. Livingston, *Anatomy of the Sacred: An Introduction to Religion* (New York: Macmillan, 4th ed., 2002), pp. 4–13.

40. James Rudin and Marcia Rudin, *Prison or Paradise: The New Religious Cults* (Philadelphia: Westminster Press, 1980). Many of these features are repeated in books that

denounce the cults. See, for example, Rachel Andres and James R. Lane, eds., *Cults and Consequences: The Definitive Handbook* (Los Angeles: Commission on Cults and Missionaries, Jewish Federation Council of Greater Los Angles, 1989), Part 1, pp. 3ff; and Lawrence J Gesy, *Destructive Cults and Movements* (Huntington, IN: Our Sunday Visitor, 1993), p. 14.

41. Rudin and Rudin, *Prison or Paradise*, p. 26ff.

42. See, for example, Edmund C. Gruss, *Cults and the Occult* (Phillipsburg, NJ: P&R Publishers, 4th ed., 2002); and H. Wayne House, *Charts of Cults, Sects, and Religious Movements* (Grand Rapids, MI: Zondervan, 2000).

43. Marc Gellman and Thomas Hartman, *Religion for Dummies* (New York: Wiley Publishing, 2002), p. 70.

44. Gellman and Hartman, *Religion for Dummies*, p. 71.

45. Benjamin Walker, *The Hindu World* (New York: Praeger, 1968), p. 419. See also Dima S. Oueine, "The Guru and His Disciple," *Unesco Courier* 45 (September 1992): 16.

46. This book has undergone several revisions and is published by the Holy Spirit Association for the Unification of Christianity (New York, 1973).

47. For a brief outline of this group see J. Gordon Melton, *Encyclopedic Handbook of Cults* (New York: Garland Publishing, 2nd ed., 1992), pp. 201–9; and Donna Wyatt, "Church Universal and Triumphant," (1997), found on Jeffrey K. Hadden's Web page, http://religiousmovements.lib.virginia.edu/nrms/cut.html (accessed June 6, 2002).

48. For a brief profile consult Shelley Perdue, "The Aetherius Society" (1998), found on Jeffrey K. Hadden's Web page, http://religiousmovements.lib.virginia.edu/nrms/aetherius.html (accessed June 6, 2002).

49. One naturally calls to mind in this context Jim Jones of the Peoples Temple in Guyana, David Koresh of the Branch Davidians in Waco, Texas, and Asahara Shoko of Aum Shinrikyo in Japan.

50. See, for instance, Anson Shupe, ed., *Wolves within the Fold: Religious Leadership and Abuses of Power* (Brunswick, NJ: Rutgers University Press, 1998).

51. People like Jimmy Swaggart and Jim Bakker are among the most glaring examples. Confer the following two reports: "More Trouble on the Broadcast Front," *Christianity Today* 32 (March 18, 1988): 47–48; and "The Bakker Tragedy," *Christianity Today* 31 (May 15, 1987): 14–15.

52. For a discussion of the Unification Church's recruitment practices see Eileen Barker, *The Making of a Moonie: Brainwashing or Choice?* (Oxford: Basil Blackwell, 1984), pp. 173ff. For an explanation by one member of the Unification Church of why "deceptive" practices have been used, even though they were never officially sanctioned, confer John T. Biermans, *The Odyssey of New Religions Today: A Case Study of the Unification Church* (Lewiston, NY: Edwin Mellen Press, 1988), pp. 245–50.

53. Confer Edgar W. Mills, "Cult Extremism: The Reduction of Normative Dissonance," in *Violence and Religious Commitment: Implications of Jim Jones's People's Temple*, ed. Ken Levi (University Park: University of Pennsylvania Press, 1982), pp. 75–87.

54. For many years New Vrindaban was a large splinter group of ISKCON. It has now been reincorporated within the mainline Hare Krishna movement and is listed in the Hare

Krishna Web page, http://www.harekrishna.com, as a "farm community." For information on New Vrindaban, see http://www.newvrindaban.com (both references accessed July 5, 2002).

55. For an analysis of this topic see George D. Chryssides, *The Advent of Sun Myung Moon: The Origins, Beliefs, and Practices of the Unification Church* (New York: St. Martin's Press, 1991), p. 131ff.

56. Samuel Wallace, "On the Totality of Institutions," in *Total Institutions*, ed. Samuel Wallace (Chicago: Aldine, 1971), pp. 1–2.

57. Erving Goffman, *Asylums* (Chicago: Aldine, 1961), p. 65.

58. For a lengthier discussion on the positive characteristics of new religions, see John A. Saliba, *Religious Cults Today: A Challenge to Christian Families* (Liguori, MO: Liguori Publications, 1983), pp. 17–24.

59. For a classic study on this topic see Ronald Knox, *Enthusiasm: A Chapter in the History of Religion* (Oxford: Clarendon Press, 1959).

60. Confer, for example, Ninian Smart, *The World's Religions* (Englewood Cliffs, NJ: Prentice-Hall, 1989), p. 10, where religious experience is included with the main dimensions of religion.

61. For several essays discussing the religious use of drugs, consult Arthur C. Lehmann and James E. Meyers, eds., *Magic, Witchcraft, and Religion* (Mountainview, CA: Mayfield Publishing Co., 5th ed., 2001), pp. 123–43.

62. The pioneering word of Robert S. Ellwood, *One Way: The Jesus Movement and Its Meaning* (Englewood Cliffs, NJ: Prentice-Hall, 1973), gives a vivid account of the centrality of the experience of Jesus in this movement.

63. See Michael West, ed., *The Psychology of Meditation* (New York: Oxford University Press, 1987).

64. J. Gordon Melton, *Encyclopedia of American Religions* (Detroit: Gale Research, 6th ed., 1999). For different typologies of new religious movements, confer Robert S. Ellwood and Harry B. Partin, *Religious and Spiritual Groups in Modern America* (Englewood Cliffs, NJ: Prentice-Hall, 2nd ed., 1988); and David V. Barrett, *The New Believers: A Survey of Sects, Cults and Alternative Religions* (London: Cassell, 2001).

65. Many scholars from different academic perspectives have pursued the study of magic and its relation to religion. See, for example, Graham Cunningham, *Religion and Magic: Approaches and Theories* (Washington Square: New York University Press, 1999).

66. For a debate on this issue, confer, for instance, the *Journal of Psychology and Theology* 20 (Fall 1992), which is dedicated to "Satanic Ritual Abuse."

67. See, for example, Mohammed Nimer, *The North American Muslim Resource Guide: Muslim Community Life in the United States and Canada* (New York: Columbia University Press, 2000); and Don Morreale, *The Complete Guide to Buddhism in America* (Boston: Shambala, 1998).

68. Melton, *Encyclopedia of American Religions*, pp. 753–55.

69. Ellwood and Partin, *Religious and Spiritual Groups in Modern America*, p. 258ff.

70. Eileen Barker, "New Religious Movements in Modern Western Society," in *The Encyclopedia of World Faiths*, ed. Peter Bishop and Michael Darton (London: McDonald Orbis, 1987), pp. 294–306.

71. Theodore E. Long, "New Religions and the Political Order," in *Religion and the Social Order: The Handbook on Cults and Sects in America*, ed. David G. Bromley and Jeffrey K. Hadden (New York: JAI Press, 1993), vol. 3a, pp. 263–92.

72. For a study of the politics of the Unification Church, consult Irving Louis Horowitz, ed., *Science, Sin, and Scholarship: The Politics of Reverend Moon and the Unification Church* (Cambridge, MA: MIT Press, 1978).

73. See David G. Bromley and J. Gordon Melton, *Cults, Religion, and Violence* (New York: Cambridge University Press, 2002).

74. Confer, for example, Mark Juergensmeyer, *Terror in the Mind of God: The Global Rise of Religious Violence* (Berkeley: University of California Press, 2000).

75. See, for example, Brian Lane, *Killer Cults: Murderous Messiahs and Their Fanatical Followers* (London: Trafalgar Square, 1997); and Larry Kahaner, *Cults that Kill: Probing the Underworld of Occult Crime* (New York: Warner Books, 1988).

76. James R. Lewis, ed., *Odd Gods: New Religions and the Cult Controversy* (Amherst, New York: Prometheus Books, 2001), pp. 53–56.

77. "Cults, Psychological Manipulation, and Society: International Perspectives—An Overview," *ISKCON Communications Journal* 7 (1999): 53–50.

78. Julia Mitchell Corbett, *Religion in America* (Upper Saddle River, NJ: Prentice-Hall, 2000), pp. 317–18, quote on p. 317.

79. David Barrett, *The New Believers: A Survey of Sects, Cults and Alternative Religions*, p. 94.

THE HISTORY OF NEW RELIGIOUS MOVEMENTS IN THE WEST

In chapter 1 it was observed that the very "newness" of contemporary religions or cults can easily be challenged and hence needs to be carefully qualified. In what sense, if any, can the worldviews and lifestyles of these new groups represent something novel? Many of the ideas that are part of the so-called new religious consciousness are not original. Even a cursory look at the history of religions would unearth similar, if not identical, beliefs and rituals in different cultures and in diverse historical eras. A good example to show that the novelty of present-day movements is, in some respects at least, questionable, is the belief in reincarnation, which is common especially among those groups that have been influenced by Eastern religious traditions.[1] The belief that the human soul will return to another human body in the future has a long history that stretches over a wide geographical area. The history of religions provides plenty of examples of the fact that the belief in reincarnation is pivotal in many of the world's religions, such as Hinduism. It can also be found, for instance, in the religion of ancient Egypt, in tribal religions of Africa, and in the religions of North American Indians.[2]

Further, traces of the belief appear in places where one does not normally expect it, namely, in Judaism, Christianity, and Islam. Belief in reincarnation was not unknown among some early Christian communities. Although the mainline Christian Churches have ignored or rejected the belief, it has resurfaced several times in the history of Christianity. Many Christians still react negatively to the resurgence of interest in reincarnation.[3] There are, however, those who argue that it can be incorporated into Christian theology.[4] Polls in the Western world over the past decade indicate that between 20–25 percent of those surveyed are disposed to accept reincarnation whether or not they have severed their adherence to Christianity.[5]

In order to understand the causes of the rise of new religions, the attractive nature of their beliefs and practices, and the influence they might have on traditional religions, it is necessary to look at the history of new religious movements in different historical periods. In this chapter several major sects or fringe religious groups that flourished in the Western world will be briefly examined. It will become evident that the emergence of new religions is not an exclusively contemporary phenomenon. A consideration of religious movements throughout history might generate insights for a better understanding of why new ones come into being and how dominant religions react to their beliefs and practices. It might also provide guidelines for formulating more appropriate social and religious reactions to their persistent presence.

New Religions in Early Western History

The missionary activities of the early Christian Church encountered many negative reactions and aroused a lot of controversy. Besides internal conflicts, which culminated in the Great Councils of the fourth and fifth centuries, Christians had to face the competition of many other religious groups that, borrowing and reinterpreting many ideas from Christianity itself, created enough disturbances to warrant imperial intervention.

Gnosticism

The first wave of religious movements that presented a formidable opposition to the Christian faith dates from the early second century. Known collectively as "Gnosticism," these religious groups were so successful that they elicited a strong apologetic response from Christian writers, who were motivated by the desire to defend their Church against what they judged to be Pagan or heretical beliefs and practices. Gnosticism[6] is a complex and varied religious phenomenon and has a long history.[7]

Understanding Gnosticism is important because many of the theological ideas and religious practices of the Gnostics have reappeared in some form or another in sects and cults throughout the centuries. For instance, the Manicheans of the fourth century, with whom St. Augustine was associated before his conversion, borrowed heavily from Gnostic teachings.[8] Medieval sects, like the Cathars, espoused beliefs that resembled the main tenets of the early Gnostics. Those post-Reformation religious groups that stressed that the knowledge of God can be achieved through direct experience (such as the Rosicrucians[9] in the seventeenth century) have been described as revivals of ancient Gnostic traditions. Since the middle of the eighteenth century influential figures, such as William Blake (1757–1827), Johann Wolfgang von Goethe (1749–1832), Herman Melville (1819–1891), Søren Kierkegaard (1813–1855), and Carl Jung (1875–1961), have all been accredited with playing a key role in the revival of Gnosticism.[10] According to some modern scholars, many of the new religious movements, including such groups as the Unification Church and the New Age movement, are revivals of the Gnostic worldview, which is "again a major competitor for the spiritual allegiance of Christians."[11] Robert Ellwood and Harry Partin maintain that there has been a continuous alternative view of reality (with Gnostic elements) in the West, a view that they trace from Hellenism up to contemporary religious movements.[12] It has also been suggested that, at present, the Western world is experiencing a rediscovery of Gnosticism.[13] There are several Gnostic Churches both in North America and in Europe, which though not large in membership, are making their presence felt.[14]

Gnosticism can best be described as a religious movement that stresses the need for salvation from the oppressive bonds of material existence, a salvation that is achieved, not by the grace of God, but rather by the individual's self-understanding or knowledge (*gnosis*) and effort.[15] It developed a complete theological system that clashed with the mainline theology that was taking shape in the early Christian era.[16] There is considerable debate among scholars regarding the origins of Gnosticism and its influence on some New Testament writings. But most seem to agree that Gnosticism borrowed ideas from Platonic philosophy, oriental religions, Judaism, and Christianity. Gnosticism is, thus, a syncretistic religion, embracing in its fold and unifying several theological systems.[17] In spite of the great diversity within the movement, there is, however, a general pattern of belief that can be ascribed to most, if not all, Gnostics. Central to Gnosticism is the belief in a dualism between God (spirit) and the material world, the former being considered good, the latter evil, and in opposition to the spirit world. Between the material universe and God, who is unknown, hidden, and not responsible for the creation of the universe, there exist many spiritual beings, some of which are fallen powers who now rule the world.

The same distinction is applicable to human beings that possess a spiritual soul and a material body, the latter being inherently evil. Gnosticism held that some human beings, namely, the Gnostics themselves, had, further, an innately divine spark, that is, a kind of inner self that was different from the soul. This spark was imprisoned in the body and could only be freed and reunited with God by means of a special revelation (*gnosis*), a secret, mystical (not intellectual) knowledge or enlightenment. This saving knowledge was said to be mediated usually by a divine being who, at times, was identified with Jesus who was not the incarnate Son of God, but rather a holy person who had the spirit of Christ, the spiritual principle inherent in all people.

Consequently, redemption, in the Gnostic system, was not a deliverance from sin and guilt achieved through the passion, death, and resurrection of Christ, but rather a form of existential self-realization. In other words, the Gnostic was able to free his or her divine spark from the confines of the material body by achieving an awareness of the divine mysteries, an awareness obtained by direct experience of the divine or by initiation into a secret, esoteric tradition of revelation.

Since the ancient Gnostics believed that not all people could reach the state of salvation, they considered themselves the privileged intellectual elite who possessed the ability to understand the most profound mysteries. Their rituals were, not surprisingly, elaborate and conducted in secret. Our knowledge of Gnostic rituals is not always very reliable, since much of it comes from Christian sources that attacked Gnosticism as a heresy. The accurate information we have about these religious rites suggests that they included highly symbolical initiation ceremonies that were deemed necessary for an individual to become a member of a Gnostic sect. Gnostics also performed rituals that prepared the living or the dying for their ascent into the realms above.

Gnostic sects (like many contemporary new religions) were often depicted unfavorably. They were said to reject traditional moral rules since these were deemed to be an obstacle to liberating the divine spark from its material prison—the body. The behavior of their members was described as antinomian, in the sense that they refused to abide by the decrees of the Church and disregarded socially accepted morality. There is no doubt that they spurned the traditional hierarchy of the Christian Church and accepted only a distinction between the chosen ones, that is, those initiated into the sacred mysteries, and outsiders. The early Christian Fathers, Epiphanius and Irenaeus in particular, wrote vehemently against the sexual symbolism and immoral practices of the Gnostics. Though most scholars today dismiss these allegations as exaggerations at best, there is evidence that a few Gnostics had a sacramental view of sex.[18] The majority of Gnostics sects, however, were rather austere in their morality and practiced vegetarianism, extreme asceticism, and/or celibacy.

Many of the accusations against the new religions (including contemporary Gnostic Churches and groups) are not very different from those made against the early Gnostics. Both have been criticized for their elitist attitudes, their nontraditional social and moral behavior, and their belief that human beings can achieve salvation and/or enlightenment through their own efforts. And both have been accused of practicing weird rituals. Kurt Rudolph remarks that many of these accusations belong "to the realm of perverted fantasy."[19]

New Religions in the Middle Ages

The period of Church history preceding the Protestant Reformation was not devoid of religious fervor and uprisings. Besides the rise of schismatic movements, this age saw the emergence of religious orders that portrayed several features usually ascribed to sects or cults. Many of these medieval sects prospered in spite of the civil and religious opposition and persecution they were subjected to. The two examples given below are the Cathars, who flourished for over two centuries, and the Flagellants, who have survived, in slightly different forms, until recent times.

The Cathars

The Cathars (often interpreted as meaning "the pure") first appeared in Cologne around the year 1143 and soon spread to southern France and northern Italy. They called themselves "good Christians," but became known by the derogatory term "Cathar." Stephen O'Shea writes:

> Their name, once thought to mean "the pure," is not their own invention; *Cathar* is now taken as a twelfth-century German play on words implying a cat worshiper. It was long bruited about that Cathars performed the so-called obscene kiss on the rear end of a cat. They were

said to consume the ashes of dead babies and indulge in incestuous orgies.[20]

Within thirty years, the number of those who joined this movement had reached such proportions that a great council of Cathars was convened in 1176 and several bishoprics were established. Those who belonged to the Cathar bishopric of Albi, a town about forty-five miles east of Toulouse, were known as Albigenses, a word also used in a derogatory meaning to label heretics.[21] They had become so influential both in the countryside and in the towns that they were considered to be a major threat to the dominant Church, and many missions were organized in an attempt to reconvert them to mainline Christianity. When, in 1208, the Cathars assassinated one of Pope Innocent III's legates, the Albigensian crusade was organized against them.[22] Although the power and influence of the Albigenses were greatly reduced by the pressures of both civil and ecclesiastical counteractivities, it took a while before their organization was effectively destroyed.

In Italy, the Cathars, who lived mainly in the cities, were riven by internal conflicts, but managed to survive because of the local opposition to both imperial and papal authority. When the wars between the popes and the emperor came to an end, legal action was taken against them, and by the beginning of the fourteenth century most of them had been literally wiped out.

The theology of the Cathars was partly based on Gnostic ideas and practices.[23] They adhered to either of two forms of dualism—one radical, another moderate. The former held that there are two principles of existence (or gods)—one spiritual and good, the other material and evil. The latter maintained that God had originally created Satan who in turn was responsible for making this material world, which, unlike the spiritual world, is intrinsically evil. Both views led to the denial of fundamental Christian beliefs, like the Incarnation and the resurrection of the body. The Cathars further denied the doctrine of the Trinity. Like Marcion in the second century of the Christian era, they rejected the Old Testament on the grounds that it reflected Satan's domain of the world. Their view that the human spiritual soul is imprisoned in a corrupt and sinful material body led them to avoid contact with anything material as much as was humanly possible. Malcolm Lambert states that "the main lines of Albigensian belief were also in vivid contrast to contemporary Catholic doctrine." He further adds:

> The Trinity was denied: Christ was either engendered or created by God and was consequently not eternal: from Mary he received no earthly body, but brought with him a heavenly one. In one account he entered and left her through the ear. He had but one, heavenly nature: his earthly body was a body through appearance and neither crucifixion nor resurrection in fact took place. He is not the Savior of mankind in the customary Catholic sense, but rather a messenger of God, an angel whose mission it was to bring knowledge of the means of salvation.[24]

The lifestyle of the Cathars was usually very austere and ascetic. They rejected marriage, practiced vegetarianism (though they ate fish, which they believed to be born in water without sexual union), spurned all material elements in worship, rejected love of material goods, and condemned all kinds of violence. All Cathars were expected to keep three Lents in the year, to fast on Monday, Wednesday, and Friday of each week, and to remain chaste. In fact, the daily life of the Cathars had much in common with the Christian monastic tradition. Consequently, the missionary endeavors of the Dominicans and Franciscans may have been a contributing factor in the Cathars' demise, since these monks provided an alternative path to Christian perfection that incorporated some Cathar practices and was recognized as orthodox by the official Church.

The ideal lifestyle of the Cathars was so rigid that, not surprisingly, only a few could follow it. These became the elite group, the "perfect," the ordained ministers who had full authority over Church matters and who demanded complete obedience from all the believers. They had more ascetical practices enjoined upon them and were expected, like those Christians who joined monastic institutions, to leave their parents and dedicate their whole lives to the task of perfection.

Two somewhat elaborate rituals dominated the liturgical life of the Cathars.[25] The first was the Transmission of the Lord's Prayer, which was held when a person wanted to become a believer and join the Cathar Church. The second was a special initiation rite that marked the superior status of the "perfect" Cathars who, as God's adopted sons and daughters, were the only ones allowed to recite the Lord's Prayer. This ritual, called the *consolamentum*, was believed to remove original sin, undo the effects of the Fall of Adam and Eve, and restore immortality. It was an elaborate ceremony, during which the candidates were given a spiritual baptism, not by water, but through the holding of the Gospels over the postulant's head and the imposition of hands by the perfect members present at the rite.

The Cathars came under attack for their doctrinal beliefs and moral practices. While many of their beliefs could not be reconciled with the major Christian doctrines as defined by the Great Councils, their moral behavior followed, generally, the standard practices of the times. The accusation that their extreme asceticism was nothing but a screen for their immoral activities has little evidence to support it.[26] Their success can be attributed to several attractive features. The high ethical standards of the perfect, the idealism that motivated them to live holy lives, the hospitality among the members, and the simplicity and confidence manifested in the ceremony of the *consolamentum* were among the more appealing characteristics of the Cathars.[27]

The Flagellants

The practice of self-flagellation is an old and widespread custom that is not restricted to Christianity, where it gradually became part of the ascetical and monastic life.[28] Various interpretations have been attached to the discipline of the whip: flagellation leads to self-conquest; it is a training program that contributes to a spiritual goal; it helps a person avoid sin by controlling one's passion; and it is a means of uniting oneself with Christ in his passion.[29] By the eleventh century the practice had already become common in the lives of individual monks. Peter Damian (d. 1072) promoted its use.[30] Both the Dominicans and the Franciscans contributed to the growing acceptance of flagellation as a form of Christian penance and mortification. The introduction, by around the middle of the twelfth century, of communal flagellation in the monasteries provided a further justification for the custom.

The first expressions of public flagellations occurred in Italy at the beginning of the thirteenth century. The year 1260 was a time of great crisis in northern Italy, brought about, in part, by the apocalyptic belief that a new age of the "Eternal Gospel" was soon to begin and by the political upheavals of the period. In the same year a public outbreak of penance that included flagellation took place in Perugia. So extensive was this manifestation that the flagellations affected all walks of life and social classes. Men, women, and children walked naked in solemn processions praying for God's forgiveness, weeping, and lashing themselves and the people nearest them with scourges until the blood ran down their bodies. Numerous people joined the throng of Flagellants as they made their way across the Alps into other parts of Europe. A spiritual renewal seemed to have accompanied the Flagellation movement. All kinds of sins were confessed, enemies made peace with one another, and people promised to reform their wayward lives. A contemporary writer describes the ferment as follows:

> The Flagellants came through the whole world. All men, small and great, noble knights and men of the people, scourged themselves naked, in procession through the cities, with the Bishops and men of religion at their head; and peace was made in many places, and men restored what they had unlawfully taken away; and they confessed their sins so earnestly that the priests had scarce leisure to eat.[31]

The practice of public flagellation, forbidden by the Holy See, waned for a while. But by the middle of the fourteenth century the movement swept throughout Germany, where the Brotherhood of the Flagellants (or of the Cross) was formed in 1349.[32] Fueled by reports that the Black Death was on its way, the movement grew and prospered. The Brotherhood was well organized under the control of able leaders. Regulations guided the lives of those who joined these penitential confraternities founded throughout Europe.

Twice daily, in public, the Flagellants stripped to the waist and, lying on the ground in various postures, performed the ritual of lashing themselves with knotted scourges that, at times, had nails embedded in them. Sometimes they allowed themselves to be whipped by the priest in charge or by another member of the Brotherhood. The singing of Psalms and the recitation of long prayers, particularly for deliverance from the plague, accompanied the ritual. These penitents believed that the blood they shed would mingle with that of Jesus, and that their penances would free them from all of their sins. This led them to feel that the sufferings they voluntarily inflicted on themselves would, if carried out for thirty-three-and-a-half days, have the effect of a second baptism that would automatically lead them to salvation and that, therefore, the mediation of the Church was not required. Some Flagellants felt that their penitential practices imbued them with great spiritual powers that would enable them to cure the sick, cast out demons, and even raise the dead.

The Flagellants were frequently greeted with public ridicule. In spite of the occasional support and encouragement they received from some of the clergy, they also faced a good deal of opposition from influential figures. In 1349, Pope Clement VI, for example, condemned the movement because of its theological views, while Emperor Charles IV (1316–1378) denounced it as a threat to public order. Two main objections to flagellation were made: (1) it led to morbid and disorderly behavior and (2) it was motivated by heretical tendencies. Civil authorities and the Inquisition thus combined their resources to effectively suppress not only the public displays of flagellations, but also the confraternities who were thought to be, not without justification, anti-authoritarian and anti-ecclesiastical. An inner core of Flagellants persisted and gradually formed a sect that was condemned by the Council of Constance in 1417 for, among other things, its contempt for the sacrament of Penance.

The Flagellants were thus driven into secrecy until the middle of the sixteenth century when the movement, with the support of the French monarchy, acquired respectability. The Brotherhood of the Annunciation Day was formed, and several eminent people, including the Cardinals of Lorraine and Guise, joined. The fanaticism for fleshly mortification in public reached a new height when noble men and women, either naked or only partially clad, paraded the streets and scourged themselves. The movement, however, encountered heavy criticism from religious leaders who declared the custom cruel and evil and claimed that it was as unlawful as castration. By the early seventeenth century public flagellation was prohibited and declared to be a heretical practice. From then onward flagellation was largely practiced in private, though, on several occasions, there were sporadic attempts to revive its public manifestation.

Until the middle of the nineteenth century, secret groups of Flagellants (or *Penitentes*) existed in some Latin American countries and in New Mexico and southern Colorado.[33] Several theories of origin have been advanced to account for their presence. One of these theories explains them as the lineal descendants of the medieval Flagellants.[34] The *Penitentes* could also have derived their customs from the *Disciplinati*, who formed confraternites in between the fourteenth and sixteenth centuries in Italy. Like the Flagellants, the *Penitentes* stressed ascetical practices, including flagellation, but they never indulged in extreme and public forms of penance and were never regarded as heretical.[35] Their rituals of flagellation by whips made of cholla cactus were observed especially during the season of Lent and when a new brother was initiated.[36] In spite of sharing some penitential customs with the Flagellants, the *Penitentes* were never judged to be heretical, even though, in the nineteenth century, the Church hierarchy looked upon them with concern and ended up denouncing them apparently because some of their rituals were performed in secret.[37] Marta Weigle writes that they were clearly not "aberrant." On the contrary, they "exist well within the history of Spanish Catholicism and its mystical, penitential, and Franciscan traditions."[38] There is evidence that these brotherhoods have survived in small numbers well into the second half of the twentieth century, though they now have both legal and ecclesiastical recognition.[39]

Like the members of so many other new religious movements, the Flagellants of the Middle Ages were in search of an ecstatic state. Flagellation, therefore, is not just a penance for one's sins or a means of purification. It is not only a test of courage and endurance, but also a technique for achieving a higher state of consciousness and for imbuing the initiate with a greater and nobler power that is believed necessary for membership in the elite community or secret society. Some scholars,[40] in their descriptions of the *Penitentes*, have focused on the meaning of their practices and have argued that joining in the ritual was an encounter with, and experience of, the sacred. Because the medieval Flagellants believed that they could achieve the new state of being and knowledge by their own endeavors, they easily acquired the attitude that they were holier than the average Christian. Consequently, they maintained that they did not have to be subject to the same Church legislation as everybody else.

Both of these religious groups, the Cathars and the Flagellants, aroused strong reactions from the prevalent culture and Church. Because both actively sought converts, they brought to the fore two main questions that the established Church had to answer: What steps could be taken to refute their teachings? And what measures could be adopted to stem their successful evangelization efforts? The Cathars and the Flagellants were not only condemned, but also pressured by the use of civil and religious edicts and physical force to abandon their faith. The resort to such measures to eradicate unconventional religious beliefs and practices was taken for granted at the time. If similar efforts were made today against any religious group, they would be denounced as barbaric and tyrannical and rejected as a violation of religious freedom. It is interesting to note that the violence against the Cathars and the Flagellants did not achieve immediate success. The Cathars were finally wiped out, but many of their ideas survived. Some ascetical practices of the Flagellants remained in existence, probably in less extreme forms. They remind us of the severe penances and/or unusual behaviors that are habitually associated with new religious movements.

New Religions in the Post-Reformation Era

The post-Reformation era saw not only the further breakup of Western Christianity into a variety of Protestant churches, but also the emergence of various religious groups that were denounced by the majority of Christian churches throughout Europe. Though many of these new movements were short-lived, they attracted a lot of attention because the theological views and lifestyles they adopted challenged traditional beliefs and morals. The blossoming of new religious movements was particularly fertile in seventeenth-century Puritan England. During this period, when the monarchy was in abeyance and Oliver Cromwell led the nation as Lord Protector (1653–1658), radical ideas in religious, social, and political matters were rampant.[41] Groups like the Muggletonians,[42] the Family of Love,[43] the Levellers,[44] and the Quakers[45] are good examples of the religious ferment and enthusiasm of the time. One of the most radical and peculiar of these countercultural movements became known as "The Ranters."[46]

The Ranters

The Ranters, a name chosen by their critics, drew adherents largely from the lowest strata of British society, mainly from around London but also from many parts of England. The first Ranters appeared in the 1640s and called themselves the "faithful and true children of God." Although they never formed an organized religious group and differed among themselves regarding matters of doctrine, preaching, and moral behavior, they shared a common opposition to the Puritan norms of the time. Their writings[47] portray a wide variety of beliefs and practices, so much so that Jerome Friedman distinguishes between five different types of Ranters: philosophers, sexual libertines, revolutionaries, divine Ranters, and gentleman Ranters.[48]

The Ranters upheld a type of primitive, apostolic Christianity free from hierarchical distinctions. Their leaders have been described as pantheists or "mystical anarchists." A. L. Morton states they brought together "pantheistic mysticism" and "rude skepticism and anticlericalism."[49] They are said to have regarded themselves as being one with God and as having an inward divinity. They claimed to be free from all forms of social restraints and moral laws. Their goal was to return to the state of the sinlessness of Adam and Eve before the Fall in the Garden of Eden. They rejected the commonly accepted Christian beliefs in heaven and hell and in the resurrection of the body on the last day. One of their main doctrines was that an individual could only become perfect if he or she had committed every sin.[50] The Ranters held their religious gatherings in taverns and encouraged those who joined the movement to smoke, to drink, to practice adultery and fornication freely and in public, and to curse and swear. They rejected both civil and ecclesiastical authorities. Their behavior was an extreme form of "antinomianism run amok into religious anarchism."[51]

Maybe partly as a reaction to the strict moral rules of the Puritans, the Ranters emphasized nakedness. Many of them were strong advocates of sexual liberty and preached a hedonistic philosophy that shocked their contemporaries. The pamphlets they published in the 1650s were decorated with crude pictures of naked people engaged in erotic dancing. One of the main Ranter writers, Abiezer Coppe, who was known as the "Great Blasphemer," preached naked and cursed constantly while delivering his rambunctious sermons.[52] His raving enthusiasm and orgiastic experiences, though hardly typical of all the influential Ranters, became synonymous with Ranterism.

The public outcry against the Ranters was expressed in several acts of Parliament that were enacted against them.[53] In 1648 Parliament forbade blasphemy and issued a proclamation of a Day of Humiliation, Fasting, and Prayer to offset the behavior of the Ranters and to make public reparation for their misbehavior. Two other acts were passed in 1648, one suppressing incest, adultery, and fornication, the other condemning atheistic and sacrilegious behavior, which was said to be not only derogatory of God's honor, but also destructive of human society. Religious antagonism and legal restrictions contributed to the demise of the Ranters, many of whom may have been absorbed into the Quaker movement, which included them in its evangelistic activity. In any case the Ranter movement seems to have died out as quickly as it came into being.

As a religious phenomenon the Ranters are particularly interesting in the context of the current rise and success of marginal religious groups in contemporary Western culture. First, historians have attempted to understand the emergence of the Ranters by investigating the historical, political, and religious conditions of the period in which they flourished. Historians do not ascribe the origins of new religious movements to be carefully devised and mysteriously organized conspiracies aimed at overturning the orthodox religion of the time. Rather, they interpret their rise as stemming from very concrete sociocultural conditions that are not very dissimilar from those that have existed in different historical periods. G. F. S. Ellens writes:

> To summarize the main causes of this widespread melancholy, at least in England, and the lack of confidence from which it sprung, we may list the following points, though not necessarily in order of importance: the war, and the execution of the king in 1649, and the subsequent internecine fighting of power-groups; the broken and confused condition of ecclesiastical authority; the ensuing doubt about the existence of a transcendent truth; widespread philosophico-religious speculation; disputes about the authority and truth of the Bible called into question by the new philosophy; fear and guilt engendered by Calvinistic preaching of predestination, not only to heaven, but to condemnation and hell; a widespread belief in the decay of the world; and, as in our times, the new astronomy which calls man's place in the universe into question.[54]

Similar attempts to understand the rise of contemporary movements in the context of social change or upheavals in modern Western societies are standard, especially among sociologists.

Second, the Ranters have been compared to modern hippies. Both were social dropouts who flourished in a period of great social conflict and cultural change. Both favored free sex and the pursuit of pleasure. Both insisted that morality is subjective and cannot be regulated by objective laws. Ellens further states that "[e]scapism, subjectivism, introversion, these are the marks of the Hippies as of the Ranters. Both groups seek an escape from harsher concepts of reality."[55] Though one can hardly call the hippies of the 1960s modern Ranters, knowledge of the latter reveals that in many respects the hippies were not very original in the beliefs and aspirations they held and in the practices they advocated. Like the Ranters they were a cultural phenomenon that must be understood in the context of a socially turbulent and changing environment.

Third, negative reactions to, and accusations against, the Ranters are not unlike those directed toward contemporary movements.[56] Psychological assessments of the Ranters are rather similar to those given to the new cults and their members. Rufus Jones, writing in the first quarter of the twentieth century, states quite categorically:

> All movements, such as this one [i.e., the Ranters], which express deep popular striving to escape from the rigidity of old systems and to secure a large area of individual freedom, tend to develop an extreme wing. Persons of unstable equilibrium are swept on by the contagion of the movement. Those who are abnormally responsive to suggestion are certain to be carried along with the movement. These psychopathic persons, lacking in perspective and balance, bring into strong light the dangers that are involved in complete religious freedom. The Ranters were largely composed of this type of person, and some of them were obviously insane.[57]

Similar assessments have been made of leaders of new religions, such as Jim Jones of the People's Temple, the Reverend Sun Myung Moon of the Unification Church, Bhagwan Shree Rajneesh of the Rajneesh Foundation, and Asahara Shoko of Aum Shinrikyo. They are seen as irrational and narcissistic fanatics who suffer from paranoia and megalomania and who indulge in psychopathological behavior.[58]

Finally, historians have been debating whether, and to what degree, the writings of the seventeenth century portray an accurate picture of the Ranters. In 1986, J. C. Davis published a book in which he argued that the Ranters did not exist as a sect or movement.[59] Ranterism was a myth, a projection of deviance, "an assertion of normative, social and ideological boundaries, in the specific context of multiplying anxieties brought to the peak by the collapse of the old order and the spectre of sectarian disintegration."[60] Historians[61] quickly rose to defend the view that, in the words of G. E. Aylmer, "the burden of proof suggests, however, that the Ranters existed."[62] F. McGregor seems to take a middle ground when he writes that there "is little objective evidence that either Seekers or Ranters formed coherent movements or that they existed in considerable numbers."[63] This debate resembles the current exchanges between scholars on the existence and proliferation of Satanism and Satanic ritual abuse in contemporary Western society.[64]

The Shabbatean Movement

The rise of new religious movements within the Christian community has its counterparts in other religious traditions besides Christianity. One of the most powerful, extensive, and important Jewish messianic revivals is known as the Shabbatean movement, which appeared in the seventeenth century and quickly spread among Jews in different parts of the world.

The leader of this movement was Shabbetai Zevi (1626–1676),[65] a Jew from Turkey, who devoted himself to ascetic exercises and to the traditional Jewish learning of the Scriptures and the Law. He immersed himself in the study of one particular school of Jewish mysticism, known as the Kabbala[66] and its most influential work, the *Zohar* ("Book of Splendor"). By 1648 Zevi had assumed a messianic role. Expelled by the local rabbinate from Smyrna (modern Izmir, in Turkey), where he was considered a lunatic and a fool, he wandered through Greece and Turkey for seven years until he found a more favorable reception in Jerusalem and Cairo. A major turning point in his career came when he went to seek the advice of a brilliant young rabbi, Nathan of Gaza. Nathan who, rather than helping Zevi with his spiritual and psychological problems, assumed the role of the prophet Elijah and hailed Zevi as the promised messiah.

The fortunes of Zevi and his movement now dramatically changed. Many leading rabbis accepted him as the messiah, and his fame and influence swept throughout the Jewish world both in the Middle East and in Europe. Zevi began acting as if he were the promised messiah by distributing the kingdoms of the Earth among the faithful and appointing counterparts of the ancient Israelite kings. Alarmed by these activities, the Turkish authorities had him arrested and imprisoned. Zevi was faced with the choice between death or conversion to Islam. In 1666 he opted to become a Muslim, even though he still continued to perform most of the Jewish rituals. His outward betrayal dismayed many of his followers who abandoned his movement and returned to Orthodox Judaism.[67] A core of followers, however, remained faithful. Nathan, in particular, defended Zevi's apostasy, which he explained as a mission to redeem the Turks. In other words, Zevi, by feigning acceptance of the Islamic faith, had succeeded in entering the enemy's camp to do battle with evil. This theological justification laid the foundation for the movement's ideology for the next hundred years. Zevi himself maintained his leadership role in the movement he founded, revealing to his elite followers the mysteries of the godhead.

After Zevi's death in 1676 the activities of the Shabbatean groups were mainly centered in Turkey, Italy, and Poland. Rejected and opposed by rabbinical authorities, the movement went underground and split into several sects. Theological speculations about Zevi and the nature of his messiahship continued. During the eighteenth century there were many of his followers who claimed to be the Messiah ben Joseph, a divinely appointed leader who was believed to fill in the period between the first manifestation of Shabbetai Zevi and his second coming. Internal controversies and factions were common in the Shabbatean movement during the eighteenth century. By the first decade of the nineteenth century Shabbateanism had disintegrated into a few small groups, some of which survived until the early twentieth century.[68]

The impact Zevi had on the Jews of his time has earned him "a ranking among the most influential Jews of all time."[69] Most Jewish commentators on the Shabbatean movement, however, are somewhat negative in their assessment of this extraordinary and unusual Jew. The majority of them agree that Zevi probably suffered from a pathological illness (probably manic-depressive psychosis with paranoid traits).[70] His behavior was erratic and antinomian; at one point, for example, he declared the abolition of the Ten Commandments. During his periods of illumination he committed acts that ran counter to religious law (like celebrating several Jewish festivals in the space of one week) and practiced bizarre rituals. Historians have pointed to a number of major factors to account, in part at least, for the rise of his movement and its initial success. The wars of religion in Europe, the popularity of the Kabbalistic (occult) doctrines, the massacres of Jews in Eastern Europe (Poland and Russia) in the middle of the seventeenth century, and the condition of the Jews in exile, coupled with their hopes for political and spiritual redemption, were all ripe conditions for the successful dissemination of the movement.[71]

Christian responses to many of the leaders of the contemporary religious movements are similar, in several respects, to the Jewish reaction to Shabbetai Zevi's theology and behavior. New claims to prophetic revelation and missionary commitment are repeatedly and vehemently denied and attacked. The moral character and behavior of new prophets are subjected to criticism and sometimes ridiculed. The majority of Christians have interpreted the alluring charismatic qualities of self-proclaimed messiahs and prophets of an impending doom, not as signs of God's presence, but rather as insane activities of mentally ill individuals or as indications of Satanic activity in the modern world.

New Religions in the Nineteenth Century

The nineteenth-century Western world, particularly in North America, experienced a dramatic rise in religious pluralism on several fronts. The first was an increase in Christian revival movements. So many new sects were spreading their evangelical message in upstate New York that historians call this geographical area the "burned-over district."[72] The second was the introduction of Eastern religions in what was largely a Christian enclave. The influence of Eastern philosophical and religious thought can be seen in the metaphysical movements (including systems like Theosophy).[73] The third was the emergence of religions or churches indigenous to the New World. One of the better examples that illustrates the presence of new religious movements in the West in this century is Mormonism (the Church of Jesus Christ of Latter-day Saints), whose continued expansion throughout the world has become a major concern of many Christians.[74]

Mormonism

One of the more successful movements of nineteenth-century America was Mormonism,[75] which was founded in 1830 by Joseph Smith who claimed to have discovered a lost Scripture, *The Book of Mormon*.[76] For the Mormons, revealed Scripture consists of the Bible, the *Book of Mormon*, and two other relatively short works by Smith, namely the *Doctrine and Covenant* and the *Pearl of Great Price*.

Most of Smith's contemporaries reacted negatively to his claim to revelation and prophethood. During the first half-century of its existence, the Mormon Church experienced ridicule and persecution. The Mormons' flight West, until they settled in Utah, is an interesting chapter of the history of nineteenth-century America. Utah was finally admitted into the Union as a state only after the Church ceased sanctioning polygamy and gave up its policy of economic separatism and a Church-sponsored political party. The development of Mormonism since then has been of steady internal growth as well as tolerance and acceptance by the rest of society. Mormonism has been transformed from a despised cult to an established church with its own religious and cultural traditions. Like the major Christian churches, it has been beset with many dissident groups over its 150-year history, the Reorganized Church of Jesus Christ of Latter-day Saints being the largest and most influential.[77]

Many writers on Mormonism have found its theology, especially its doctrine of God, difficult to understand.[78] Mormon writings speak openly in terms of many gods, even though sometimes one is left with the impression that these gods are but aspects of one divine being.[79] God is said to be a spirit in the same sense that a resurrected person is a spirit. God the Father is a glorified and perfected man, a person of tangible flesh and bones in which an eternal spirit is housed. Christ was literally the Son of God, in the sense that he was conceived of the Virgin Mary and born like any other human being. The Holy Ghost is a spirit person who has the functions of comforter, revealer, and sanctifier. Mormons also believe in a duality of God, namely, that of fatherhood and motherhood. In Mormonism, God is not the ultimate being, but rather a spirit who, like human beings, is subject to a superior principle of growth and development.

God created an infinite number of universes, in the sense that he organized them out of existing chaotic matter. Many earths exist; every one of which is inhabited by God's spirit children and has been given its own particular divine law. The human soul enjoyed a preexistent life before it took human flesh. Adam was the first human being to fall, both spiritually and temporally, from the immortal state, bringing suffering and death into this world. Christ, the firstborn of the Father, was chosen to execute the whole plan of redemption. His sacrifice atoned for the human condition, restoring the spiritual and temporal conditions human beings had before the Fall. Salvation enables human beings to become gods, like their heavenly Father, and to rule over a planet just as Jesus rules over the Earth.[80]

The Mormons believe that their Church is the true Church of Jesus Christ.[81] They maintain that Jesus founded a church while on earth, but it became very corrupt soon after he died. The revelation of Joseph Smith restored the Church with a new dispensation that includes the reintroduction of prophetic leadership, the reinstitution of the priesthoods of Aaron and Melchizedek, and the gathering of the saints (true believers).

The Mormon Church is hierarchically organized with a prophet, the successor of Joseph Smith, and two counselors at the top of the organization. A council of Twelve Apostles helps and advises these main leaders, while a First Quorum of Seventy is mainly concerned with missionary activity. The priesthoods of Aaron and Melchizedek are open to Mormon men, the former being concerned with preparing members to be worthy and faithful ministers, the latter for those elders who are invested with power and authority in the Church. On a local level, the Church is divided into wards (parishes) and stakes (dioceses).[82]

The ward church is the center of Mormon life and culture. Regular Sunday services include the commemoration of the Lord's Supper at which bread and water (not wine) are blessed and received. The ritual of baptism is carried out by immersion. The heart of Mormon worship is, however, the Temple, which is open only to Mormons who are in good standing. In the Temple the most significant rituals take place, namely, baptism of the dead (by proxy), endowments (spiritual blessings), and sealings (of marriages).[83] The secret initiation ritual, at which a person is ritually washed, anointed with oil, and dressed in white Temple garments, is said to be similar to Masonic rites. Mormons further adhere to a rigid moral code. Sex is strictly limited to marriage partners. Modesty of dress and abstinence from alcohol, tobacco, tea, and coffee are the norms.

Given the uniqueness of Mormon beliefs and practices, many scholars have debated whether Mormonism can be called a Christian Church. Some have labeled it a marginal Protestant Church, or an alternative

Christian movement. Others see it as an entirely new religion or a mixture of Judaic, Christian, and Pagan ideas and practices. Jan Shipps refuses to make a judgment on the matter and counts "within the definition of Christian any church, sectarian movement, liberal or conservative coalition, or new religious tradition that gathers persons together in the name of Christ."[84] Whatever the correct answer might be, Mormonism has definitely introduced a number of beliefs and practices that were either unheard of in, or rejected by, traditional Christianity. Mormonism has certainly inherited a lot from the Judeo-Christian tradition, which, together with ideas taken from elsewhere and with different interpretations of several basic Christian tenets, has made it a unique American religion. Its appeal does not seem to have subsided. Rodney Stark, a leading sociologist of religion, thinks that it is the fastest growing new religion in the world and is well on the way to becoming a universal faith.[85]

The reaction to Mormonism by most Christian Churches has always been negative. Like many contemporary religious movements, it has been attacked as a system that promotes heresy and immorality,[86] and it has been criticized for building a financial empire.[87] Yet the story of Mormonism can be cited as an excellent illustration of how new religions can manage to survive over a period of time by actually changing and adapting, under social pressure, to more conventional standards. There is some evidence that several of the new religious movements might be undergoing a similar process. In the modern world, where individual freedom and independence are cherished virtues, new religious movements cannot convert populations by physical force; in an open society, psychological and intellectual pressures to accept a new faith can hardly produce many conversions. Consequently, the new religions are faced with the options of adapting, in part at least, to the dominant culture, remaining an insignificant minority, or simply ceasing to exist.

The Lessons of History

This brief survey of select major religious movements throughout Western history leads to the conclusion that these groups have shared similar ideologies and behavioral patterns. Even though there are significant differences between contemporary religious movements and those that preceded them in the past,[88] alternative (unorthodox) and marginal religious systems of all ages have exhibited similar trends. Patterns of strictness or laxity in lifestyle have appeared again and again in new movements. Secrecy, enthusiasm, a sense of elitism, and a quest for an experiential knowledge of the divine have been features recurring with almost uncanny regularity. The reaction of the established traditions to their beliefs and activities has always been one of fear, suspicion, antagonism, and persecution. Christianity itself was subjected to a similar treatment in the Roman Empire before the Emperor Constantine, by his Edict of Milan (A.D. 313), tolerated Christian worship. In fact, it has been argued that Christianity in its first three centuries was a "high intensity cult movement."[89]

Not many new religious movements, however, have survived the course of history. Many of those that did went through a process of change that eventually led them to adopt rather traditional religious forms of behavior and activity. The main lesson of history is that the presence of new religions should not be a cause for fear and panic. New religious groups more often than not present a challenge rather than a threat to mainline society and religion. Their presence might appear menacing because they succeed in capturing the imagination and attention of many young adults, and their activities and beliefs are, at times, shrouded in mystery. Moreover, since there are no antidotes to the rise of new religious movements, no established and proven ways to respond to them effectively, and no known techniques for suppressing them or curtailing their activities without endangering religious liberty, many people might feel intimidated or alarmed by their modest successes. History shows, however, that the number of new religious movements that have developed into world religions have been few. Those that survived have offered spiritual alternatives that have attracted relatively few people. The enthusiasm they generated waned in a rather short period of time. Few, if any, became a major threat to the dominant religious traditions.

Another lesson of history suggests that new religions are part and parcel of human cultural evolution. They are the natural outgrowths of social and religious developments, rather than sinister plots of evil cult leaders or Satanic concoctions aimed at the spiritual destruction of the human race. Their beliefs and practices may still be judged to be unacceptable by the mainline churches, but their presence might indirectly serve the function of keeping the major faiths alive. In other words, cults and sects could urge people to reexamine their own belief systems and moral standards. The religious faiths of the majority run the risk of being taken for granted, of becoming a matter of cultural routine, with the result that their adherents easily settle down to stagnant and uninspiring ideologies and lifestyles. The enthusiasm and devotion of members of new religious movements can be interpreted as a warning that traditional faiths could become too complacent.

Finally, history points to the evolving nature of religion and leads us to take a fresh look at religious change. In some Christian traditions (particularly Roman Catholicism) this is sometimes referred to as the "development of doctrine."[90] The new religions may point to future trends that could eventually be incorporated into the mainline churches. In the past, Western Christianity adopted and transformed Pagan philosophical ideas, beliefs, and customs of the ancient world. Can it also do the same with some of the values and practices that the new religious movements are propagating?

An example of this would be the current concern with the environment. Many New Age groups base their interest in preserving the Earth from pollution on a pantheistic view of the universe, a view that is not reconcilable with orthodox Christianity. It is quite possible, however, that such a concern with the environment can be based on quite traditional theological reflections. Rather than condemning those involved in the New Age movement for their unorthodox beliefs, one can attempt to harmonize environmental concern with a more traditional Judeo-Christian concept of a personal God who cares for creation and who has created human beings as stewards, rather than destroyers, of the Earth. A historical study of alternative religions in the West hints that, instead of adopting a belligerent attitude toward them, one can respond more reflectively and constructively to their presence and influence.

Notes

1. For a description of different kinds of beliefs regarding reincarnation, see E. C. Parrinder, "Varieties of Belief in Reincarnation," *Hibbert Journal* 5 (1957): 260–66.

2. A brief survey is provided by J. Bruce Long, "Reincarnation," in *Encyclopedia of Religion*, ed. Mircea Eliade (Chicago: Macmillan, 1987), vol. 12, pp. 265–69.

3. A typical example of this is Mark Albrecht, *Reincarnation: A Christian Appraisal* (Downers Grove, IL: Inter-Varsity Press, 1982). William J. Whalen, in his popular article,

"Reincarnation: Why Some People Expect to Make a Comeback," *US Catholic* 53 (August 1988): 33–39, observes, perhaps with a slight exaggeration, that the Catholic Church and its theologians have shown little interest in pursuing the matter. For various discussions on whether reincarnation could be harmonized with the Christian belief in the resurrection, see *Reincarnation or Resurrection?*, ed. Herman Haring and Johann-Baptist Metz (London: SCM Press, 1993).

4. Qunicy Howe, *Reincarnation for Christians* (Philadelphia: Westminster Press, 1974); and Geddes McGregor, *Reincarnation as a Christian Hope* (Totowa, NJ: Barnes and Noble/London: Macmillan, 1982).

5. See, for instance, George Gallup and Frank Newport, "Belief in Paranormal Phenomena Among Adult Americans," *Skeptical Inquirer* 15 (1991): 138, where it is recorded that 21 percent of the population in the United States of America believes in reincarnation. More recently, the Gallup Poll found that 24 percent believe in it. See *Index to International Public Opinion 1997–1998*, ed. Elizabeth Hann Hastings and Philip K. Hastings (Westport, CT: Greenwood Press, 1999), p. 392. The 1990 European Values Survey concluded that one-fifth believe in it. Confer Eileen Barker, "Whatever Next?: The Future of New Religious Movements," in *Religions Sans Frontières?: Present and Future Trends of Migration, Culture and Communication,* ed. Roberto Cipriani (Rome: Istituto Poligraphico e Zecca dello Stato, 1994), p. 371. For research on this issue done in England, see Tony Walter and Helen Waterhouse, "A Very Private Belief: Reincarnation in Contemporary Britain," *Sociology of Religion* 60 (1999): 187–97; and Tony Walter, "Reincarnation, Modernity, and Identity," *Sociology* 35 (2001): 21–38. See also Helen Waterhouse, "Reincarnation Belief in Britain: New Age Orientation or Mainstream Opinion," *Journal of Contemporary Religion* 14 (1999): 97–110.

6. For a short profile on Gnosticism, see Erin Potter, "Gnosticism" in Jeffrey K. Hadden's Web page http://religiousmovements.lib.virginia.edu/profiles (accessed December 15, 2002). For a brief, though somewhat sketchy, summary see B. A. Robinson, "Gnosticism: Ancient and Modern," http://www.religioustolerance.org/gnostic.htm (accessed December 15, 2002).

7. See, for example, R. Van den Broek and Wouter J Hanegraaff, *Gnosis and Hermeticism from Antiquity to Modern Times* (Albany: State University of New York, 1998).

8. Geo Windergren, *Mani and Manichaeism* (London: Weidenfeld and Nicolson, 1965).

9. Christopher McIntosh, *The Rosicrucians: The History, Mythology, and Rituals of an Occult Order* (Wellinborough, UK: Crucible, 1987).

10. See, for example, Stuart Holroyd, *The Elements of Gnosticism* (Shaftesbury, UK: Element, 1994), pp. 62ff.

11. Mary Carman Rose, "Christianity and the Gnostic Challenge," *Christian Century* 102 (November 13, 1985): 1030. Confer Ralph Moellering, "Ancient and Modern Gnosticism," *Currents in Theology and Mission* 10 (August 1983): 222–32; and Ellen Hinlicky and Paul Hinlicky, "Gnosticism: Old and New," *Dialog* 28, no. 1 (1989): 12–17. James M. Powell, "Gnosticism in the Thickets of Academe," *America* 165 (September 5, 1991): 194–95, maintains that Gnosticism is experiencing a revival in colleges and universities.

12. Robert Ellwood and Harry Partin, *Religious and Spiritual Groups in Modern America* (Englewood Cliffs, NJ: Prentice-Hall, 2nd ed., 1988), pp. 30ff.

13. Stephen A. Hoeller, "What Is a Gnostic?," *Gnosis: A Journal of Western Inner Traditions,* no. 23 (Spring 1992): 24. This quarterly journal, published since 1985, sometimes contains articles on Gnosticism and its Spring 1992 issue was dedicated to the subject. *Gnosis* ceased publication in 1999. Its publisher, the Lumen Foundation, still publishes several books on Gnosticism. See also Christopher Lasch, "Gnosticism, Ancient and Modern: The Religion of the Future?," *Salmagundi 96* (Fall 1992): 29–42.

14. For examples of these churches, consult the Web pages of the First Gnostic Church, http://www.1gnostics.com and Ecclesia Gnostica, http://www.gnosis.org/eghome.htm (accessed December 15, 2002). Both churches have several branches. Gordon Melton, in his *Encyclopedia of World Religions* (Detroit: Gale Research, 1999), pp. 736, 738, 761 describes several Gnostic Churches.

15. For descriptions of Gnostic beliefs and practices, see the following works: Kurt Rudolph, *Gnosis: The Nature and History of Gnosticism* (San Francisco: Harper and Row, 1983); Giovanni Filoramo, *A History of Gnosticism* (Oxford: Basil Blackwell, 1990); Gilles Quispel, "Gnosticism from Its Origins to the Middle Ages," in the *Encyclopedia of Religion,* vol. 5, pp. 566–74; John Glyndwr Harris, *Gnosticism: Beliefs and Practices* (Portland, OR/Sussex: Academic Press, 1999), pp. 87–125; and Holryod, *The Elements of Gnosticism.* For the major Gnostic writings consult Bentley Layton, ed., *The Gnostic Scriptures* (Garden City, NJ: Doubleday/London: SCM Press, 1987); and Willis Barnstone, ed., *The Other Bible* (San Francisco: Harper and Row, 1984).

16. See, for example, Alastair H. B. Logan, *Gnostic Truth and Christian Heresy: A Study in the History of Gnosticism* (Peabody, MA: Hendrickson, Publishers, 1996), where Gnostic theogony, cosmogony, anthropology, soteriology, and eschatology are dealt with in some detail.

17. There is a lot of debate as to how much syncretism is actually found in Gnosticism. See, for example, Simon Pétrement, *A Separate God: The Christian Origins of Gnosticism,* translated by Carol Harrison (San Francisco: HarperSanFrancisco, 1990).

18. Chas S. Clifton, "The Seed of Light: Gnosticism and Sacramental Sex," *Gnosis,* no. 23 (Spring 1992): 30–31.

19. Rudolph, *Gnosis,* p. 249.

20. Stephen O'Shea, *The Perfect Heresy: The Revolutionary Life and Death of the Medieval Cathars* (New York: Walker, 2000), p. 13.

21. O'Shea, *The Perfect Heresy.*

22. For an account of this crusade, see Zoé Oldenbourg, *Massacre at Montségur: A History of the Albigensian Crusade* (New York: Pantheon Books/London: Weidenfeld and Nicolson, 1961); Joseph R. Strayer, *The Albigensian Crusades* (New York: Dial Press, 1971); Jonathan Sumption, *The Albigensian Crusade* (London: Faber, 1978); and M. D. Costen, *The Cathars and the Albigensian Crusade* (Manchester, UK: Manchester University Press, 1997).

23. For a description of Cathar belief see Oldenbourg, *Massacre at Montségur,* pp. 28ff; Strayer, *The Albigensian Crusades,* pp. 26ff; and Harris, *Gnosticism,* pp. 87ff. See also Jacques

Madaule, *The Albigensian Crusade: An Historical Essay* (New York: Fordham University Press/London: Burns and Oates, 1967), pp. 30ff.

24. Malcolm Lambert, *The Cathars* (Oxford, UK: Blackwell, 1998), pp. 197–98.

25. See Strayer, *The Albigensian Crusades*, pp. 33–34; and Oldenbourg, *Massacre at Montségur*, pp. 44–48. Both books reproduce the rituals in appendices (Strayer, pp. 175–82; and Oldenbourg, pp. 369–70). Confer also Madaule, *The Albigensian Crusade*, pp. 45–50.

26. Strayer, *The Albigensian Crusades*, pp. 34–35.

27. Lambert, *The Cathars*, pp. 73ff.

28. Joseph McCabe, *The History of Flagellation: The Whip as an Instrument of Punishment, Torture, Self-Beatings, Religion and Erotic Stimulation* (Girard, KS: Haldeman-Julius Publications, 1946).

29. F. J. Courtney, "Flagellants" in the *New Catholic Encyclopedia*, ed. David Eggenberger (New York: McGraw-Hill, 1967), vol. 5, pp. 594–95; and Kenneth C. Russell, "Asceticism," in *The New Dictionary of Catholic Spirituality*, ed. Michael Downey (Collegeville, MN: Liturgical Press, 1993), pp. 63–65.

30. Russell, "Asceticism," p. 64.

31. Quoted by Rufus M. Jones, "Flagellants," in *Encyclopedia of Religion and Ethics*, ed. James Hastings, John Alexander Selbie, and Louis H. Gray (New York: Charles Scribner's Sons, 1925–35), vol. 6, p. 50.

32. Norman Cohn, *The Pursuit of the Millennium* (London: Secker and Warburg, 1957), especially pp. 131–33.

33. See Carlos E. Caries, ed., *The Penitentes of New Mexico* (New York: Arno Press, 1974). This book reprints three major studies on the *Penitentes* of New Mexico: (1) Alex M. Darley, *The Passionisis of the Southwest, or The Holy Brotherhood* (1893); (2) Alice Corbin Henderson, *Brothers of Light: The Penitentes of the Southwest* (1937); and (3) Dorothy Woodward, *The Penitentes of New Mexico* (1935).

34. See Woodward, *The Penitentes of New Mexico*, pp. 100–103. Woodward gives six theories that have been proposed to explain the presence of these brotherhoods in the southwestern parts of the United States and finds them all wanting. Her view is that their origin should be traced to religious confraternities. See also Marta Weigle, *The Penitentes of the Southwest* (Santa Fe, NM: Ancient City Press, 1970), pp. 3–13.

35. Confer Courtney, "Flagellants," in *The New Catholic Encyclopedia*, vol. 5, p. 595.

36. For the ritual observances of these *Penitentes* see Weigle, *The Penitentes of the Southwest*, pp. 26ff.

37. Nichole L. Ashby, "En Divina Luz: In Divine Light," *Humanities* 16 (July–August 1995): 31.

38. Weigle, *The Penitentes of the Southwest*, p. 13.

39. See Charles Aranda, *The Penitente Papers* (published privately in Albuquerque, NM, c. 1960). This booklet contains the constitutions of, and ecclesiastical documents relating to, one particular *Penitente* organization, the Brothers of Our Lord Jesus the Nazarene. In spite of their reputation to the contrary, this brotherhood has been declared to be in good standing in the Catholic Church.

40. See, for example, Alberto l. Pulido, *The Sacred World of the Penitentes* (Washington, DC: Smithsonian Institute Press, 2000).

41. Confer Michael Mullet, *Radical Religious Movements in Early Modern Europe* (London: George Allen and Unwin, 1980); Christopher Hill, *The World Turned Upside Down: Radical Ideas During the English Revolution* (New York: Viking Press/London: Temple Smith, 1972); and F. D. Dow, *Radicalism in the English Revolution, 1640–1660* (Oxford: Basil Blackwell, 1985), especially chap. 4, "The Religious Situation," pp. 57–73.

42. Christopher Hill, Barry Reay, and William Lamont, *The World of the Muggletonians* (London: Temple Smith, 1983).

43. Alastair Hamilton, *The Family of Love* (Cambridge, UK: J. Clarke, 1981); and Christopher W. Marsh, *The Family of Love in English Society, 1550–1630* (Cambridge: Cambridge University Press, 1994).

44. See Henry Noel Brailsford, *The Levellers in the English Revolution* (Stanford, CA: Stanford University Press, 1961); and D. B. Robinson, *The Religious Foundations of Leveller Democracy* (New York: King's Crown Press, 1951).

45. Elbert Russell, *The History of Quakerism* (New York: Macmillan, 1942).

46. For some basic works on the Ranters, see Norman Cohn, "The Ranters: The 'Underground' in the England of 1656," *Encounter* 34 (April 1970): 15–25, and Cohn, *The Pursuit of the Millennium*, pp. 315–72; G. F. S. Ellens, "The Ranters Ranting: Reflections on a Ranting Counter-Culture," *Church History* 40 (1971): 91–107; A. L. Morton, *The World of the Ranters: Religious Radicalism in the English Revolution* (London: Lawrence and Wishart, 1970); Jerome Friedman, *Blasphemy, Immorality, and Anarchy: The Ranters and the English Revolution* (Athens: Ohio University Press, 1987).

47. For a collection of Ranter writings see Nigel Smith, ed., *A Collection of Ranter Writings from the 17th Century* (London: Junction Books, 1983).

48. See Friedman, *Blasphemy, Immorality, and Anarchy*, where several chapters are devoted to each type of Ranter distinguished by the author.

49. Morton, *The World of the Ranters*, p. 75.

50. Cohn, "The Ranters," pp. 19–20.

51. Leonard W. Levy, *Ranters Run Amok: And Other Adventures in the History of Law* (Chicago: Ivan R. Dee, 2000), p. 6.

52. Ellens, "The Ranters Ranting," p. 98. For a study of Coppe's preaching as a form of rhetoric of "manic enthusiasm," see Clement Hawes, *Mania and Literary Style: The Rhetoric of Enthusiasm from the Ranters to Christopher Smart* (Cambridge: Cambridge University Press, 1996), pp. 77–97.

53. Confer Morton, *The World of the Ranters*, pp. 102–3; and Smith, *A Collection of Ranter Writings from the Seventeenth Century*, pp. 14ff.

54. Ellens, "The Ranters Ranting," p. 97.

55. Ellens, "The Ranters Ranting," p. 107. Cohn, "The Ranters" (p. 25), compares the Ranters not only with the hippies but also with the Manson cult.

56. Morton, *The World of the Ranters*, pp. 101ff. The doctrines of the Ranters, for example, were attacked in many pamphlets. Some of the accusations against them, which

included the far-fetched views that they were Royalist agents or Jesuits in disguise, could hardly be backed by concrete evidence.

57. "Ranters," in *Encyclopaedia of Religion and Ethics,* ed. James Hastings, vol. 10, p. 587.

58. Confer, for example, André Haynal, Niklós Molnár, and Gerard de Puvmêge, *Fanaticism: A Historical and Psychoanalytic Study* (New York: Schocken Books, 1983); and Ronald 0. Clarke, "The Narcissistic Guru: A Profile of Bhagwan Shree Rajneesh," *Free Inquiry* 8 (Spring 1988): 33–35.

59. J. C. Davis, *Fear, Myth and History: The Ranters and the Historians* (Cambridge: Cambridge University Press, 1986).

60. J. C. Davis, "Fear, Myth, and History: Reappraising the 'Ranters'," *Past and Present,* no. 129 (1990): 79–103.

61. See J. F. McGregor, Barnard Capp, Nigel Smith, and B. J. Gibbons, "Debate: Fear, Myth and Furore: Reappraising the 'Ranters,'" *Past and Present,* no. 140 (1993): 155–94; and J. C. Davis, "Reply," *Past and Present,* no. 140 (1993): 94–210.

62. G. E. Aylmer, "Did the Ranters Exist?," *Past and Present,* no. 117 (1968): 208–19.

63. F. McGregor, "Seekers and Ranters," in *Radical Religion in the English Reformation,* ed. J. F. McGregor and B. Reay (New York: Oxford University Press, 1984), p. 122.

64. For examples of writers who believe that there are many Satanic cults today who practice the most heinous rituals, see Carl A. Raschke, *Painted Black: From Drug Killings to Heavy Metal: The Alarming Story of How Satanism Is Threatening Our Communities* (San Francisco: Harper and Row, 1990). Almost all of the contributors to the Spring 1994 issue of the *Journal of Psychohistory* insist that disclosures of Satanic rituals are describing actual occurrences. On the other side, many have argued that beliefs expressed in these rituals are mythological or folkloristic in nature. Confer James T. Richardson, Joel Best, and David G. Bromley, eds., *The Satanism Scare* (New York: Aldine de Gruyter, 1991); Jeffrey S. Victor, *Satanic Panic: The Creation of a Contemporary Legend* (Chicago: Open Court, 1993); and Philip Jenkins, *Intimate Enemies: Moral Panics in Contemporary Britain* (New York: Aldine de Gruyter, 1992). Various views surrounding the controversy of Satanic beliefs and practices can be found in Tamara L. Roleff, ed., *Satanism* (San Diego, CA: Greenhaven Press, 2002).

65. The most thorough treatment of this Jewish religious movement and its founder is Gershom Scholem's massive work, *Sabbatai Sevi: The Mystical Messiah, 1627–1676* (Princeton, NJ: Princeton University Press, 1973). See also his shorter essay "Shabbatai Zevi" in *Encyclopaedia Judaica,* ed. Cecil Roth (Jerusalem: Keter Publishing House, 1972), vol. 14, pp. 1219–54; and Joseph Kastein, *The Messiah of Ismir: Sabbatai Zevi* (New York: Viking Press, 1931).

66. Zevi delved more precisely into Lurianic Kabbala, which represented the original and novel teachings of Issac Luria Ashkenazai (1534–1572). See Scholem, *Sabbatai Sevi,* pp. 23ff. Scholem provides an overview of the Kabbala in his essay, "Kabbalah," in *Encyclopaedia Judaica,* vol. 10, pp. 649–54.

67. For various reactions to this apostasy, see Scholem, *Sabbatai Sevi,* pp. 691ff.

68. One such group has been traced to Greece where a small band of followers continued to pray to him in secret ceremonies. Confer Michael Shapiro, *The Jewish 100: A Ranking of the Most Influential Jews of All Time* (New York: Citadel Press, 2000), p. 242.

69. Shapiro, *The Jewish 100*, pp. 239–42.

70. See Scholem, *Sabbatai Sevi*, p. 126.

71. Confer, Scholem, *Sabbatai Sevi*, pp. 1–8, for a discussion of the causes leading to the rise of Zevi's movement.

72. Whitney B. Cross, *The Burned-Over District: The Social and Intellectual History in Western New York, 1800–1850* (Ithaca, NY: Cornell University Press, 1950); and Michael Barkum, *The Crucible of the Millennium: The Burned-Over District of New York in the 1840s* (Syracuse, NY: Syracuse University Press, 1986).

73. J. Stillson Judah, *The History and Philosophy of the Metaphysical Movements in America* (Philadelphia: Westminster Press, 1967).

74. See, for instance, Joe Maxwell, "New Kingdom of the Cults," *Christianity Today* 36 (January 13, 1992): 37–40. The author examines the missionary work of many Christian sects and new religions in Eastern Europe and accuses the Mormons of deceiving would-be Christians.

75. For a brief summary of the origins and history of the Church and its various institutions see Dean L. May, "Mormons," in *Mormons and Mormonism: An Introduction to an American World Religion*, ed. Eric A. Eliason (Chicago: University of Illinois Press, 2001), pp. 47–75.

76. For a history of Mormonism, the following works may be consulted: James B. Allen and Glen B. Leonard, *The Story of the Latter-day Saints* (Salt Lake City, UT: Desert Book, 1976); Leonard J. Arrington and David Bitton, *The Mormon Experience: History of the Latter-day Saints* (New York: Alfred Knopf/London: Allen and Unwin, 1979); and Jan Shipps, *Mormonism: The Story of a New Religious Tradition* (Champaign: University of Illinois Press, 1985). *The Encyclopedia of Mormonism*, ed. Daniel Ludlow (New York: Macmillan, 1992), vol. 2, pp. 598–647, provides several relatively short surveys of the history of Mormonism. For recording, cataloguing, and assessing historical interpretations of the Church of Later-day Saints see the works of Ronald W. Walker, David J. Whittaker, and James B. Allen, *Studies in Mormon History, 1830–1997: An Indexed Bibliography* (Chicago: University of Illinois Press, 2000) and *Mormon History* (Chicago: University of Illinois Press, 2001).

77. Steven Shields, *Divergent Paths of the Restoration* (Bountiful, UT: Restoration Research, 1985), gives a comprehensive account of the over one hundred Mormon sects that have come into being over the years.

78. For a summary of Mormon beliefs, Thomas F. O'Dea's *The Mormons* (Chicago: University of Chicago Press, 1957) is still one of the better books on the subject.

79. See Stephen E. Robinson, "God the Father" in *Encyclopedia of Mormonism*, vol. 2, pp. 548–51.

80. Several short articles covering different aspects of Mormon Christology can be found in the *Encyclopedia of Mormonism*, vol. 2, pp. 723–53.

81. See Bruce Douglas Porter, "Church of Jesus Christ of Latter-day Saints" in *Encyclopedia of Mormonism*, vol. 1, pp. 276–80.

82. O'Dea, *The Mormons*, pp. 155ff. See also: William C. Hartle, "Organizational and Administrative History," and Lee Tom Perry, Paul M. Bons, and Alan L. Wilkins, "Con-

temporary Organization," both in *Encyclopedia of Mormonism*, vol. 3, pp. 1035–44 and 1044–49 respectively.

83. For a short descriptions of these rituals see, H. David Burton, "Baptism of the Dead," Alma P. Burton, "Endowment," and Paul V. Hyde, "Temple Sealings," in *Encyclopedia of Mormonism*, vol. 1, pp. 95–96, vol. 2, pp. 454–54, and vol. 3, pp. 1289–90, respectively.

84. Jan Shipps, "Is Mormonism Christian?: Reflections on a Complicated Question," in *Mormons and Mormonism*, ed. Eric A. Eliason (Chicago: University of Illinois Press, 2001), p. 97.

85. "The Rise of a New World Faith," *Review of Religious Research* 26 (1985–86): 18–27. Confer William M. Kephart, *Extraordinary Groups: An Examination of Unconventional Lifestyles* (New York: St. Martin's Press, 1987), pp. 262–63.

86. Gary L. Ward, ed., *Evangelical Christian Anti-Mormonism in the Twentieth Century* (New York: Garland, 1990). See also John A. Saliba, "Mormonism in the Twenty-First Century," *Studia Missionalia* 41 (1992): 59–62.

87. John Heinerman and Anson D. Shupe, in the preface to their book *The Mormon Corporate Empire* (Boston: Beacon Press, 1985), p. x, write: "The Mormon financial/political enterprise is not simply an American success story but rather an ongoing crusade to reshape our society and its democratic traditions."

88. See Bryan Wilson, "Historical Lessons in the Study of Sects and Cults" in *Religion and the Social Order: The Handbook of Sects and Cults in America*, ed. David C. Bromley and Jeffrey K. Hadden (New York: JAI Press, 1993), vol. 3A, pp. 53–74.

89. D. James Atwood and Ronald B. Flowers, "Early Christianity as a Cult Movement," *Encounter* 44 (Summer 1983): 245–61.

90. Thomas P. Rausch, "Development of Doctrine," in *The New Dictionary of Theology*, ed. Joseph A. Komonchak, Mary Collins, and Dermot A. Lane (Wilmington, DE: Michael Glazier/Dublin: Gill and Macmillan, 1987), pp. 280–83; and Candido Pozo, "Development of Dogma" in *Sacramentum Mundi: An Encyclopedia of Theology*, ed. Karl Rahner et al. (New York: Herder and Herder, 1968), vol. 2, pp. 98–102. For a Protestant perspective consult Nicholas Lash, "Development, Doctrine," in *The Westminster Dictionary of Christian Theology*, ed. Alan Richardson and John Bowden (Philadelphia: Westminster Press, 1983), pp. 155–56.

THE NEW RELIGIOUS MOVEMENTS IN PSYCHOLOGICAL PERSPECTIVE

One of the most frequently asked questions about the new religions is what kind of person is attracted to their ideals, beliefs, and practices. Many people find it hard to understand the factors and motives that might lead young adults to abandon a traditional and respected religious faith community in order to accept an unconventional ideology and to adopt an unusual religious lifestyle.

Professional psychologists and psychiatrists who have studied involvement in fringe religions have also directed their queries to the type of person who is attracted to them. Is there a "cult" personality? Is there a specific temperamental and attitudinal makeup that renders an individual liable to seek membership in groups such as the Hare Krishna movement, the Unification Church, The Children of God ("The Family"), Scientology, or a fundamentalist Christian Church? One might further ask what kind of training or education a person receives once he or she has joined a new religion. Is this training comparable to the normal socialization or enculturation[1] one goes through in any society or educational system?

A second area of investigation deals with the way in which a young adult joins a new movement. Does the decision to become a member constitute a free choice? Or is the individual in such a psychological condition that his or her powers of making an autonomous, knowledgeable choice are severely impaired? Or are there outside pressures that bear so heavily upon an individual's judgment that one's entrance into a new religion is accomplished by means of subtle manipulation and/or coercion?

These questions bear on the ongoing debate about the mental health of those who opt for life in a new religion and who have been members for a while.[2] Do the new religions attract the weak and vulnerable who are unable to cope with the problems of life? In other words, is entry into a marginal religious group symptomatic of unresolved psychological problems? Moreover, one often hears of the drastic changes that people undergo after they have joined an alternative religion. What effects can a rigid, strict, and tightly controlled communal regime have on the well-being of its members? Is the radical change in ideology and lifestyle beneficial or detrimental to one's mental and emotional development?

There is also evidence that sexual and other forms of abuse have been observed in a few new religious movements. The case of the treatment of children in some of the schools run by the International Society for Krishna Consciousness in the 1970s and 1980s is well documented.[3] Even fundamentalist Christian Churches have been criticized for being abusive toward their members not only in their efforts to achieve total control over their lives but also in the harsh punishments often inflicted upon children.[4] These cases must be taken into account even though they may well be exceptions, rather than the rule. Studies by Lawrence Lilliston and Gary Shepherd[5] on children in the Hare Krishna movement and in the Church Universal and Triumphant found no fewer psychological problems than those recorded among children in the general population.

Psychological and psychiatric studies present conflicting answers to these nagging questions. One the one hand, there are many reports, confirmed by scholarly research, that members of new religions have given up the use of drugs, alcohol consumption, and other harmful habits to which they were previously addicted. This is especially the case with groups fostering some kind of meditation technique, often borrowed from Eastern religions. Studies on the positive psychological and mental effects of meditation are numerous.[6] Devoted members give testimony to these kinds of achievements. Some new movements, in fact, attempt to attract candidates by the promise of a happier and healthier life free of all personal and social problems.

One the other hand, many ex-cult members insist that membership in a new religious movement produced deleterious effects on their personalities and intellectual performances.[7] Further, some psychologists and psychiatrists are concerned about the psychological and social changes that follow entry to a new religious movement. They have routinely diagnosed ex-members as psychologically weak or sick individuals who, because of their commitment, have lost interest in both intellectual and mundane matters and become slavish followers of their religious leaders or superiors.

The popular image of cult members, an image heavily influenced by Flo Conway and Jim Siegleman's book[8] on conversion to the new religions, is that of "hypnotized" or "brainwashed" individuals or mindless robots who are in an induced trance state.[9] Members of new religious movements are depicted as young adults who have been rendered unable to think for themselves and to make the simplest decisions about their own lives. This caricature of "glassy-eyed zombies" has survived both in the media, pop culture, and in psychiatric literature. It has, however, found little acceptance by sociologists. Robert Balch,[10] writing on a UFO religion, thinks that the zombie look of its members was actually a front purposely put on by its members to ward off evil spirits. Fred Emil Katz, reflecting on the tragedy of Heaven's Gate, remarks that "by all evidence, the Heaven's Gate cultists did not act like zombies, devoid of all will of their own."[11]

The view that draws attention to the destructive effects that result from membership in new religions must be seen in the context of the negative evaluation of religion that has dominated the psychological disciplines for decades. Recent research has shown, however, that religion may be a constituent element in one's mental and psychological health.[12] Changes in the evaluation of the effects of cult membership are in harmony with the changing attitude toward religion among many psychologists. This is evidenced in the more positive treatment of both religion and cults in the most recent edition of the *Diagnostic and Statistical Manual of Mental Disorders IV.*[13]

The Psychological Profile of a "Cult" Joiner

The study of personality is a major research area in psychology. The structure and development of personality, the cataloging of human motives, the listing of various character typologies, and the criteria for mental health have all been of continuing psychological interest.[14] Among the many factors that are usually considered are early childhood, unconscious processes, intrapsychic conflicts, structural constructs, and anxiety and defense mechanisms.[15] Psychologists studying the new religions have used most of these elements in their efforts to profile those individuals who join new religions. Many cult members, with apparently little evaluation of the change they were contemplating and with even less advice from peers or experts, have embarked on a lifestyle that might drastically change their behavioral patterns, modes of thought, and interpersonal relationships. Is it possible to delineate the personality features and issues that lead a person to go in search of a "deviant" lifestyle and/or to respond positively to the recruitment efforts of the new religions?

Reactions to the new movements vary enormously. Many people seem to ignore their presence and most are unresponsive to their overtures. Their knowledge about them might be limited to what they read in an occasional magazine article or a newspaper or television report. It would appear that the proselytizing efforts of the new movements elicit more feelings of revulsion, ridicule, or sheer curiosity, then fanatic admiration, irresistible attraction, sincere concern, or genuine interest. A majority of those who are inquisitive enough to follow up their first contacts with members of the new religious movements with a closer look at their activities and living conditions never actually join.

Reports from scholars who have investigated defections from the new religions indicate that the turnover rate in the majority of them is rather high.[16] What psychological factors influence defections from new religious movements? Why is it that others persevere in their new vocational callings? And are personality traits one of the factors that must be taken into account when studying the reasons why people stay or leave? Several efforts have been made to create a psychological profile of a young adult who is more likely to be drawn to the new movements. Representative of such profiles is the one suggested by the American Psychiatric Association:[17]

> The white middle-class, idealistic young people who form the majority in most contemporary cults are often lonely, depressed, and fearful of an uncertain future. They tend to be dependent. They have strong needs for affection. Unable to provide for their own emotional sustenance, they need external sources for a feeling of self-worth, a sense of belonging, and a reason for living. They feel resentful and are often openly hostile towards society at large; it has disappointed them and does not value them. The freedoms as well as the demands of young adulthood, eagerly awaited by many, may be overwhelming to them.

It is generally assumed that a combination of the following and possibly other overlapping factors could lead a person to search for an alternative lifestyle and/or render him or her more open to the recruitment techniques and evangelization efforts of the new religions.

The Deprived Individual

One of the common theories of cult formation, accepted by many psychologists and sociologists, is that members of new religions are deprived young adults who are seeking satisfaction for their various needs.[18] This approach starts with a functional definition of religion and argues that religious revivals and movements come into being to satisfy practical human needs that are not being met, to help people cope with new problems, and to act as a catalyst for religious change.[19]

A typical psychological application of the functional theory is exemplified by Frank MacHovec who maintains that participation in a marginal religious group satisfies the need for safety and security as well as the human longing for emotional support and approval. He writes:

> Uncertain of the future, with career and life goals neither clearly seen nor firmly established, cults provided a packaged personality, and the illusion of security in a comfortable, orderly structure and safe, nonthreatening, noncompetitive, predictable, repeated routine. Acceptance, approval, and affection from self-assured, enthusiastic, persuasive "new friends" with answers and commitment seem to fill the void and give life new meaning.[20]

If one tries to locate the social deprivations that may influence the individual to join a new religion, one runs into some serious difficulties. Most members of these religions come from an economically advantaged family background. Unlike the many sects and cults of the nineteenth century that, generally speaking, attracted the uneducated and socioeconomically underprivileged, contemporary groups have recruited their adherents largely from the middle and upper social strata. Members of new religions typically come from families that have all the material benefits of modern culture. Their parents are well educated and they themselves have either begun or completed their college education. They have been brought up thinking in terms of following a career, getting married and raising a family, and finding a respectable and comfortable niche in society. They are not economically, socially, or educationally deprived.

It is precisely this advantageous background of the members of new religious movements that makes it even harder to explain why people become involved with them. From the point of view of contemporary culture, new religions appear to have little to offer. The rejection of one's family ties and culture for commitment to a seemingly bizarre religious group that curtails or cuts off completely the neophytes' links with their past, seems, not surprisingly, both rash and unintelligible. Such behavior appears irrational and clamors for an explanation that exonerates the individual from his or her choice and the parents from any blame.

It is also arguable that contemporary young adults may have all the material benefits society can offer and still be disadvantaged or deprived in many other respects. An individual who is highly educated can be searching for truth and meaning in his or her life. Those who have grown up in a family where finances were never a problem might find themselves lacking in genuine caring for the needy and for those who are the victims of social injustice. It is possible that the young adult who pledges commitment in a new religious movement is both ethically and spiritually deprived.

The theory that individuals join new religions because they suffer from various deprivations is far from self-evident. One of its main difficulties is that it fails to take into account the fact that many people still find support and security in more traditional religious and social institutions, which have, after all, been satisfying human needs for centuries. Christian missionaries have preached their faith among many deprived people, of whom only a relatively small number converted.[21] Even though a person might be considered deprived by most members of society, she or he might not *experience* deprivation.[22]

The theory of deprivation, however, has attractive features and has been repeatedly employed by scholars with diverse academic backgrounds to explain why people join new movements in different cultural situations and historical periods. Some researchers have argued that, in spite of its invalidity as a social theory, deprivation can be used to explain why people join some new religions. S. Dein and H. Barlow have applied the theory to explain conversions to the Hare Krishna movement, whose members do not suffer from a higher rate of mental illness than is found in society at large. They point out that members "do not speak in terms of beliefs such as freedom from reincarnation, but rather in terms of vague psychological *experiences* of the psychological benefits which include sense of meaning, sense of belonging, peace and harmony, and freedom from material desires." And they conclude "that some form of *existential* deprivation (sense of anomie, lack of meaning in life) may be important for joining the movement."[23] The same theory has its adherents outside the field of the psychological sciences. It has been adopted by some mainline churches,[24] to account for, in part at least, the success of the marginal movements in contemporary culture.

The Alienated Individual

Alienation, especially social and political dissatisfaction, in modern Western society has been the subject of intensive studies by both psychologists[25] and sociologists.[26] Its causes include sociological factors, psychological disturbances, and religious aspects.[27] Fritz Pappenheim maintains that there are three related types of alienation—from the self, from other people, and from the world. In modern societies alienation has become "more intense and widespread, actually turning into a dominant trend."[28] Some scholars[29] have suggested that adolescents from traditional families with strong religious backgrounds were more alienated than their peers and, therefore, might be more open to consider religious options different from those in which they have been reared. Others[30] think that alienation among adolescents is influenced more by religious factors than by gender and ethnicity.[31] Adolescents appear to be more prone to alienation, which might explain why the majority of those attracted to new religious movements are young adults.

Alienation refers primarily to the experience of strangeness or separateness. It is a feeling that one doesn't belong to, nor has warm relationships with, one's peers, family, or society. Low self-esteem, lack of primary relationships, and personal failure and dissatisfaction are the main elements that have been linked with alienation. Marginal groups, such as Satanic cults, violent street gangs, neo-Nazi skinhead movements, terrorist organizations, and gay people are said to be havens for alienated people.[32]

People who join new religions can be characterized as having gone through a socialization process marred by discord. The young adult who is attracted to a marginal religion is one whose socialization in the values and mores of society has been far from smooth. This painful introduction to the culture of one's birth could have been the result of a variety of factors, including insecurity, tension, and conflict within the family, inappropriate educational training, and unpleasant experiences in the context of the family's religious practices. The presence of these unfavorable conditions may have caused the young adult to become an alienated, disgruntled individual who does not feel at home in his or her family, religion, or society.

It is important to stress that alienation is perceived as preceding and not following involvement, even if this involvement may render the sense of alienation more acute and sharply defined. The acceptance of a substitute family that new religions offer, the demand of total allegiance, and a different sociocultural milieu that stresses separation from the rest of society follow the partial or complete rejection of, or dissatisfaction with, the culture of one's upbringing. The new religions simply provide an alternative to an individual who has already lost, or is seriously questioning, his or her roots.

The concept of alienation is particularly useful when examining the family problems that come to the fore whenever a family member joins a new religion. There is no doubt that membership in a new religion either creates or aggravates family problems and tensions. A crisis in family relationships can come to a head when a family member converts to another church or religion. One still hears of the occasional case when parents break off all contact with their offspring who marry outside the church or religion in which they were raised. The new religions have added a new dimension to the family situation, not only because they are perceived as atypical and aberrant forms of human behavior, but also because they have been causally connected with mental illness or psychological weakness.

It would, however, be naive to conceive of the new religions mainly as disrupters of family life. Joining a new movement might be an indicator that all is not well at home. While there is an ongoing debate about the ideal form of family life, there is little argument that the institution of the family has undergone, for better or for worse, substantial changes over the past few decades. Empirical research has established that the form, role, and functions of the family are in the process of change. There seems to be agreement on several areas related to the family. First, many of the traditional functions of the family, such as education and social control, have been transferred to, or are shared with, other institutions in society. Second, the roles of men and women have been altered considerably, particularly because of the increasing number of women entering the workforce and pursuing educational and professional careers. And third, modern medicine has increased control over human sexual functions and indirectly buttressed the conviction that sex should not be limited to married couples or necessarily linked with procreation. The consequences of these and other changes that are influencing family life have been enormous. The traditional institution of the family has been showing signs of a breakdown long before the new religions emerged as a problem in the early 1970s. The contemporary family faces many difficulties or crises that are unrelated to the rise of new religions.[33]

Given this situation, joining an alternative religious group could be but one expression of current family issues. It might connote a rejection of parental authority and value systems as well as a need for a strong, male authority that the family might not have provided. It would be an oversimplification to assert that adverse family relations are always the direct or immediate cause of involvement in an alternative religion. Those seeking an explanation of why people join cults should, however, carefully investigate the family conditions that definitely affect children. Many people actually find in their new faith communities substitute families and parents who are considered better than the natural ones. Although one might disagree with the young adults' evaluation of their family lives, one cannot dismiss the fact that the changing institution of the family in the Western world has contributed to the alienation of young men and women who might seek refuge in different religious or social groups.

The theory of alienation may also throw light on the seemingly abrupt manner in which many young adults reportedly join a new religious movement. It explains why parents, relatives, and friends are repeatedly caught unaware when they find out that the people they thought they knew so well have decided to become members of a new religion or have joined a religious commune. Young adults who are alienated from their families or in conflict with their parents do not normally discuss their personal difficulties at home. Nor do they mention to their parents their interests in exploring the nontraditional lifestyle of a particular new religious movement or commune.

CHAPTER THREE

The Religiously Inclined Person

Another psychological trait of those who seek entrance in new cults is their interest in religious and philosophical matters. Although ideology may not be the main feature that first attracts a person to a new religion, there are some indications that would-be cult members are more religiously inclined than their peers. Many adolescents have a need to adhere to definite beliefs and to belong to a community of faith that enables them to cope better with the difficulties they encounter during the course of their lives.[34] Some scholars have suggested that the person who joins a new religion may be motivated by the desire to be a "world saver."[35] In other words, he or she feels that the world is in need of salvation and that something must be done to avoid a disaster. Utopianism and millenarianism are two ways in which such a concern has frequently expressed itself. The coming of the millennium or the golden age and the imminent advent of a catastrophe have been proclaimed innumerable times over the past thirty-five years by prophets, religious leaders, psychics, and astrologers. Whether such religiously motivated and inspired concerns and emotionally charged preoccupations are healthy, and whether the enthusiastic, and at times frantic, response to such prophecies of doom denote a serious mental and/or psychological weakness, are debatable.

In order to understand how an individual develops such a religious attitude, one has to look briefly at the cultural condition of the second half of twentieth century. Several distinctive qualities of the contemporary scene are obvious. Most people today cannot live in isolation from other faiths or religions. Mass communications, increased mobility, and a shared educational system have made it inevitable that people learn about, and sometimes confront, alien religious traditions. The manner in which religion is taught in many contemporary schools exposes many children and young adults to different religious options before they are securely grounded in one faith.[36] Besides, many people, who have little knowledge about their own faith and less expertise about defending it, have to face enthusiastic evangelizers seeking to convert them to alternative lifestyles and spiritualities.

Moreover, Western culture places a great stress on individual choice. Young adults are encouraged to be independent and to make their own decisions, even if they are expected to consult and inform their parents. Religious freedom could easily be expressed in rebellion against the religion of one's upbringing. For many people, especially young adults, religion has become a commodity that one investigates, explores, and chooses, and not just accepts from one's parents or teachers. One's own personal experience is accorded priority over conformity.

When studying Western society one must also consider the process of secularization, which removes or dissociates religious expressions, beliefs, and symbols from public life. Religiously inclined individuals may find it hard to express openly their religious ideas and spiritual experiences. They might feel pressured to live a dual existence. On the one hand, they pursue a private one that is religious and concerned with the sacred. On the other hand, they follow a civil one that is not only disinterested in such matters, but also seemingly based on the assumption that there is no place for religion in modern life.

Given these cultural conditions, it is not surprising that many people, young and old, find themselves religiously insecure and confused. Religion offers definite and absolute answers to those persistent human questions about the meaning of life and the morality of one's behavior. It is possible that once a religion is no longer perceived as providing the answers to the major human concerns and as being relevant to one's daily activities, it loses a lot of its attractiveness. A person educated in Western culture can grow up with a very negative view of religion, even if one's parents are regular churchgoers. It is quite possible that many young adults at the start of their careers are not yet committed to the religion of their parents and are ready either to give up the beliefs and practices they have been taught or to embark on a religious quest of their own initiative.

The rise of fundamentalism over the past few decades appears to be a worldwide trend present in many of the world religions and affecting both social and political life.[37] In the Western world Christian fundamentalist churches and many of the new religious movements tend, as a rule, to propose their belief systems in a rather dogmatic and absolute fashion. Similarly, many proponents of Eastern meditation techniques insist that what they have to offer is the best way to achieve peace of mind, happiness, and security. Some new religions propose specific programs both to save the world and to develop the individual's natural spiritual and intellectual talents, programs that the religion of one's birth seems to lack or to have discontinued. The person who heeds the appeal of the new evangelizers might be reacting to a society that tends to deny, ignore, or be unconcerned with, traditional religious concerns, values, and interests.

The Individual in Search of an Identity

One finds in psychological literature a lively debate about today's identity crisis.[38] Adolescents in particular may experience an "identity deficit," which can occur also in adults especially when they go through important transitions in their lives. Roy Baumeister states that an identity crisis "refers to an inadequacy of the self to make the decisions that confront it." This type of crisis is linked to the rejection of parental authority. He writes:

> In adolescence, the crisis appears to rise when the young person rejects parental teachings, values, and plans, in order to decide for him- or herself what course to take toward adulthood. This rejection of parental input creates an inner vacuum that must be filled before decisions can be made about adult life. The rejection of parental teachings is typically followed by a stage of exploring new ideas, life-styles, and/or modes of relating to other people.[39]

An identity crisis could have a great impact on the individual. D. Motet points out that a "severe, acute identity diffusion is linked with the inability to make decisions, confusion, loss of identity in a crowd, difficulty in establishing satisfying relationships with a tendency toward isolation, difficulty in work, and poor concentration." He adds that in some cases "the identity confusion finds expression in a 'negative identity' in which a dangerous or socially undesirable role is adopted."[40] One can easily conclude that joining a new religious movement, considered by many a "dangerous and socially undesirable" group, is directly linked with an identity crisis that is pathological and hence can only be dealt with in therapy.

Many young adults, brought up in a religiously and ethically insecure world, may experience a loss of their sense of identity, a lack of the normal feeling that one has a historical continuity. They may have modified or altered their attitude toward life several times and tried out so many different experiences that they have become aware that their identity has changed dramatically over a relatively short period of time. One could probably describe this feeling as that of being lost, of having no moorings, and being unconnected with both one's past and present surroundings.

The experience of a lost and vague identity is related to the fact that contemporary Western culture tends to treat people rather impersonally, as if they are numbers in a computer bank and not unique individuals of worth. One can easily end up feeling like a mere cog in a dehumanized and blundering social machine. Although this feeling of depersonalization does not necessarily denote a psychological disorder, it may become such if it is accompanied by a loss of contact with one's own personal reality and by feelings of strangeness and unreality of experience.

Although religion has been seen as promoting personal identity, it is possible that many large churches might also be, unwittingly, contributing to this depersonalization process. They could be failing not only in ministering to the individual needs of their members but also in providing them with a faith-sharing environment. Traditional churches tend to stress the observance of rules and uniform behavior more than the satisfaction of the individual needs of their members. Preoccupation with conformity and the pressures of religious institutions could have a negative impact on one's sense of identity. Such depersonalized treatment is related to alienation in the sense that it leads a person to feel separate from his or her "real" or "deeper" self. Many of the new religions seem to cater to the needs of the self and have been labeled cults of personality or even narcissistic cults.[41] Such a connection between the new religions and narcissism is an application of the view that narcissism and religion often go together. John Shaw, for example, in discussing the issue of personal significance, suggests that narcissism is "a motivational structure" that ensures a feeling of personal significance and worth.[42]

In like manner John Battista has introduced the concept of an "offensive spirituality." He maintains that spiritual awakenings and crises are not to be equated with psychotic states. But, reflecting on the importance of spirituality in many of the new religious movements, such as the New Age, he writes: "Offensive spirituality may be considered the narcissistic use of a spiritual persona or spiritual identification." The spiritual aspirant who joins a new religion is "engaged in narcissistic self-absorption, mistaking spiritualized self-gratification for self-fulfillment." His examples of such narcissistic indulgence include not only new religions but also fundamental Christian Churches. He writes:

> Common forms of offensive spirituality involve spiritual name dropping or spiritual testing. For example, some "spiritually identified" people appear to test the "spiritual development" of others using a "higher consciousness

scorecard" that includes frequency of mediation, depth of experience, status of teacher, adherence to vegetarianism, and spiritual demeanor. Alternatively, some fundamentalist Christians simply insist on acceptance of Christ as one's personal savior as the prerequisite for association. Such standards are thinly disguised forms of narcissism.[43]

People who join new religions exhibit masochistic, spiritual defenses, such as submission to an authority, "failure to ask for or receive nurturance from another human being," "failure to deal with interpersonal or sexual needs," and the inability to deal with various problems such as depression.[44]

Many of the new religions attract individuals by the promise of peace of mind, spiritual well-being, gratifying experiences, and material success. In so doing they stress their concern for the individual and highlight one's personal worth and self-development. This is especially so in human growth movements such as Scientology, The Forum (previously known as Erhard Seminar Training [EST]), and quasi-religious encounter groups. Here the focus is on the individual's need to enhance one's own sense of identity, independence, spirituality, and personal talents. Some new religions seem to provide some relief for those who are plagued by an identity crisis.

Sherman Feinstein, for example, states that young adults attracted to new religious movements are characterized by a dissatisfaction with their status quo and with a slow resolution of their identity crisis. While conversion does bring some relief, he maintains that the very resolution of their existential anxiety is pathological and cannot be sustained for any length of time.[45]

The Individual in a General State of Crisis

The above reflections on the characteristics of cult members leave us with a picture of a person who is religiously and emotionally deprived, who feels alienated from self and society, who is in a state of personal crisis, and who has already embarked on a religious quest. Eagan Hunter, for instance, describes young people attracted to the new religions as characterized by "identity confusion, alienation from family members, weak cultural, religious, and community ties, and feelings of powerlessness in a seemingly out-of-control world."[46] Marc Galanter found that members of new religions frequently suffered from psychological distress or some major pathology before they embraced marginal beliefs and lifestyles.[47] And Chana Ullman, writing about conversion in general, states:

> The emotional turmoil that characterized converts' descriptions of their childhood and adolescence was also apparent in the immediate antecedents to the conversion experience. About 80 percent of the religious converts in my study were judged as describing considerable distress during the two-year period prior to their conversion. They described their preconversion absorption in anxiety, anger, or desperation and cited the release from the upheavals of their emotional life as the most important consequence of their change of heart.[48]

Experiences of misfortune or failure are common explanations of why one starts looking for alternative solutions to one's difficulties. Many embark on a search, religious or otherwise, when family life is faltering, when future political, social, or economic prospects are perceived as disheartening, or when a death of a close relative or friend has created a deeply felt void in one's life. It is not surprising that new religious movements have also been called "crisis cults," even though this phrase was originally coined to describe the rise of new religious movements in nonliterate societies.[49] In times of crises a person is more open to listen to the message of renewal and to the promise of salvation from a problematic situation that is beyond one's control.

But these are features that can be ascribed to many more young adults who are repulsed rather than attracted by the activities of the new religions, and who successfully cope with their personal problems and adapt to modern conditions in ways other than abandoning their religious and/or cultural heritage. Given the changing sociocultural conditions of our times, these features are normal not only in the sense that they are average or typical, but also in that they are not necessarily indicative of mental disease or disorder, emotional imbalance, or psychological dysfunction. Unless the above-mentioned features prevail in an extreme form, they do not appear to render an individual incapable of making free choices. The question that needs to be answered is under what precise conditions some young adults, instead of seeking the support offered by traditional religions or the availability of psychological counseling, decide to join a new religion.

Moreover, there are moral pressures that individuals experience whenever they are faced with making important decisions, but the pressures, by themselves, do not render a person mentally ill, nor do they destroy human freedom, even though they might, regrettably, lead one to make the wrong choice. The cult-personality type turns out to be fairly common among, and easily applicable to, many young adults who live in a highly mobile society and a fast-changing cultural scene. The characteristics discussed above are too general and cannot, by themselves, lead to a reliable and distinctive profile of a prospective cult member. One must, therefore, explore other psychological factors that might explain why young adults join new religious movements.

Both popular literature and some psychological studies typically draw an elaborate picture of how members of new religions go out on an aggressive search for new recruits. Psychological weaknesses of the individual and the often chance contact with cult members are seen as sufficient causes for the successful recruitment methods employed by some of the new movements. These conclusions, however, seem to assume that everybody is easy prey for the happy smiles and enticing promises of enthusiastic recruiters. Nothing could be further from the truth.

Recruitment to a religious cause is, in fact, a complex process. Those people who join a new religion have been described as "seekers."[50] They tend to view religion as a "spiritual quest" and not an unquestioned acceptance of the beliefs and practices of the organized churches in which they were raised.[51] Most of them have already embarked on a search for an alternate lifestyle and different religious beliefs and commitments before being approached by evangelizers. Recruitment methods have little effect on those who are settled in life and who feel secure, content, and fulfilled in their respective religious traditions and professional careers. It is, therefore, necessary to stress that some measure of choice is present when a person joins a new religious movement.

The Psychopathology of Cult Leaders and Members

The psychological evaluation of cult leaders and members has not, in general, been positive. Drastic changes in belief system and lifestyle are often viewed as resulting from serious personality flaws or problems that tend to be aggravated or concealed rather than solved with cult membership.

Gurus and other cult leaders, in particular, have been lumped together and labeled as insincere con artists or psychopaths. Colin Wilson, for example, examines a range of leaders of new religious movements throughout history and does not hesitate to call them "Charlatan Messiahs."[52] In his survey he includes, among others, David Koresh of the Branch Davidians and Jim Jones of the Peoples Temple, leaders of communes, like John Humphrey Noyes, Rudolph Steiner of Anthroposophy, and self-proclaimed messiahs, like Sabbatai Zevi. He finds that many of the leaders of new religions are driven by power and sex beyond the normal limits and dismisses them as "demented messiahs." He even draws parallels between the serial killer and the "manic messiah." He also discusses the psychiatrist as a messiah and selects Freud and Jung as examples. All these leaders draw people who crave an authority figure.

Equally devastating is Anthony Storr's study of gurus.[53] Besides several leaders of relatively new religious movements, such as Gurdjieff, Rajneesh, and Rudolph Steiner, Storr includes Ignatius of Loyola and Paul Brunton. He starts by pointing out that integrity, virtue, and goodness are the qualities one should look for when examining gurus, most of whom he finds unworthy of the veneration accorded them. Gurus tend to be friendless and narcissistic, intolerant of criticism, elitist, and anti-democratic. They risk becoming corrupted by power and engage in sexual conduct that is held to be reprehensible by other people, and they frequently exploit their followers. Like Wilson, he includes Freud and Jung in his analysis, though these do not receive the same harsh criticism accorded to religious gurus. Among the many similarities he notices between these psychoanalysts and gurus is their inability to tolerate views that differ from their own. Some of the views of human personality propounded by various gurus are bizarre. Thus, for instance, Steiner proposed the view that a person has three bodies—the physical body, the etheric body, and the astral body. But, according to Storr, Freud's theory also looks strange. His division of the personality in the Ego, the Superego, and the Id "has no anatomical or physiological existence." Storr concludes: "we are justified in assuming that mental illness due to brain damage or disease plays little part in the guru phenomenon. The mental disturbances displayed by gurus are more closely related to manic-depressive illness or to schizophrenia."[54]

Not all gurus, according to Storr, are, however, dangerous pathological persons. Steiner and Brunton, though delusional, were well meaning and harmless. And while Freud had many of the characteristics of a guru, he did not possess many of the disreputable qualities of some modern gurus. Storr softens his negative depiction of the guru by stating that "paranoid delusions have a positive function. They make sense out of chaos within, and also preserve the subject's self-esteem."[55] Gurus often go through a "creative illness" that leads to novel ideas and visions. Not all gurus are psychotic, unless there is evidence of "mental malfunction or social incompetence." Thus believers in UFOs and alien abductions, like the Harvard psychiatrist John Mack, are not psychotic, though their beliefs are delusional.

The diagnosis of narcissism seems common in many psychiatric evaluations of the gurus and the relationship they establish with their devotees. Such a relationship is similar to the transference that occurs between narcissistic patients and their group therapist. Moreover, there seems to be a general tendency among psychiatrists to see cult leaders as having pathological narcissistic personalities.[56]

A further critique of cult leaders is that they manipulate their members through heightened dissociation. Hanna Hyams asserts that cult leaders "elicit in dissociated persons the projections of the ideal, mythical, good-father/mother, heightening dissociation through memories of old, repetitious abuse, lack, and loneliness."[57] Among the common characteristics of cult leaders she lists is that, as children, they were unloved loners. They further are unable to tolerate criticism and suffer from delusions, hallucinations, and paranoia. Moreover, they "are corrupt, abusive, violent, and manipulative, with extremely narcissistic personalities."[58]

In an extensive study of charisma, Len Oakes examined many charismatic leaders from various traditions, including new religious movements. He thinks that charisma is probably "a necessary and inevitable part of human growth, albeit a transitory part."[59] He finds that narcissism is a common trait in the early development of these personalities. An unrestrained and overinflated ego is typical of charismatic leaders whose relationship with their followers is based on the latter's "extraordinary needs and ultimate concerns." As regards these leaders, Oates writes:

> The leader also is on a quest, but of quite a different sort. His earliest history has left him with a "memory and vision of paradise" and a personality adept at manipulating others. He retains his infantile grandios-

ity and exhibitionism by skillful use of empathy and memory, traits that are acute in young children but have been socialized down in the normal adult. . . . As an adult he has become a charismatic leader at least in part because he is afraid that if he doesn't, nobody will love him.[60]

Oakes finds the relationship between the leaders and their devotees psychologically unhealthy, if not pathological. He states:

But is the prophet really an enlightened, spiritual being? If this question asks whether the prophet has personally experienced with the fullness of his being—with his feelings and in his relationships—a spiritual reality, then the answer seems to be no. Indeed, quite the opposite is true; it is the very shallowness of the prophet's feelings and relationships, his pervasive narcissism, that prevents him from ever entering into a genuine relationship with another, or ever having anything other than pseudo feelings for others.[61]

One must note, however, that several psychologists have challenged the view that the guru–disciple relationship is pathological. Thus, Anthony Martignetti compares three groups, including a nonreligious one, and concludes that the guru–devotee relationship is not indicative of pathology.[62]

Some attempts have been made to link pathological personality types with specific religious movements. One of the pioneering and comprehensive efforts in this field has been a study of the members of the International Society for Krishna Consciousness by Tommy and Frank Poling.[63] The conclusion reached by these researchers was that, besides having many of the features discussed above, those who join this Hindu group are characterized by a "sensate personality." The ISKCON preconvert is one who seeks sensual pleasure but is afraid of becoming a victim of sense gratification for its own sake. The movement itself promotes a sensate orientation in, for instance, the centrality of food in its ritual, its belief that the deities are contained in clay images, and in its tendency to interpret myths, like those regarding Krishna, in literal concrete terms.

The prospective Hare Krishna devotee is described as an emotionally frustrated and dependent person who has a growing sense of alienation and identity confusion. He or she is one who, most probably, has had a traumatic childhood experience and later began to develop a religious orientation. Experimenting with drugs and then with yoga and other Asian religious practices are sensate ways in which the individual seeks an outlet for sensual desires. Unsatisfied with this secular lifestyle, the pre-convert enters a period of confusion and anomie, during which time contact with Hare Krishna devotees is made. The attraction to the Hare Krishna movement validates the sense orientation in religious terms and at the same time provides the mechanisms for controlling one's sensual inclinations.

Another study of the Hare Krishna movement suggests that pathological family relationships might explain the reason why some youths join the movement. In a case study (unfortunately based on therapeutic intervention of just one fifteen-year-old male), Ittameveetil Kutty and his co-researchers write:

> The complete identification with the father made the task of withdrawing libidinal cathexis from the parents more difficult in the middle phase of adolescence. The narcissistic blows experienced in his attempts at heterosexual relationships led to a feeling of inadequacy. . . . He was vulnerable and the accidental contact with a religious movement presented an opportunity for resolving these conflicts. . . . Identifying with the HKM provided some answers, for example, denial of sexuality and therefore avoidance of heterosexual narcissistic blows; approval of dependent relationships; anti-materialistic and anti-establishment beliefs which helped him in de-idealizing his parents in the process of separation.[64]

The depressive personality is another type associated with some of the new movements. The person who can be categorized as "depressive" is one who has a sense of inadequacy and feelings of despondency, pessimism, and sadness. The feeling of dependency is also a central ingredient in this type of person who tries to relieve one's feelings of inadequacy by adopting an unquestioning obedience to external authority, a dogmatic belief system, and a lifestyle that fosters a strong group identity. The inadequacies of this personality lead the individual to find refuge in a reduction of one's personal satisfactions, in passive conformity to a structured system of authority, and in hostility toward outsiders.

Peter Magaro and his associates,[65] for example, compared two religious movements, namely ISKCON and the InterVarsity Christian Fellowship (an evangelical group that concentrates its activities on college campuses) and concluded that their members tend to be predominantly depressive personalities. ISKCON is a "total" institution, in the sense that its members are expected to renounce all outside ties and loyalties, to observe a rigorous communal lifestyle, and to adopt an unquestioning attitude to the dogmas of their new faith. Similar rigidity was observed among those committed to the InterVarsity Christian Fellowship, where worldly pleasures are denounced as sinful and the Bible is interpreted literally and accepted as the only path to salvation.

The same scholars[66] linked yet another negative personality characteristic, namely, catatonia, with those who practice Transcendental Meditation and with the members of the Divine Light Mission (a meditation group of Hindu origin that has undergone some radical changes over the past two decades and adopted the name of "Elan Vital").[67] Each group promotes its own special kind of meditative experience that is initially imparted individually to the neophyte in a secret ceremony.

Catatonia is a disorder that reflects a dissociation or cleavage between the functions of feelings and those of thinking or cognition. In this particular form the patient tends to remain in a stupor-like state during which he or she might sit or lie in the same posture for long periods. Strong needs to establish passivity are prominent in this kind of personality, which seeks a symbiotic union with a powerful protector and master of the self, primarily through motor control. Both the Divine Light Mission and Transcendental Meditation stress meditation or yogic techniques during which the practitioner might sit alone and immobile for specified periods of time. Meditation, according to some researchers,[68] could also produce minor epileptic-like fits. These defects could offset the much-touted benefits of relaxation, peace, and happiness that attract new members.

Dissociation is also a fairly common pathology noticed especially among ex-cult members who needed therapeutic intervention. It includes among other things depersonalization disorder and de-realization, and feelings of mistrust and fear. Hanna Hyams, in her study of ex-members of the Order of the Solar Temple[69] who were traumatized when the sect leader and their adepts committed suicide, concludes:

> Most were victims of serious psychological and psychical sexual abuse in childhood and now showed severe symptoms of dissociation, including

some DID. In joining the Sun Sect they had been in search of hope and miracles from outside.[70]

Another personality trait often common to members of new religions is narcissism. Human potential movements, such as Silva Mind Control, in the opinion of Francis Westley, use techniques that focus on narcissistic elements and are just as liable to compensate for structural defects as they are to exacerbate them.[71] Ann Braden Johnson has examined several groups, including Zen Buddhism, ISKCON, the Divine Light Mission, and the Meyer Baba movement, and concluded that they are characterized by a rejection or avoidance of the adult world through a regressive, narcissistic retreat from reality.[72] This trait is confirmed by the study of Daniel Kriegman and Leonard Solomon who think that the appeal of the structure and process of the Divine Light Mission matches the needs of the narcissistic personality.[73]

Many studies of ex-members have led therapists to conclude that involvement in new religions has deleterious effects. Thus Irene Gasde and Richard Block evaluated former members of the Church Universal and Triumphant who reported a high level of psychological stress.[74] Involvement in this church, they concluded, led to the deterioration of personal relationships. The authors maintain that cults may have a negative impact on the well-being of their members. Such a conclusion is in sharp contrast to studies of active members of the same church.[75]

Those involved in various groups that promote occult and paranormal practices, such as out-of-the-body experiences,[76] have also received negative psychological evaluations. A study of nine occult groups in England found a connection between magical and paranormal phenomena and schizotypal thinking, which is both eccentric and erratic.[77] Since psychologists and psychiatrists have linked the belief in magic with mental and developmental abnormalities,[78] it is not surprising that those involved in occult groups are often diagnosed as having personality disorders that require professional treatment.

The Normality of Cult Members

Not all studies, however, confirm this grim picture that those who join new religions suffer from defective personalities.[79] On the contrary, many psychiatrists, who have tested members of various new religious groups, have reached the conclusion that some of them have benefited psychologically from membership.

In a protracted study of members of the Unification Church and of the Divine Light Mission, Marc Galanter[80] did not record any serious psychological malfunctions that seemed typical of their committed members. He did, however, observe that there are certain pre-cult conditions commonly shared by all the individuals he studied. The pre-cult state was generally found to have been one in which members experienced a troubled family life where personal autonomy was missing. They frequently suffered from psychological distress. Limited social ties contributed to their loneliness and alienation. Preoccupation with one's purpose and destiny was prevalent. The state of unhappiness could have been a major factor leading to their conversion experiences. But there was no evidence of insanity or mental illness caused or aggravated by their new lifestyles.

Membership in a cult or sect, rather than induce psychological problems for members, seems to ameliorate one's previous condition and is reflected in a decline in perceived psychotic symptoms and in drug use. Membership has the beneficial effects of easing tensions and relieving anxiety and stress. Three main areas, namely, the general well-being of members of marginal religious groups, their improved sense of purpose, and their sense of belonging, were especially explored in members of the Unification Church and the Divine Light Mission. The results definitely point to an improvement that had to be attributed to their new lifestyles. Members in both groups felt better and healthier; their preoccupations and worries diminished in intensity; their goals in life became sharper; and they experienced strength because they were part of an organization that valued their commitments and promoted shared tasks and recreational activities. Cult membership seems to offer a solution to many familial and social conflicts and might be usurping the functions of traditional counseling and therapy. Galanter, who prefers to call these new religions "charismatic groups," states:

> Members of such groups typically (a) adhere to a consensual belief system, (b) sustain a high level of social cohesiveness, (c) are strongly influenced by group behavioral norms, and (d) impute charismatic or divine power to the group and its leadership.[81]

Galanter further suggests that membership in the new religions should not be readily judged as detrimental to one's mental and psychological well-being. He writes:

> Charismatic groups appear to offer succor and the promise of resolution of many of these developmental conflicts, particularly in respect to identity and participation in a viable peer group. Such groups may also hold particular appeal to youth and other members of society who are socially alienated or suffer from psychiatric distress.[82]

Other independent studies of members of the Hare Krishna movement seem to buttress the results reached by Galanter. Michael Ross conducted psychological research on Hare Krishna devotees in Australia and discovered that they were, in general, within the normal psychological range.[83] There was no evidence of psychopathological symptoms, no sign of thought disorder, and no indication of emotional instability even after years of involvement. In a follow-up study Ross[84] discovered several changes in the members' personality profile, but all were in a positive direction, except in the anxiety level, which registered an increase.

In the United States, Arnold Weiss and Andrew Comrey subjected Hare Krishna members to a number of standard tests and their results were largely positive.[85] The scores of Hare Krishna devotees on mental inventory tests showed little difference between them and the general population. The male members of ISKCON exhibited a higher sense of well-being; their level of psychological distress and rate of mental disorder were average. Women's scores did indicate that they felt more stressful and less happy than their male confreres. Their scores, however, were typical of all women in the general population. The personality structure of all Hare Krishna members was within the average range with two major differences: they were more compulsive and less trusting in the society at large, with men having more idiosyncratic traits. This compulsiveness is interpreted as necessary for a lifestyle that combines the practice of a highly structured religion with the secular endeavors of promoting business and achieving financial success. It also explains why devotees have a narrowly focused worldview and restricted personal opinions, why they expound their beliefs dogmatically, and why they engage in strong evangelizing efforts.

The majority of studies on the effects of the practice of meditation, which so many of the new religions encourage in one form or another, do not support the view that those who meditate are rendered psychologically inferior or mentally weaker than those who do not.[86] On the contrary, they uphold the position that regular meditation contributes to the betterment of one's physical, mental, and psychological conditions. Practitioners of three forms of meditation—TM, Yoga, and Buddhist meditation—have been subjected to numerous experiments, which, by and large, endorse the claim that meditation reduces stress and leads to mental and emotional catharsis. The following outcomes of meditation have been repeatedly recorded: reduced anxiety; heightened awareness; increased self-knowledge, self-control, and self-acceptance; reduction in the level of hostility and aggression; and the cure of drug and alcohol addictions. There is some evidence that not everybody has benefited from the practice of meditation and that in some cases meditation created rather than relieved anxiety. Also many advantages of sitting down in quiet meditation are short-lived or can be achieved by more ordinary relaxation methods. Yet, the research results seem to establish the much-acclaimed spiritual usefulness and psychological efficacy of meditation. People who embark on a meditation program within a religious group end up feeling calmer and happier, exhibiting greater strengths, and enjoying life to a fuller degree. To what extent these effects of meditation are contingent on membership in a religious or quasi-religious movement that offers a philosophy of life requires further study.

Similarly magical beliefs and practices are not always judged to be pathological and/or maladaptive. Stuart Vyse, for example, states that believe in magic is superstitious and all superstitions are irrational because they are not based on scientific evidence. He observes, however, that "common superstitious behaviors and paranormal beliefs are not abnormal. One need not seek psychological services for the treatment of belief in astrology."[87] One can further argue that such beliefs can, at times, have positive functions if for no other reason than that they may provide the individual with a sense of purpose and direction.

One of the most outspoken proponents of the view that members of new religions are not psychologically impaired is James Richardson. Reviewing various studies of the Rajneesh movement, the Hare Krishna movement, and the Jesus movement, he concludes by stating that "it seems time to admit that participation in the new religions is similar to participating in other, more 'normal' religious groups."[88]

Evaluation of Psychological Studies

The above studies indicate that assessing the personality traits of members of new religions and measuring the influence of membership on one's character and behavior are far from easy. Many of the psychological studies on cult members suffer from unacceptable methodological weaknesses. They rely on poor and insufficient sampling, they fail to realize that the research assumptions can influence the results, and they at times betray both uneasiness with, and misunderstanding of, religious beliefs and practices. Studies on ex-cult members appear to be equally unreliable. Jodi Aronoff, Steven Jay Lynn, and Peter Malinowksi state that perhaps "the most common symptom reported by clinicians treating former cult members is dissociation," which is exhibited in various ways, such as the floating phenomenon, cognitive deficiencies, and depression. But they also observe:

> It is important to bear in mind that these symptoms are based on clinician's impression and not on empirical research using standardized psychometric instruments and diagnosis interviews. Also, it should be noted that former members studied had all sought treatment from reporting clinicians.[89]

Aronoff and her coresearchers conclude that those who join new religions are not necessarily suffering from some form of pathology, and current cult members appear to be psychologically well-adjusted and free from psychopathology. They still maintain, however, that a minority of ex-members experience serious difficulties in adjusting, which may not be surprising given the change they go through when leaving and the pressure applied by family members and exit counselors.

Moreover, those scholars who consider the various lifestyles of new religions deviant and conducive to psychopathology are predisposed to start with negative assumptions about religion itself. If one maintains that asceticism, vegetarianism, and celibacy are outward manifestations or direct causes of personality disorders and dysfunctions, then many religious organizations, traditional or new, can be said to worsen rather than ameliorate the psychological and mental states of their members. And if one holds that any serious religious commitment betrays a psychological weakness, then the total dedication of members of any religion can be readily judged to border on the pathological and to justify therapeutic intervention.

One of the difficulties that permeates the studies that link membership in a new religion with some kind of pathology is their failure to specify in a convincing manner the nature of the connection between the observed psychological flaws and membership in the new religions. There are conflicting views about whether pathology existed before or after membership. The negative traits discussed above—catatonia, depression, and narcissism—are not limited to members of new religions. Some scholars,[90] for example, have suggested that even traditional monasticism could become a narcissistic escape from reality. Others[91] have argued that Western culture is itself narcissistic.

The more positive studies that conclude that the participation in the new religions relieves stress and anxiety can be criticized for depending too much on self-reports. They, further, make little attempt to explore whether these reports owe their origin partly to the socialization process itself. Moreover, they have not sufficiently evaluated the long-term effects on those who have voluntarily defected from a new religious movement after years of membership.

Psychological studies on the new religions are, at best, conflicting. There seems to be, however, a general, popular assessment that those who join new religions have a deviant personality in the sense that their patterns of behavior are not just markedly different from the accepted social, ethical, and religious standards of society. Members of new religions are held to be deviant in the sense that there is something so basically wrong with their ideology, values, and mores, that their psychological welfare is thus impaired. Seen from this perspective, new religious movements do not propose an alternative lifestyle, another possible philosophical outlook on life, or a feasible rearrangement of social relations. The behavior they espouse is deviant in the same way that certain forms of crime are, hence it cannot be condoned nor tolerated, even though it might not be easily eradicated.

The overall negative psychiatric assessment of new religions could easily lead one to conclude that their members are mentally and emotionally sick and in need of psychiatric intervention and care. New religions become a refuge for those who could not survive in a regular society and who are looking for justification and respectability for their irreligious and illegal behavior. Or one can take the position that normal young adults are so negatively influenced by the lifestyles of the new religions that their mental and psychological states deteriorate. Some members may even degenerate into psychopaths or criminals.

Such a view, however, does not withstand much scrutiny. There is little evidence, if any, that the new religions *as a whole* condone crime, much less encourage criminal behavior. On the contrary they have tended to stress the need to abandon drugs and have largely (with some notable exceptions) accepted the prevalent moral values of Western society. The deplorable mistakes of individual members and leaders of new (or traditional) religions are by no means necessarily indicative of the official policy of their institutions or of the general practices of their members.

How and Why Does a Person Actually Join a New Religious Movement?

The above discussion has concentrated on the character traits that can be linked with membership in new religions or that are believed to render an individual suitable for recruitment. But it does not quite explain why and how a person joins a fringe religious group. What are the mechanisms and the processes that would lead an individual to become a member of an alternative religion?

The Psychology of Conversion

In dealing with the current controversy over contemporary fringe religions one cannot avoid discussing the nature of religious conversion, which is open to a variety of theological, sociological, and psychological considerations. The psychological study of conversion began toward the end of the nineteenth century.[92] Research was channeled into three major areas. The first dealt with the time frame within which conversion takes place. The debate centered about sudden or gradual personality changes, sometimes called respectively "self-surrender" and "voluntary" conversions. Psychologists showed more interest in, and were fascinated by, conversions of a sudden nature that usually occurred at a crucial turning point in life. The second examined the age at which people usually experienced a religious conversion. Adolescence was found to be the most common period in one's life when conversion could transpire, with sudden conversions tending to take place earlier than gradual ones. And, finally, the possible explanatory factors and causal antecedents that account for conversions were discussed. Although both sudden and gradual conversions result in the awareness of a transformed self, they differ significantly in several main aspects. Sudden conversions are passive and highlight the converts' experiences of being influenced by outside forces or confronted by "otherness." Gradual conversions, on the other hand, are achieved by the individual's active search for meaning in one's life, a search that can take a long time before the convert becomes aware of his or her transformation. Sudden conversions are also accompanied by a feeling of self-surrender to the "otherness," which converts immediately accept. Gradual conversions denote a continual process through which one's faith is deepened. Sudden conversions, unlike gradual ones, are further accompanied by a sense of unworthiness, sin, and guilt. They are experienced at a time of emotional upheaval during which cognition plays a minor role. In spite of the inclination of researchers to spend more time on sudden conversions, all seem to agree that the frequency of gradual conversions by far outnumbers that of sudden ones.

The rise of new religious movements has rekindled, to a limited degree, psychological interest in the study of religious conversion,[93] especially among sociologists and social psychologists. It is important, however, to bear in mind that the study of religious conversion is much broader. Lewis Rambo, for example, has distinguished between "traditional transition" (from one major religion to another), "institutional transition" (from one subgroup to another within a particular transition), "intensification" (when there is an increase and commitment within one tradition), and "affiliation" (conversion to new religious movements).[94] It is probably the latter type of conversion that has led scholars both to rethink the meaning of conversion and to reconstruct models of the conversion process. This recent tendency follows to some degree the well-established psychological tradition that defines conversion as a radical, sudden shift in one's religious beliefs, values, and practices linked with the acceptance of a new faith commitment. The conversion process itself, however, is being approached from quite a different perspective. The major change has been the adoption of an activist-oriented theory to explain how an individual ends up in a new religious group. The personal psychological state of the prospective devotee and the intense proselytization by zealous members do not by themselves explain the actual entry and involvement. The convert plays a key role in his or her own conversion process. Various sociocultural conditions also come into play to influence one's decision. Thus the impact of one's prior socialization and education, peer and family pressures, and stress situations should all be considered necessary for interpreting the experience of conversion.

Moreover, the tendency among contemporary psychologists is to see conversion as a process that takes place over time. Lewis Rambo has outlined this process as occurring in seven distinct stages.[95] The first is the context, "the dynamic forces fields," which stands for "the overall environment in which change takes place." The second is the crisis, "the catalysts for change," that triggers the third stage, that of the quest for salvation. The fourth stage is the encounter, which refers to the contact made between the seeker and the missionary or evangelizer. The fifth is the interaction between the converting person and the members of the other faith, during which time the neophyte learns more about the teachings, lifestyle, and duties of the new tradition. Commitment is the sixth stage, during which the convert consolidates his new status. And finally, there is the seventh stage in which the convert assesses the consequences of his or her new commitment.

Models of Conversion to the New Religions

Two main models of conversion dominate contemporary studies.[96] The first stresses the independent, active role of converts who responsibly commit themselves to a new faith. The second sees the individual as playing the dependent, passive, and negative role of a victim who succumbs to carefully planned recruitment tactics that solicit his or her commitment.[97] In the activist theories of conversion the convert is an individual who looks for, or is confronted with, a new faith perspective and makes a free, deliberate choice, even though there might be psychological and social factors that affect the final decision. In the passive theories of conversion, converts do not freely choose their new faiths. They are rather cajoled into accepting them and then molded into typical adherents. They do not change their religious orientation by a thoughtful and evaluative procedure, but are rather "brainwashed" into accepting a whole lifestyle and value system. These two models endorse diametrically opposed interpretations of cult involvement: the passive model considers such involvement as pathological and detrimental, while the activist model tends to see it as largely therapeutic or beneficial.

The Brainwashing Model

The theory of brainwashing, also referred to as "coercive persuasion" or "thought reform," has become the most popular perception of what happens when a young adult joins a new religious movement.[98] Relying heavily on studies of Chinese and Korean communists' treatment of prisoners of war, who were apparently convinced to accept their captors' ideology, proponents of the brainwashing theory of cult induction have insisted that members of new movements undergo a process similar, though obviously not identical, to what prisoners of war went through. In spite of the attempts[99] made to refine it, the brainwashing theory has remained essentially the same.

Central to this theory is the assertion that the evangelization techniques used by these groups to attract members and to maintain their allegiance are forceful and deceptive and largely responsible for the success they have had over the past thirty-five years. The susceptible individual who happens to meet recruiters at the right time and place can easily fall victim to their engaging propaganda and be lured to make a sudden, hasty decision to become a member. The reason why people join is that they have been skillfully led to believe that membership in a new religion solves the emotional and intellectual problems they have been experiencing. Once they join, members are taught cult ideology that explains the noble goals of the organization and the motivations that attract people to commitment. They are not just socialized or educated into their new belief system and lifestyle, but rather skillfully indoctrinated, or brainwashed, into it. Their previous ideologies and value systems are recast by subtle methods that are beyond their control. The same indoctrination techniques serve as a maintenance mechanism that shelters them from the outside world and continuously inculcates the virtues and benefits of their new lifestyles.

Some scholars see little difference between the methods used by the Chinese on their prisoners of war and those employed by the Unification Church of the Reverend Moon and by the now-defunct Peoples' Temple of Jim Jones and David Koresh's Branch Davidians. Though they admit that in the Unification Church there is little evidence of physical coercion, they appear to hold that this exception (which is, in fact, typical of the new religions) doesn't make much of a difference. On a psychological level, the convert goes through a sudden personality change called "snapping," which is a kind of "information disease" characterized by impaired awareness, irrationality, disorientation, and delusion. The individual loses one's free will and is unable to reevaluate one's position in the cult, unless explicit pressures are initiated on one's behalf from outside the group.

The comparison between cult recruitment and socialization methods with brainwashing techniques used on prisoners of war in communist countries has become one major disputed area in the study of the phenomenon of new religions. Most scholars agree that five major ingredients of coercive persuasion are central in the transformation of the individual. These are: (1) total control and isolation; (2) physical debilitation and isolation; (3) confusion and uncertainty; (4) guilt and humiliation; and (5) release and relaxation. The debate in scholarly literature has concentrated around three major points. The first concerns the meaning of coercive persuasion. The five factors mentioned above do not always occur together and at the same level of intensity. One could, therefore, talk of degrees of coercive persuasion ranging from the extreme Chinese communist brainwashing techniques to military indoctrinations or religious summer-camp programs. The second is related to the effectiveness of coercive persuasion. People tend to react differently to various forms of indoctrination procedures and one is left with the problem of whether one can talk of brainwashing as a universal technique that always produces the same results. The third challenges the assumption that the brainwashing model can be applied to the new religions at all. It would be difficult to find a new religious movement where all or most of the determinants mentioned above exist and are strong enough to warrant the accusation of "brainwashing."

One can, further, raise formidable objections to the brainwashing theory of cult conversion. First of all it renders the pre-cult members passive participants in the recruitment process. The initiative is put totally in the hands of the recruiter. One important aspect, namely, that the person who joins a new religious movements is, more often than not, an active seeker, is completely ignored. Second, this analysis fails to explain two main undeniable facts, namely, that (1) the majority of young and seemingly vulnerable adults, who have had contact with members of new religions, do not succumb to the allegedly irresistible, alluring techniques; and (2) many of those who have joined leave on their own accord without family pressures or exit counseling. Third, many studies of members of new religions do not support the hypothesis that they are disoriented individuals who have more psychological problems than the average person. Fourth, recent psychological studies on conversion tend to show that the conversion process can be a lengthy one that spans many stages and extends over a period of months, if not longer.

The Drift Model of Conversion

One major theory aimed at unraveling the process of conversion to new religious movements is based on two observations on their members. First, those attracted to a new religion have been, as a rule, involved in countercultural activity before their conversion; and, second, they have at times tried different faith commitments, long before they appear to have settled down in one particular religious movement. Rather than a sudden conversion to one particular cult, these individuals have experienced a gradual change that included partial or complete involvement in more than one nontraditional religious group. They had embarked on a "conversion career,"[100] and their final involvement in a new religion was not a sudden decision made on the spur of the moment and under outside pressure, when they were unable to cope with a difficult period in their lives. They went through a gradual transformation. People do not jump into new religions, they drift almost imperceptibly into them over a period of time. Lewis Rambo has developed a seven-stage model of religious conversion that usually has the following sequence: (1) context; (2) crisis; (3) quest; (4) encounter between the potential convert and an evangelist or advocate; (5) interaction between both parties; (6) commitment; and (7) consequences.[101] This model may be applicable to conversions from one religion or church to another and also to conversions to new religions.

One of the most elaborate expositions of the drift model has been made in connection with conversions to the Divine Light Mission ("Elan

Vital"). This theory argues that the "premies," or "lovers of God" (as initiates are called), did not experience a radical personality change but an evolutionary development of their egos. Based on intensive interviews with followers of Guru Maharaj Ji (the founder and leader of the Mission), James Downton, a sociologist, identified ten stages in the process of conversion to the worldview of this movement. These stages are reproduced here intact, since they portray a developmental model of personality change that stretches over a period of time during which the individual exercises both reflection and free decision making:

Stage 1: General disillusionment with conventional values, social, organization, and solutions to problems.

Stage 2: Deepening or developing faith in a spiritual solution to problems.

Stage 3: Growing determination to take spiritual direction, reflected in the development of a new spiritual ego-ideal and self-image.

Stage 4: Increasing sense of personal futility, leading to a greater psychological receptivity to the appeals of unconventional spiritual leaders or followers who make bold promises of change.

Stage 5: Contact and increasing attraction to an unconventional spiritual movement as a result of positive interactions with members and ideological compatibility with the movement's beliefs.

Stage 6: Acceptance of a problem-solving perspective of the movement, strengthening the determination to join.

Stage 7: Initiation and conversion: the transformation of awareness resulting from a shift in identity from the personality (ego) to the spirit (Life force, God).

Stage 8: Surrender to the spirit (God) and to a spiritual leader, characterized by idealization of the leader, identification with him, conformity to his initiatives, and loss of capacity to criticize him (features of the role of "devotee").

Stage 9: Intensification of commitment through increasing investments and sacrifices, greater social communion with members, reduction of social ties with outside world, and mortification of the ego.

Stage 10: Gradual modification of identity, beliefs, and behavior through commitment, which secures the individual's adherence to the movement's norms and practices and, therefore, ensures the accumulation of experiences considered by the movement to be essential for a thoroughgoing change of character and outlook.[102]

Although Downton's theory has not been tested on members of other new religions, it does challenge the popular "snapping" theory of conversion that conceives of personal change in religious orientation as taking place suddenly and solely through outside pressures. And while it admits that enculturation or socialization takes place within a new religion, it allows for the converts' active and conscious participation in their reeducation.

It should be stressed that membership and/or commitment in a religious organization do not necessarily require that the adherent know everything about one's new faith. Neither does genuine conversion necessitate complete awareness of all the implications that flow from membership and of the difficulties that commitment might eventually entail. These limitations do not automatically make one's decision to enlist in a new religion hasty, unwise, or forced. People who make important decisions (like getting married and making a career change) that affect their lives do not normally foresee or consider all the possible outcomes of their behavior. They are nonetheless free agents and are held responsible for their actions, even if later on they have to admit they had been mistaken and must endure the unpleasant consequences of their errors.

Combination of the Two Models

The above-mentioned paradigms of conversion have habitually been seen as incompatible ways of explaining how young people join "deviant" religious groups. It is possible, however, that these two models are not as irreconcilable as they appear to be at first sight. People can experience sudden and unexpected conversions within the religion in which they have been raised from infancy. Many of the mainline churches are not satisfied with their religious education and socialization programs that start from early childhood; they encourage their adult members both to reform and to deepen commitment. There are also religious groups that initiate adult members by sudden conversions, but then expect them to raise their children in the faith by the gradual process of socialization. The classic example of sudden conversion experienced by Saul (later changed to Paul) on the road to Damascus (Acts 9) may not have been that sudden. The reader of the account of Saul's dramatic change of heart is left to wonder whether he had already reflected on, and maybe doubted the righteousness of, his fanatic persecution of Christians before his conversion experience. Sudden and gradual conversions are possibly complementary and could represent two ways of viewing the same religious and personality change.

Two sociologists, John Long and Jeffrey K. Hadden, have thus argued that one can better understand the conversion sequence if one starts from a general theory of socialization that implicitly relies on both the brainwashing and drift models.[103] There are two aspects of the socialization process that are applicable to conversion: there is first the group's effort to mold or form the new member (brainwashing or indoctrination), and then the new member's "journey" toward affiliation with the group (drift or free conscious search). Socialization is conceived of as the social process of creating and incorporating new members into a group. It instructs the new members not only in the ideology of the group, but also in the manner they should behave and feel.

Any theory of conversion must, therefore, take into account three components of the socialization process: (1) the nature and requirements of membership; (2) the participants; and (3) the creating and incorporating activities. Knowledge and understanding of a new religion's membership requisites, as well as the ability to fulfill the requirements of commitment, are certainly needed for conversion. But the determining element in becoming and remaining a member is the relationship of trust that exists between the novice and those who accept him or her in the group. For socialization, a bonding between new members and the group is required, a bonding that can take the form of separating newcomers from the outside world and of inculcating the distinction between insiders and outsiders. Once members, the converts take part in activities that are geared to the realization of the movement's goals and, at the same time, they become incorporated into the movement's hierarchical system.

This model of conversion, applied to the members of the Unification Church, led to the conclusion that the church's socialization process encouraged quick, short-lived commitments but created difficulties for long-term affiliations for most converts. The reason for this is that the church offers insufficient opportunities for advancement within the movement. Many of the Unification Church's recruits, who come largely from a social background, where upward mobility formed part of their ideology, often lose interest in the ideals, goals, and programs of the church. They become increasingly aware that they will probably remain stuck at the level of novices (who do most of the recruiting and street fundraising) with no prospect for advancement. That so many of them opt out of the system is an indication that the indoctrination methods used by the Unification Church, no matter how strong they might be, do not destroy its members' ability to think critically and to make decisions for themselves.

While this model of conversion still needs to be tested in the context of other new religious movements, it does clarify some of the issues that are still the subject of heated exchanges between scholars. The accusation, for instance, that many young adults join new religions without knowing what they are getting into is only partially correct. The person who commits oneself to a new church or religious group is far from being completely in the dark about its beliefs and practices. What triggers the conversion, however, is not a dispassionate, impartial, intellectual inquiry into the theological and philosophical system of the group, nor is it a careful and thorough examination of its manifold activities. It is the social networks within the group that lead the individual to make the initial commitment and to retain membership. In this view, the emotional ties between members are more important than the intellectual acceptance people eventually make of their new faiths. Although emotional commitment comes first, it does not necessarily invalidate the later theological adherence to the movement's ideology.

Conversion Motifs

The dichotomy between sudden and gradual conversions could also be a rather naive way of looking at a complex phenomenon that consists of a great variety of religious experiences, personality types, and transformatory expressions. John Lofland and Norman Skonovd have united sociological and psychological elements in their attempt to decipher the process of conversion, which is described as a radical reorganization of one's identity, meaning, and life.[104] They do not focus on the planned activities or programs employed by new groups to induce or encourage conversion, or on the individual's subjective life, which stresses the self-induced aspect of conversion. Instead they distinguish six conversion motifs and five levels of intensity that go with each of the motifs. The motifs are: (1) intellectual; (2) mystical; (3) experiential; (4) affectional; (5) revivalist; and (6) coercive. The following major variations are said to interact with the motifs: (1) the degree of social pressure; (2) temporal duration; (3) the level of affectional arousal; (4) affective content; and (5) the belief-participation sequence.

Seen in schematic form the relationship between the motifs and variations is amenable to several combinations that represent many kinds of conversions. The level of intensity of the conversion tactics, the socialization procedures, and the response of converts vary greatly. It would be unwise and unrealistic to choose one label, namely, that of "brainwashing," as an encompassing description of all conversions to the new movements. Lofland and Skonovd's judgment is that the concept of coercive persuasion should be restricted to those situations where there is a high degree of long-term external pressure coupled with an intense arousal of fear and uncertainty, culminating in empathetic identification and even love.

Conversion, therefore, is not exactly the same phenomenon for every individual, and the process of commitment also depends on the character and nature of the particular religious movement. Thus, to give a couple of examples, the degree of social pressure is rather low when the conversion motif is intellectual, mystical, or experiential, while the level of affective arousal tends to be the highest where revivalist and coercive patterns predominate. When applied to the current debate on the process of affiliation to a new religion, the theory of Lofland and Skonovd eschews generalizations about the cult-induction process. It further allows for a wider variety of interpretations depending on the particular movement under study and the individual's own intellectual and emotional state of being.

The conclusion that one should draw from these studies is that there is no one generally accepted theory that satisfactorily explains the mechanism of conversion that leads a young adult to join a new religious movement. One can find individuals who entered a new movement after a relatively short period of consideration and others who had been shopping for years before settling down to a particular marginal lifestyle. The motivations that lead a person to commit oneself to a specific religious group are also diverse and complex. And though, in most cases, participation in a new religion usually precedes acceptance of its belief system, there could also be instances when an intellectual examination of the theology of a cult could lead to a decision to involve oneself in the group's rituals and activities. Similarly, one comes across members of new religious movements who have serious psychological problems, as well as others who are as "normal" as the average person who has never considered becoming a member of an alternative religious group.

There is also the possibility that different lifestyles might not have the same effects on their members. "High-demand sects," as the new religious groups have sometimes been called, are more likely to have a deleterious effect on those members whose level of commitment does not go deep enough and who, therefore, discover that more is being asked of them than they are able and/or willing to give.

Understanding the New Religions as Rites of Passage

What has been largely lacking in psychological studies is a general theoretical model to understand the new religions as sociocultural institutions that have a bearing on an individual's psychological and spiritual growth and development.

The most original and provocative approach to the cults along these lines has been that of J. Gordon Melton and Lawrence Moore[105] who have borrowed the anthropological concept of "rites of passage" from the works of Arnold van Gennep[106] and Victor Turner[107] and applied it to the new religions. The transition from childhood to adulthood is never an easy process and societies throughout the history of the human race have created socially sanctioned rituals to make the passage easier and to imbue it with meaning.

The traditional anthropological analysis divides rites of passage into three distinct stages. The first stage has been called "preliminal" and involves the separation or segregation of young adults from the rest of the community. The second stage is the actual period of separation during which young adults are stripped of their previous identities and enculturated into the new condition to be assumed at initiation. This is the marginal or "liminal" stage. In the final stage, called "aggregation," "reintegration," or "postliminal," the individuals are accepted anew into the community as transformed people with new rights and responsibilities. The liminal period can be compared to the grief process and other important and demanding life changes (like divorce) in that it might be bizarre in form and traumatic to both those in transition and to their relatives and friends. Liminal stages can be considered dangerous because they can be compared to a kind of "no-man's-land" through which individuals are traveling. They are also necessary steps that all people go through with varying degrees of difficulty.

Applying this theory to members of new religions, Melton and Moore argue that the conversion or sudden personality change that accompanies entrance into a new religion is comparable to the stage of liminality or transition. Ascetical practices, long hours of work, dangerous and apparently inane activities, total obedience to authority, and an austere lifestyle are all characteristics of this marginal phase. The so-called trance-like stare that cult members are said to manifest is not a sign of brainwashing or hypnotism, but rather an indication that they are still in the state of shock that accompanies the trauma of any major life transition.

A comparison of the conversion process to new religions with other transition stages might provide useful insights. Coming to terms with a grief situation, adopting a completely new lifestyle or profession, coping with divorce, going through the middle-age crisis, and adapting to retirement are all stages in life that can be accompanied by rites of passage. One can understand involvement in a new religion better if one saw it as a rite of passage that might, at times, require therapeutic intervention. One can also understand why some cult members remain committed for many years or for life. There are people who take longer than the average individual to solve a personal problem and others who never seem to be able to make the transition from one stage to another. People are sometimes accused of never having grown up, that is, of having remained in a kind of transitional stage between childhood and adulthood. The widow or widower who spends the rest of her or his life in mourning and the divorced couple who are still enmeshed in court battles decades after their divorce was finalized are examples of people who are stuck in the stage of transition.

While the above approach illuminates the process of becoming a member of a new religion, it leaves open for contention a number of important issues. The first is that the liminal stage theory treats religious conversion, just as many psychological theories have done in the past, merely as an adolescent or transient state, a sort of childhood behavior that one eventually will grow out of. However, not all converts to the new religions are young adults and some of them have now been members for over twenty years.

Second, Melton and Moore's model disregards the fact that many of the unusual and/or dangerous practices associated with cult membership can be found among the major religious traditions, especially monastic and religious institutions. Are we to conclude that the Christian monk or nun, secluded in a remote and cloistered monastery, is a person fixated in the liminal stage because of defects grounded in early childhood experiences? If celibacy and chastity are liminal stages what are we to make of the celibate clergy in the Catholic Church? If the arranged marriages in the Unification Church are liminal rites, what about cultures where such marriages are the norm? And lastly, why is it that only a relatively small number of individuals make their transition to full adulthood by way of a new religious movement? It is reasonable to presume that many young adults, who have the same family backgrounds as those who join new religions, make the transition through other less unusual and traumatic liminal stages. What other factors might influence those who take the cult route?

The application of the theory of rites of passage to the new religious movements, in spite of its weaknesses, opens for us the possibility of making a better assessment of the problems the new religions have raised. If rites of passage are necessary or useful devices that enable human beings to make transitions from one important stage of life to another, it is reasonable to conclude that alternative religions can provide certain benefits for some individuals.

Much of the controversy on the new religions has, with due reason, centered on the question of whether they are harmful or therapeutic. If membership in an alternative religion is a temporary condition that enables a person to pass from one state of life to another, then it might be said that, for some at least, membership might actually contribute to the individual's growth. There are many advantages that belonging brings to an individual in a state of critical transition. First, the community and controlled environment provide security and support. Second, the experience of sharing a lifestyle de-emphasizes competition and stresses acceptance and cooperation. Third, a well-defined and disciplined daily schedule of work and other activities contributes to the development of one's self-control. And, fourth, the performance of distasteful activities (such as fund raising) might contribute to one's new confidence.

These are all features and conditions of cult life that might help people overcome their problems and later reenter the mainstream better equipped for success in living. It is definitely possible that in certain cases membership in a new religious movement does have a healing effect on individuals who could not resolve crises generated by a highly mobile society and a rapidly changing culture. This does not mean that some psychologists and psychiatrists are ready to recommend membership in a new religion as a viable alternative to traditional therapy. It rather suggests that the controlled environments of new religions can, like those of monastic institutions, have positive effects on some individuals at certain critical stages of their lives and maybe also for the duration of their lives.

The rigidity and demands of membership in new religions do, however, raise pressing problems for those psychologists who maintain that they have therapeutic effects. One might dismiss the exotic and fantastic elements of the new religious movements as relative perceptions of features common to most, if not all, religions. However, the fanatical, authoritarian, and intolerant stance one finds in the membership of several new religions (and, one might add, in some traditional Christian churches) has never been taken as a sign of psychological well-being. Further, the treatment of children in a number of cults and fundamentalist Christian churches has been criticized especially when it resulted in grievous bodily harm.[108] Some Christian fundamentalist churches, citing the authority of the Bible, have pursued harsh authoritarian and disciplinary measures in their dealing with young members of their community. Contemporary psychologists do not recommend such treatment of children. They further maintain that both parents and educators who inflict extreme physical harm on youngsters may themselves be suffering from severe psychopathology. The assertion that cults are "dangerous detours for growing up" appears to sum up the dilemma one faces when evaluating both the advantages and disadvantages of membership in some of the new religions. Whatever the benefits of membership, however, joining a new religious movement is definitely not a recommendable and preferred solution to adolescent problems nor a panacea for all mental and psychological problems that one experiences in times of crises.

Conclusion: Are the New Religions Therapeutic or Destructive?

Psychological studies on new religious movements are not conducive to sweeping generalizations about the beneficial or deleterious effects they might have on the mental and emotional well-being of their members. They lead inevitably to unpopular conclusions. Membership in new religions is, at best, ambivalent and ambiguous; it can contribute to one's mental and spiritual health and social stability, serve as a meaningful (and temporary) stage in one's life, expose and exacerbate one's innermost problems, or be the direct cause of pathological and self-destructive behavior. The evidence adduced to support the tenet that new religious movements in general are destructive organizations that invariably ruin one's life and warp one's personality is just not strong enough. And the statement that they function as alternative therapies relies too optimistically on reports of members themselves. Both approaches tend to ignore studies that do not confirm their own individual hypothesis. Consequently, one has to examine each religious group on its own merit without any preconceived notions of the evils of cultism or the benefits of commitment. And one must consider carefully both what members and ex-members have to say.

One must stress, however, that the advantages of traditional therapy would seem to override whatever indirect treatment and temporary comfort membership in the new religious movements might offer. Although there are some similarities (such as the authoritative roles assumed by therapists and gurus) between traditional psychiatry and the indirect therapy one might receive in a new religion, the differences between the two are substantial. The former is a conscious, formalized, and planned treatment that is open to improvement and critique by peers in the same field. There are academic and social boundaries that confine and monitor counseling and therapy. There is a code of professional ethics. Legal procedures, independent of the counseling profession, can be initiated if counselors or therapists are not properly trained and/or if they abuse their position of trust. Unlike membership in a new religion, involvement in therapeutic sessions does not demand total allegiance or commitment, nor does it prescribe an absolute system of religious beliefs and rituals.

One of the major problems with traditional therapy seems to be its neglect of the spiritual or religious dimension of life. Conversion or religious involvement, especially if the level of emotion is rather high, is customarily dismissed as a childish stage in one's life, a phase out of which any healthy individual will automatically grow. Most therapists and counselors do not require any knowledge of religious matters to qualify for their respective profession. It is not surprising that, as a rule, they have manifested an insensitivity and lack of empathy when religious topics emerge in therapy. There are signs, however, that psychiatry is acquiring greater awareness of the importance of the spiritual and religious aspects of human life.[109] If this trend actually transpires, then psychiatrists and psychologists will be able to deal, both perceptively and effectively, with religious issues in therapy and with problems that arise when evaluating and counseling members and ex-members of the new religious movements.

Notes

1. These two terms used, respectively, in sociology and anthropology, are closely related. *Enculturation*, "which refers to the process of learning one's culture, is often (but by no means universally) distinguished from *socialization*, which means the general process of learning culture. Enculturation is more often applied to childhood learning. In anthropology, enculturation is not limited to childhood but is a life-long process." MaryAnn Foley, "Enculturation," in *Encyclopedia of Anthropology*, ed. David E. Hunter and Phillip Whitten (New York: Harper and Row, 1976), p. 143.

2. For materials on this issue see John A. Saliba, *Psychiatry and the Cults: An Annotated Bibliography* (New York: Garland, 1987); "The New Religions and Mental Health," in *Religion and the Social Order: The Handbook of Cults and Sects in America*, ed. David G. Bromley and Jeffrey K. Hadden (Greenwich, CT: JAI Press, 1993), vol. 3, part B, pp. 99–113; and "Psychology and the New Religious Movements," in *The Oxford Handbook of New Religious Movements*, ed. James R. Lewis (New York: Oxford University Press, 2003). See also Lawrence Lilliston and Gary Shepherd, "New Religions and Mental Health," in *New Religious Movements: Challenge and Response*, ed. Bryan Wilson and Jamie Cresswell (New York: Routledge, 1999), pp. 123–39.

3. See E. Burke Rochford, with Jennifer Heinlein, "Child Abuse in the Hare Krishna Movement, 1971–1986," *ISKCON Communications Journal* 6, no. 1 (1998): 43–69. See also the report in the *New York Times* (October 9, 1998): Aa.

4. Ronald Enroth, *Churches that Abuse* (Grand Rapids, MI: Zondervan, 1992).

5. Lilliston and Shepherd, "New Religious Movements and Mental Health," p. 129.

6. See Saliba, *Psychiatry and the Cults*, pp. 400ff. For a comprehensive review, confer Michael Murphy and Steven Donovan, *The Physical and Psychological Effects of Meditation* (San Raphael, CA: Esalen Institute, 1988). For more recent studies see Roger Walsh, "Asian Contemplative Practices, Clinical Applications, and Research Findings," *Journal of Transpersonal Psychology* 31, no. 2 (1999): 83–107; G. Alan Marlett and Jen L. Kristeller, "Mindfulness and Meditation," in *Integrating Spirituality into Treatment: Resources for Practitioners*, ed. William R. Miller (Washington, DC: American Psychological Association, 1999), pp. 67–84; and Keith G. Lowenstein, "Meditation and Self-Regulatory Techniques," in *Handbook of Complementary and Alternative Therapies in Mental Health*, ed. Scott Shannon (San Diego, CA: Academic Press, 2002), pp. 159–81.

7. Several ex-members of the Unification Church, for example, have denounced their previous commitment not only in public talks but also in books about their experiences in

the Church. See, for instance, Barbara Underwood, *Hostage to Heaven* (New York: C. N. Potter, 1979); and Christopher Edwards, *Crazy for God* (Englewood Cliffs, NJ: Prentice-Hall, 1979).

8. Flo Conway and Jim Siegleman, *Snapping: America's Epidemic of Sudden Personality Change* (New York: A. B. Lippincott, 1978).

9. See Jack Sparks, *The Mind Benders: A Look at Current Cults* (Nashville, TN: Thomas Nelson, 1977), p. 17; Joel A. McCollam, *Carnival of Souls: Religious Cults and Young People* (New York: Seabury Press, 1979), pp. 106–8; and Willa Appel, *Cults in America: Programmed for Heaven* (New York: Holt, Rinehart and Winston, 1983), p. 133.

10. Confer Robert W. Balch, "Looking Behind the Scenes in a Religious Cult: Implications for the Study of Conversion," *Sociological Analysis* 41 (1980): 137–43.

11. Fred Emil Katz, *Immediacy: How Our World Confronts Us & How We Confront Our World* (Raleigh, NC: Pentland Press, 1999), p.18.

12. Consult, for example, Bernard Spilka, Ralph W. Hood, and Richard L. Gorsuch, *The Psychology of Religion: An Empirical Approach* (Englewood Cliffs, NJ: Prentice-Hall, 1985), esp. 287ff; John F. Schumaker, ed., *Religion and Mental Health* (New York: Oxford University Press, 1992); Edward P. Schfranske, ed., *Religion and the Clinical Practice of Psychology* (Washington, DC: American Psychological Association, 1996); and Diane Jonte-Pace and William B. Jones, eds., *Religion and Psychology: Mapping the Terrain. Contemporary Dialogues, Future Prospects* (London: Routledge, 2001).

13. Confer John A. Saliba, "Psychology and the New Religious Movements," in *The Oxford Handbook of New Religious Movements*, where the differences between the treatment of religion and cult in different editions of DSM are briefly outlined. For a critical appraisal of the DSM-III, see James T. Richardson, "Religiosity as Deviance: Negative Religious Bias in and Misuse of the DSM-III," *Deviant Behavior: An Interdisciplinary Journal* 14 (1993): 1–21.

14. See Robert B. Ewen, "Personality Theories," in *Encyclopedia of Psychology*, ed. Raymond J. Corsini (New York: John Wiley and Sons, 1994), vol. 3, pp. 52–58. For more in-depth studies of the various theories of personalities, see Robert B. Ewen, *Personality: A Topical Approach. Theories, Research, Major Controversies, and Emerging Findings* (Mahwah, NJ: Erlbaum Associates, 1998); Lawrence A. Pervin and Oliver P. John, *Personality: Theory and Research* (New York: John Wiley and Sons, 2001); and Jess Feist and Gregory J. Feist, *Theories of Personality* (Boston: McGraw Hill, 5th ed., 2002).

15. See Ewen, *Personality: A Topical Approach*, pp. 275–78.

16. Saul Levine, in his book *Radical Departures: Dangerous Detours to Growing Up* (New York: Harcourt Brace Javanovich, 1984), p. 15, states that over 90 percent of those who join leave within two years. Studies of individual movements have also noticed the high rate of defection. See, for example, Eileen Barker, *The Making of Moonies: Brainwashing or Choice* (Oxford, UK: Basil Blackwell, 1984).

17. Committee on Psychiatry and Religion, *Leaders and Followers: A Psychiatric Perspective on Religious Cults* (Washington, DC: American Psychiatric Association, 1992), p. 28.

18. Anson D. Shupe, in his volume *Six Perspectives on New Religions: A Case Study Approach* (Lewiston, New York: Edwin Mellen Press, 1982), discusses several models

(including that of deprivation) that have been employed by social psychologists to understand the new religious movements. Rodney Stark and William Bainbridge, in their book, *A Theory of Religion* (New York: P. Lang, 1987), adopt a deprivation theory of cult formation.

19. See John A. Saliba, *Social Science and the Cults: An Annotated Bibliography* (New York: Garland, 1990), xxxi–xxxiii.

20. Frank MacHovec, *Cults and Personality* (Springfield, IL: Charles C. Thomas, 1989), p. 71.

21. Paul Heelas and A. M. Haglung, "The Inadequacy of 'Deprivation' as a Theory of Conversion," in *Vernacular Christianity: Essays in the Social Anthropology of Religion Presented to Godfrey Lienhardt,* ed. James Wendy and Douglas H. Johnson (Oxford: JASO, 1988), pp. 113–19.

22. Roy Wallis, *Salvation and Protest: Studies of Religious Movements* (New York: Harper and Row, 1979), pp. 5–6.

23. S. Dein and H. Barlow, "Why Do People Join the Hare Krishna Movement: Deprivation Theory Revisited," *Mental Health, Religion & Culture* 2 (1999): 82.

24. See, for instance, "The Vatican Document on Sects and New Religious Movements," *Origins* 16 (May 22, 1986): 1–9.

25. Patrick C. Heaven and C. L. Bester, "Alienation and Its Psychological Correlates," *Journal of Social Psychology* 126 (1986): 593–98; and S. Long, "Alienation (Political)," in *Encyclopedia of Psychology,* pp. 54–55.

26. Adam Sharif, *Alienation as a Social Phenomenon* (Oxford: Pergamon Press, 1980); and Clarence Y. H. Lo, "Alienation," in *Encyclopedia of Sociology,* ed. Edgar F. Borgatta and Marie L. Borgatta (New York: Macmillan, 1992), vol. 1, pp. 48–54.

27. See Gregory Baum, *Religion and Alienation: A Theological Reading of Sociology* (New York: Paulist Press, 1975), p. 71ff. Baum discusses the possibility that alienation can be produced by "bad religion" itself.

28. Fritz Pappenheim, "Alienation in American Society," *Monthly Review* 52 (June 2000): 36–53.

29. Raymond L. Calabrese and Edgar J. Raymond, "Alienation: Its Impact on Adolescents from Stable Environments," *Journal of Psychology* 123 (1989): 397–404.

30. Raymond L. Calabrese, "Adolescence: A Growth Period Conducive to Alienation," *Adolescence* 22 (1987): 283–93.

31. Iain Williamson and Cedric Cullingford, "Adolescent Alienation: Its Correlates and Consequences," *Educational Studies* 24 (1998): 333–43.

32. Cynthia M. Clark, "Deviant Subcultures: Assessment Strategies and Clinical Interventions," *Adolescence* 27 (1992): 283–93. See also Michael Sullivan and John S. Wodarski, "Social Alienation in Gay Youth," *Journal of Human Behavior in the Social Environment* 5 (2002): 1–17; and Saul Levine, "Youth in Terrorists Groups, Gangs, and Cults: The Allure, the Animus, and the Alienation," *Psychiatric Annals* 29 (1999): 342–49.

33. See, for example, Neil Freude, *Understanding Family Problems: A Psychological Approach* (New York: John Wiley and Sons, 1991); Kurt Finsterbusch, *Taking Sides: Clashing Views on Controversial Social Issues* (Guilford, CT: McGraw-Hill/Dushkin, 11th ed., 2001), especially issue 6, "Is the Decline of the Traditional Family a National Crisis,"

pp. 90–109; and R. P. Kappenberg, "Family Crises," in *Encyclopedia of Psychology*, ed. Raymond J. Corsini, vol. 2, pp. 8–9.

34. Saul Levine, "Adolescents: Believing and Belonging," *Annals of the American Society of Adolescent Psychiatry* 7 (1979): 41–53. See also Saul Levine, "Youth and Contemporary Religious Movements: Psychosocial Findings," *Canadian Psychiatric Association Journal* 21 (1976): 411–20.

35. John Lofland and Rodney Stark, "Becoming a World-Saver: A Theory of Conversion of a Deviant Perspective," *American Sociological Review* 30 (1965): 862–74; and John Lofland, "'Becoming a World-Saver' Revisited," *American Behavioral Scientist* 20 (1977): 805–19.

36. This is especially true in those educational systems where religion is taught in the public schools. The United Kingdom is an excellent case in point. Those high school students preparing for the GCSE exam in religious studies are expected to follow the descriptive and historical methodology common in the field of religious studies, a methodology that treats religions on a par and avoids making judgments regarding truth claims. See, for example, J. Glyn Harris, *GCSE: Religious Studies* (London: Longman, 2nd ed., 1995); and Catherine Lane, *GCSE: Religious Studies* (London: Letts Educational, 1997). Confer also Michael Keene, *Seekers After Truth: Hinduism, Buddhism, Sikhism* (Cambridge, UK: Cambridge University Press, 1993), and *Believers in One God: Judaism, Christianity, Islam* (Cambridge, UK: Cambridge University Press, 1993). In the United States courses on world religions are taught in most private and state colleges and universities.

37. Scholarly studies on fundamentalism over the past two decades have increased. See, for example, *The Fundamentalism Project*, ed. Martin Marty and E. Scott Appleby (Chicago: University of Chicago Press, 5 vols., 1991–1995); Brenda E. Brahser, *Encyclopedia of Fundamentalism* (New York: Routledge, 2002); and Richard T. Autoun, *Understanding Fundamentalism: Christian, Islamic, and Jewish Movements* (Walnut Creek, CA: AltaMira Press, 2001).

38. Erik H. Erikson, *Identity: Youth and Crisis* (New York: W. W. Norton, 1968) is an excellent example.

39. Roy Baumeister, "Identity Crisis," in *Encyclopedia of Adolescence*, ed. by Richard M. Lerner, Anne C. Petersen, and Jeanne Brooks-Gunn (New York: Garland, 1991), vol. 1, p. 519.

40. D. Motet, "Identity Crisis," in *Encyclopedia of Psychology*, ed. by Raymond J. Corsini, vol. 2, p. 203.

41. See, for instance, W. W. Meisner, "The Cult Phenomenon: Psychoanalytic Perspective," *Psychoanalytic Study of Society* 19 (1980): 91–111.

42. John Shaw, "Narcissism as a Motivational Structure: The Problem of Personal Significance," *Psychiatry: Interpersonal and Biological Processes* 63 (2000): 219–30. For a discussion on Shaw's view see Richard M. Waugaman, "Religion—The Last Taboo," *Psychiatry: Interpersonal and Biological Processes* 63 (2000): 234–38.

43. John Battista, "Offensive Spirituality and Spiritual Defenses," in *Textbook of Transpersonal Psychiatry and Psychology*, ed. Bruce W. Scott, Allan B. Chinen, and John R. Battista (New York: Basic Books, 1996), p. 255.

44. Battista, "Offensive Spirituality and Spiritual Defenses," p. 259.

45. Sherman Feinstein, "The Cult Phenomenon: Transition, Repression, Regression," *Adolescent Psychiatry* 8 (1980), p. 18.

46. Eagan Hunter, "Adolescent Attraction to Cults," *Adolescence* 33 (1998): 709.

47. Marc Galanter, "Charismatic Religious Sects and Psychiatry: An Overview," *American Journal of Psychiatry* 139 (1982): 1539.

48. Chana Ullman, *The Reformed Self: The Psychology of Religious Experience* (New York: Plenum Press, 1989), p. 18.

49. Weston La Barre, "Materials for a History of Studies of Crisis Cults: A Bibliographic Essay," *Current Anthropology* 12 (1971): 3–27.

50. Robert W. Balch and David Taylor, "Seekers and Saucers: The Role of the Cultic Milieu in Joining a UFO Cult," *American Behavioral Scientist* 20 (1980): 847ff.

51. Wade Roof Clark, "The Baby Boomers' Search for God," *American Demographics* 14 (December 1992): 50–56.

52. Colin Wilson, *The Devil's Party: A History of Charlatan Messiahs* (London: Virgin Publishing, 2000).

53. Anthony Storr, *Feet of Clay: Saints, Sinners, and Madmen: A Study of Gurus* (New York: Free Press, 1996).

54. Storr, *Feet of Clay*, pp. 77–78, 151–52.

55. Storr, *Feet of Clay*, p. 161.

56. Ruth G. Newman, "Thoughts on Superstars of Charisma: Pipers in Our Midst," *American Journal of Orthopsychiatry* 53 (1983): 201–8; Alexander Deutsch, "Psychological Aspects of Cult Leadership," in *Cults and New Religious Movements: A Report of the American Psychiatric Association*, ed. Marc Galanter (Washington, DC: American Psychiatric Association, 1989), pp. 147–63; and Ronald O. Clarke, "The Narcissistic Guru: A Profile of Bhagwan Shree Rajneesh," *Free Inquiry* 9 (Summer 1989): 41–48.

57. Hanna Hyams, "Dissociation: Definition, Diagnosis, Manifestation, and Therapy with Special Reference to Cults/Sects," *Transactional Analysis Journal* 28 (1998): 239.

58. Hyams, "Dissociation," p. 240.

59. Len Oakes, *Prophetic Charisma: The Psychology of Revolutionary Religious Personalities* (Syracuse, NY: Syracuse University Press, 1997), p. 192. See Michael H. Stone, "Normal Narcissism: An Etiological and Ethnological Perspective," in *Disorders of Narcissism: Diagnostic, Clinical, and Empirical Implications*, ed. Elsa F. Ronningstam (Washington, DC: American Psychiatric Press, 1998), p. 14, where the author relates charisma to "the quality of supernormal narcissism."

60. Oakes, *Prophetic Charisma*, p. 187.

61. Oakes, *Prophetic Charisma*, p. 188.

62. Anthony Martignetti, "Gurus and Devotees: Guides or Gods? Pathology or Faith?" *Pastoral Psychology* 47 (1998): 127–44.

63. Tommy Poling and Frank Poling, *The Hare Krishna Character Type: A Study of the Sensate Personality* (Lewiston, NY: Edwin Mellen Press, 1986).

64. Ittamveetil N. Kutty, Arthur P. Froese, and Quentin A. F. Rae-Grant, "Hare Krishna Movement: What Attracts the Western Adolescents," *Canadian Journal of Psychiatry* 24 (1979): 607.

65. Peter B. Magaro, Ivan W. Miller, and Thomas Sesto, "Personality Style in Post-Traditional Religious Organizations," *Psychology: A Journal of Human Behavior* 21:3–4 (1984): 10–14.

66. Magaro, Miller, and Sesto, "Personality Style in Post-Traditional Religious Organizations," pp. 12–14.

67. For a short profile of this group see Eugene M. Elliott, III, "Elan Vital" (2001), found at Jeffrey K. Hadden's Web page, http://religiousmovements.lib.virginia.edu/nrms (accessed December 22, 2002).

68. M. A. Persinger, "Transcendental Meditation-Super and General Meditation Are Associated with Enhanced Complex Partial Epileptic-Like Signs: Evidence for 'Cognitive' Rekindling," *Perceptual and Motor Skills* 76 (1993): 179–200.

69. For a profile of this group, see Jennifer Sloan, "Order of the Solar Temple," (1999), found at Jeffrey K. Hadden's Web page http://religiousmovements.lib.virginia.edu/nrms (accessed December 22, 2002).

70. Hanna Hyams, "Dissociation: Definition, Diagnosis, Manifestation, and Therapy," *Transactional Analysis Journal* 28 (1998): 239.

71. Francis Westley, "Ritual as Psychic Bridge Builder: Narcissism, Healing, and the Human Potential Movements," *Journal of Psychoanalytic Anthropology* 6 (1983): 179–200.

72. Ann Braden Johnson, "A Temple of Last Resorts: Youth and Shared Narcissism," in *The Narcissistic Condition*, ed. Marie Coleman Nelson (New York: Human Sciences Press, 1977), pp. 27–75.

73. Daniel Kriegman and Leonard Solomon, "Cult Groups and Narcissistic Personality: The Offer to Heal the Defects of the Self," *International Journal of Group Psychotherapy* 25 (1985): 238–61.

74. Irene Gasde and Richard Block, "Cult Experience: Psychological Abuse, Distress, Personality Characteristics, and Changes in Personal Relationships Reported by Former Members of Church Universal and Triumphant," *Cultic Studies Journal* 15 (1998): 192–221.

75. See B. A. Sowards, M. J. Walser, and R. H. Hoyle, "Personality and Intelligence Measurement of the Church Universal and Triumphant," in *Church Universal and Triumphant in Scholarly Perspective*, ed. James R. Lewis and J. Gordon Melton (Stanford, CA: Center for Academic Publications, 1994), pp. 55–56.

76. Susan L. Blackmore, *Beyond the Body: An Investigation of Out-of-the-Body Experiences* (Chicago: Aldine, 1992).

77. John Rust, "Schizotypal Thinking among Members of Occult Sects," *Social Behavior and Personality* 20 (1992): 121–29.

78. For a discussion on the various psychological models of magic, see John A. Saliba, "Magical Thinking in Contemporary Western Culture: A Psychological View," in *Le Défi Magique: Esotérism, Occultisme, Spiritisme*, ed. Jean-Baptiste Martin (Lyons: University of Lyons Press, 1994), vol. 1, pp. 249–63.

79. Brock K. Kilbourne and James T. Richardson, "Social Experimentation: Self-Process or Social Role," *International Journal of Social Psychiatry* 31 (1985): 13–22.

80. See, for instance, Marc Galanter, "The 'Relief Effect': A Sociobiological Model for Neurotic Distress and Large-Group Therapy," *American Journal of Psychiatry* 135

(1978): 588–91, *Cults: Faith, Healing, and Coercion* (New York: Oxford University Press, 1989), and "Cults and Zealous Self-Help Movements: A Psychiatric Perspective," *American Journal of Psychiatry* 147 (1990): 543–61.

81. Marc Galanter, "Cults and Charismatic Group Psychology," in *Religion and the Clinical Practice of Psychology*, ed. Edward P. Shafranske (Washington, DC: American Psychological Association, 1996), p. 270.

82. Galanter, "Cults and Charismatic Group Psychology," p. 271.

83. Michael Ross, "Clinical Profiles of Hare Krishna Devotees," *American Journal of Psychiatry* 140 (1983): 416–20, and "Mental Health and Membership in the Hare Krishnas: A Case Study," *Australian Psychologist* 18 (1983): 543–51.

84. Michael Ross, "Mental Health in Hare Krishna Devotees: A Longitudinal Study," *American Journal of Social Psychiatry* 4 (Fall 1985): 65–67.

85. Arnold Weiss and Andrew Comrey, "Personality Factor Structure among Hare Krishnas," *Educational and Psychological Measurement* 14 (1987): 317–28, "Personal Characteristics of Hare Krishnas," *Journal of Personality Assessment* 51 (1987): 399–413, "Psychological Distress and Well-Being in Hare Krishnas," *Psychological Reports* 61 (1987): 23–35, and "Personality and Mental Health of Hare Krishnas Compared with Psychiatric Outpatients and 'Normals,'" *Personality and Individual Differences* 8 (1987): 721–30.

86. For a brief summary of studies on the effects of meditation, confer John A. Saliba, "The New Religions and Mental Health," in *Religion and the Social Order*, vol. 3, part B, pp. 104–6.

87. Stuart Vyse, *Believing in Magic: The Psychology of Superstition* (New York: Oxford University Press, 1997), p. 176.

88. James Richardson, "Clinical and Personality Assessment of Participation in New Religions," *International Journal for the Psychology of Religion* 5 (1995): 165.

89. Jodi Aronoff, Steven Jay Lynn, and Peter Malinowski, "Are Cultic Environments Psychological Harmful?," *Clinical Psychology Review* 22 (2000): 100.

90. Consult, for example, Walter Capps, *The Monastic Impulse* (New York: Crossroads, 1983).

91. Christopher Lasch, *The Culture of Narcissism: American Life in an Age of Diminishing Expectations* (New York: W. W. Norton, 1978). See also, Claudio Laks Eizirik, "Psychoanalysis and Culture: Some Contemporary Challenges," *International Journal of Psycho-Analysis* 78 (1997): 789–800.

92. Confer Spilka, Hood, and Gorsuch, *The Psychology of Religion*, p. 199ff. Lewis R. Rambo has done some major work on the subject. Confer his article "Conversion: Towards a Holistic Model of Religious Change," *Pastoral Psychology* 38 (1989): 47–63. See also his book, *Understanding Religious Conversion* (New Haven, CT: Yale University Press, 1993). Saliba, *Psychiatry and the Cults*, pp. 40ff, dedicates a section to studies on religious conversion before the rise of the new movements.

93. See, for instance, Rambo, *Understanding Religious Conversion*; and Natalie Isser and Lita Linzer Schwartz, *The History of Conversion and Contemporary Cults* (New York: Peter Lang, 1989).

94. Confer Rambo, *Understanding Religious Conversion*. For a short summary of Rambo's view see Raymond F. Paloutzian, James T. Richardson, and Lewis R. Rambo, "Religious Conversion and Personality Change," *Journal of Personality* 67 (1999): 1052–53.

95. Louis Rambo, "Converting: Stages of Religious Change," in *Religious Conversion: Contemporary Practices and Controversies*, ed. Christopher Lamb and M. Darrol Bryant (London: Cassell, 1999), pp. 23–34.

96. See Saliba, *Psychiatry and the Cults*, p. 531ff.

97. See Martin Eggleton, "Belonging to a Cult or New Religious Movement: Act of Free Will or Form of Mind Control?" and Lorne L. Dawson, "Cult Conversions: Controversy and Clarification," both in *Religious Conversion*, ed. Lamb and Bryant, pp. 263–77 and pp. 287–314 respectively.

98. For some of the more elaborate articulations of this model confer Thomas W. Keiser and Jacqueline Keiser, *The Anatomy of Illusion: Religious Cults and Destructive Persuasion* (Springfield, IL: Thomas, 1987); and Steven Hassan, *Releasing the Bonds: Empowering People to Think for Themselves* (Sommerville, MA: Freedom of the Mind Press, 2000). Margaret Singer has been one of the more vociferous proponents of the brainwashing theory. See, for example her book, coauthored with Janja Lalich, *Cults in Our Midst* (San Francisco: Jossey-Bass, 1995). Confer also Margaret T. Singer and Richard Ofshe, "Thought Reform Programs and the Production of Psychiatric Casualties," *Psychiatric Annals* 20 (1990): 188–93; and Margaret T. Singer and Marsha Emmer Addis, "Cults, Coercion, and Contumely," *Cultic Studies Journal* 9 (1992): 163–89.

99. See, for example, Benjamin D. Zablocki, "Hyper Compliance in Charismatic Groups," in *Mind, Brain, and Society: Toward a Neurosociology of Emotion*, ed. Thomas S. Smith (Stanford, CT: JAI Press, 1999), pp. 287–310.

100. James T. Richardson, "Conversion Careers," *Society* 17, no. 3 (March–April 1980): 47–50.

101. Rambo, *Understanding Religious Conversion*, pp. 20–21. Each model is described separately at length in one or more chapters.

102. James Downton, "An Evolutionary Theory of Spiritual Conversion and Commitment: The Case of the Divine Light Mission," *Journal for the Scientific Study of Religion* 19 (1980): 392–93. See also Downton's monograph, *Sacred Journeys: The Conversion of Young Americans to the Divine Light Mission* (New York: Columbia University Press, 1979).

103. John Long and Jeffrey K. Hadden, "Religious Conversion and the Concept of Socialization: Integrating the Brainwashing and Drift Models," *Journal for the Scientific Study of Religion* 22 (1983): 1–14.

104. John Lofalnd and Norman Skonovd, "Conversion Motifs," *Journal for the Scientific Study of Religion* 20 (1981): 373–85.

105. J. Gordon Melton and Lawrence Moore, *The Cult Experience: Responding to the New Religious Pluralism* (New York: Pilgrim Press, 1982), p. 47ff.

106. Arnold van Gennap, *The Rites of Passage* (Chicago: University of Chicago Press, 1960).

107. Victor Turner, *The Ritual Process: Structure and Anti-Structure* (Chicago: Aldine, 1969). See also his essay, "Betwixt and Between: The Liminal Period in Rites of Passage," in his book, *The Forest of Symbols* (Ithaca, NY: Cornell University Press, 1967), pp. 93–111.

108. There is great debate about how members of new religions are rearing their children. Some maintain that the children are being abused. Confer Arthur A. Dole and Steve K. Dubrow Eichel, "Some New Religions are Dangerous," *Cultic Studies Journal* 2 (1985): 17–30; and David A. Halperin, "Cults and Children: The Role of the Psychotherapist," *Group* 11, no. 1 (1987): 47–53. Other studies of some controversial movements, however, have reached quite different conclusions. See, for instance, Gary Shepherd and Lawrence Lilliston, "Children of the Church Universal and Triumphant," in *Church Universal and Triumphant*, pp. 67–95.

109. The new edition of the diagnostic and statistical manual of mental diseases, DSM-IV includes a completely new section titled "Religious or Spiritual Problems." For a report on DSM-IV see the *New York Times*, February 10, 1994, p. A16. For a more detailed study consult Robert Turner, David Lukoff, Ruth Tiffany Barnhouse, and Francis G. Lu, "Religious and Spiritual Problem: A Culturally Sensitive Diagnostic Category in DSM-IV," *Journal of Nervous and Mental Disease* 183 (1996): 435–44. For recent approaches to the psychology of religion, see Bernard Spilka and Daniel N. McIntosh, eds., *The Psychology of Religion: Theoretical Approaches* (Boulder, CO: Westview Press, 1997).

THE NEW RELIGIOUS MOVEMENTS IN SOCIOLOGICAL PERSPECTIVE

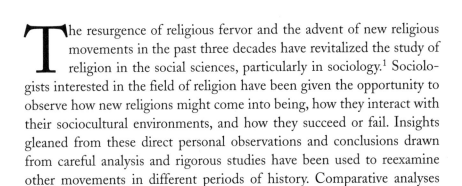

The resurgence of religious fervor and the advent of new religious movements in the past three decades have revitalized the study of religion in the social sciences, particularly in sociology.[1] Sociologists interested in the field of religion have been given the opportunity to observe how new religions might come into being, how they interact with their sociocultural environments, and how they succeed or fail. Insights gleaned from these direct personal observations and conclusions drawn from careful analysis and rigorous studies have been used to reexamine other movements in different periods of history. Comparative analyses have been employed to determine the degree to which the new movements of the second half of the twentieth century can be considered a unified phenomenon sharing similar features among themselves and with other alternative groups that came before them.[2]

The sociological study of the new religions differs from the psychological approach in that it looks on them as social movements, affecting not just individuals but society as a whole.[3] Sociologists focus on the existence of these new religious entities as marginal subcultures or units that are in conflict with society at large. They examine the way diverse religious institutions and organizations are formed and maintained. They explore the internal dynamics that make them viable social units, their economic and political structures, the type of charismatic leadership that provides divine legitimacy for their beliefs and practices, and the levels and types of commitment demanded of their devotees. They further observe the social correlates that go with membership and the cultural factors that influence recruitment policies. They are also interested in the conflicts that exist between the new groups and the mainline religious traditions and the effects such conflicts might have on both. And they follow the evolution of particular movements that eventually cease to exist, undergo radical changes, acquire respectable, though still marginal, niches in society, or sometimes become institutionalized and established religions spread in different parts of the world.

But the sociology of new religious movements has not been a smooth undertaking. Contemporary sociologists quickly found themselves engaged in heated debates with some psychiatrists and counselors who maintain that involvement in a new religion is either an expression or a direct cause of pathology. They also failed to have much impact on the parents of cult members and on the general public, because their reflections do not directly address four main, practical, and commonly asked questions: (1) How should society react to the apparent threat of a rising new religious subculture? (2) How can parents best respond to their offspring's involvement in alternative belief systems? (3) What can be done to prevent people from joining them? (4) How can their members be persuaded to return to their natural family ties and previous religious affiliations? Further, most sociologists have defended religious freedom and have tended to support the position of the new religions in legal suits. Consequently, sociologists have not been very successful in influencing people's attitudes toward, and responses to, the new religions.

The sociological method has been another hindrance to the public's acceptance of sociological understandings of the phenomenon of new religions. Sociologists aim at studying religions as objectively and impartially as possible. They tend to put all religions on the same level. They are not interested in establishing which religion is true or false or in defending any one particular religious tradition or innovation. Besides, they make no moral judgments about religious behavior. Their aims are to explore how and why new values, beliefs, and lifestyles emerge, how new religious concepts become popular, and how experimental communities are formed. Further, sociologists have assumed that the new religions, while existing in various levels of friction with their surroundings, are genuine religious expressions. This perspective is foreign to most members of traditional religions, who might interpret it either as an endorsement of the cults' belief systems and activities and/or a challenge to the believer's stance that new religions and spiritualities must be judged in the light of true religion.

It does not come as a surprise, therefore, that there have been serious disagreements and clashes between sociologists and other observers of the contemporary religious scene. At least six issues can be identified in the current debate about the new religious movements. The first deals with the definition of a cult. The second questions the reasons for studying the new religious movements and the methods that should be used to examine them. The third concerns their variety and hinges on whether any generalizations can be made about them. The fourth centers on their distinguishing characteristics. The fifth focuses on the models that are devised to understand why they come into being and to explain their significance for, and impact on, modern Western culture. The sixth discusses the societal response that is appropriate to their persistent presence, a response that is determined by the answers that are given to the first five issues.

The Definition of a New Religion

The definition of religion has been a subject of debate in sociological literature since the nineteenth century.[4] It is thus not surprising that new movements have come under scrutiny and their claim to being "religions" has been challenged or denied. In chapter 1, several different definitions were identified and it was shown that whether one calls the new movements religious or not is closely linked with an evaluation of the movement's authenticity as a religion and the leader's genuineness. The issue of authenticity is important because it is not restricted simply to new religious movements. It has been raised between members of the same religion who split on matters of orthodoxy as well as between members of different religions who often reject, for instance, each other's claim to divine revelation. Whether any particular religious group is religious or not has been the subject of debate especially when the question is raised in regard to the new cults, since these may not fit easily into the traditional mold of what constitutes religious belief and practice.[5] The question is important and cannot be ignored or downplayed. Lewis Carter correctly remarks that

> to exclude authenticity issues from the domain of secular scholarly discourse would likely prevent that discourse from understanding the "sound of fury" of religious conflicts, understanding the basis for accommodation of competing traditions, or examining some of the mechanisms by which social and moral order are grounded in human systems.[6]

Whether a new movement is labeled a religion or not is not simply a matter of academic interest. In fact, there are both practical advantages and disadvantages that can be accorded to the status of a religion. Alan Aldridge points out that there are four main benefits to being recognized as a legitimate religion: (1) gaining legal protection, (2) gaining tax benefits, (3) establishing a link to an ethnic community, and (4) achieving respectability.[7] However, the title "religion" may also carry with it some disadvantages, such as (1) legal restrictions, (2) negative images of mainstream religion, and (3) identification as a cult. Not all movements want to be listed with the world's religions. Scientology has fought for years to gain tax exemption by insisting that it is a religion. Those defending Transcendental Meditation in court argued in vain that TM was essentially a program designed to increase one's creativity and not a religious institution. The Hare Krishna movement has strengthened its ties with the ethnic community from which it originally rose by stressing its roots in the Hindu Vaishnava tradition. It has further emphasized the spiritual functions it performs to the Hindu community.[8] Several religious movements stemming from the East, such as Brahma Kumaris and Ananda Marga, prefer to be known as spiritual and/or educational organizations.

By training, sociologists are inclined to be dispassionate and open-minded and, hence, they normally adopt a neutral position to the phenomenon of new religions. From a sociological point of view, theories and classifications of religions are all-inclusive; no religion is given a special status or prestige or used as a paradigm for understanding or evaluating other religions. Because of the familial, social, and religious conflicts that new religions have brought, one, however, wonders whether a nonpartisan definition of a marginal religious group is at all possible.

Although an impartial approach to the study of the new religions may be highly commendable, it is certainly fraught with difficulties. Treating cults on par with established religious groups could easily lead to a relativistic and noncommittal approach that conflicts with the truth claims and the commitment demands of all religions. Besides, sociological attempts to give a nonjudgmental, factual definition may not be as value-free as they might appear to be at first sight. All scholars are faced with the initial task of identifying and defining the various kinds of religious groups they are studying. In so doing, they cannot avoid making an implicit evaluative statement on the movement under study. Neutral definitions of cults or sects may not incorporate a religious appraisal of their orthodoxy, but they might indirectly state something about them that contributes to their acceptance as credible and respectable religious options in a pluralistic society. Sociologists may further influence public opinion both with regard to cults' importance and worth and in the kind of responses that can be made to their challenging presence. A definition of a new religion, for instance, may steer away from the question as to whether its claim to be within the Orthodox Christian or Judaic traditions is a legitimate one. But it can hardly avoid making a statement on its nature and/or functions and selecting certain constitutive features that determine its makeup. One can also observe that the scholars' own religious backgrounds or lack of them, their academic training, and their own attitudes toward religion are bound to influence their definitions and evaluations of the new religions.

Sociologists have been active participants in the public debates on the new movements for the simple reason that they view a new religion as just one type of socioreligious group and organization. Cults (and sects) seem to share at least some features with other religious organizations and traditions—a position that contrasts sharply with the conviction that a cult is a pseudo-religion and, therefore, should in no way be compared and confused with the major traditions and their main branches. Sociologists also contend that contemporary new religions share several characteristics with religious movements in other periods of Western history. On the other hand, there are those who argue that the majority of new movements use the label "religion" to acquire legal and social acceptance, when in fact they are destructive entities that are intrinsically different from the traditional majority of religious groups that came into being in previous centuries.

Social scientists also disagree about the religious significance of the new religious movements, whether they are labeled sects or cults. From a sociological viewpoint, the new religions may be seen as natural processes that have taken place several times in the history of the human race and that will occur again, given the correct sociocultural conditions. From this general picture it is easy to conclude that the rise of new religious movements is an interesting but unremarkable event in a society that is changing rapidly under the influence of modern technology. This does not logically lead to the view that sectarian developments are necessarily good in themselves or beneficial to the individual and society, but it certainly leans toward the position that alternative religious groups should not be the subject of overwhelming concern, much less fear. It follows, therefore, that most sociologists[9] do not exhibit the same level of anxiety, apprehension, and panic that one finds among some psychiatrists and psychologists, certain segments of the Christian community, parents of cult and ex-cult members, self-styled deprogrammers, and news media reporters.

Yet sociologists, as well as other scholars (such as historians of religion) who study religious phenomena, are aware that not all new religious movements can be easily categorized as "religions" in the traditional meaning of the term. Various terms, such as "implicit religion," "quasi-sacred," and "secularized" or "secular" religion have been applied to some of the new movements.[10] Bryan Wilson, for example, describes Scientology as a "secularized religion."[11] Ninian Smart points out that religious dimensions, such as myth and ritual, can be found outside the mainline traditions and in areas, such as sports, that are not usually linked with religion.[12] Malcolm Hamilton sees the concept of implicit religion as a notion that includes elements that appear to be religious, but in fact are not.[13] Other terms, such as "invisible religion," "surrogate religion," "quasi-religion," and "parareligion," are often employed to describe organizations and/or institutions that adopt many transcendental or ultimate values and ritual practices comparable to those in traditional religions. Under the label of implicit religion many political, spiritual, and social groups could be included. Thus, Maoism has been viewed as having several religious dimensions even though it rejects commonly held religious beliefs, such as the existence of God and the afterlife.[14]

Some scholars, such as Richard Fenn, include among "the quasi-sacred forms of religiosity" various therapies, spiritual disciplines, and twelve-step programs that are dedicated to enhancing the self.[15] Others prefer to use the somewhat vague term "quasi-religion." John Steadman Rice, for example, prefers to call twelve-step programs quasi-religions and then goes on to show how the two groups he compared—Co-dependency Anonymous and Alcoholics Anonymous—have a different conception of God.[16] Similarly, Humanism, Marxism, and Nationalism,[17] and some corporations, like Amway,[18] have been called "quasi-religions." Mary Jo Neitz defines quasi-religions as those groups whose beliefs and practices are "spiritual at the core, but which lack the structure of conventional religion and religious movement organizations."[19] A. Greil and D. Rudy apply the term "quasi-religions" to those out-of-the-mainstream "organizations which either see themselves or are seen by others as sort-of religious."[20] David Bromley and Mitchell Bracey adopt the same term and point out that some of the new religions "straddle the boundary between sacred and secular groups within a society, and have a nonreligious as well as a religious character."[21] They include the New Age movement, Transcendental Meditation, certain therapies, and Scientology as quasi-religious movements. They explore Scientology in some detail and conclude that it is a combination of religion and therapy. They write:

> Today, Scientology has as much a therapeutic look as a religious look. For example, clergy and traditional ceremonies are not central to the religious lives of Scientologists. There are no traditional church buildings at which the faithful regularly gather. Scientology operates on a fee-for-service basis, providing services to clients. The Church is not financed through gifts and offerings from members. From the perspective of the outsider, members more closely resemble consumers than parishioners. Finally, Scientology uses scientific research to measure its benefits. It urges practitioners to evaluate any results they experience. Conventional Churches, on the other hand, are based on faith and results are not examined critically.[22]

Scientology brings into focus the difficulties one encounters when evaluating whether some of the new movements could be called "religions." Though Scientology may be an exceptional case, it is not unique. Transcendental Meditation and some Yoga groups raise the same issue.

Why and How Should One Study the New Religions?

Many of the new religious movements have been subjected to intensive research from different academic perspectives. Traditional religious groups have added to the voluminous literature by their apologetical responses and frequently vehement denunciations. But since the number of those who have become involved in these new religions is relatively small, one could certainly question whether they have been given more attention than they actually deserve. Thus, a second major issue regards both the reasons why and the manner in which new religions should be studied.

Reasons for Studying the New Religions

The reasons for studying the new movements seriously are very similar, if not identical to, the reasons advanced for studying other religions besides one's own.[23] One might add that the rise of the new religions might also be indicative of religious and spiritual trends that will influence both the cultural and religious landscape of the future.[24]

While the majority of sociologists and students of religions support the continued research into the new movements, some Christian writers[25] have argued that the study of the cults does not deserve the prominence it has been given. Since cults cannot be reconciled with Christianity, they should be simply dismissed as pseudo-religious or non-Christian organizations. Others[26] seem to engage in the study of new religions with the intention of counteracting their alleged manipulative techniques and pervasive influence.

Sociologists are interested in the new religions because they are a specific form of human social behavior and an expression of religious, social, and cultural dynamism. They are not primarily dedicated to the investigation of the new movements for personal reasons. Their research is not an aspect of their involvement in, or reaction to, a new religion, nor is it directly related to their own personal quest for religious meaning and experience, even though there might be some exceptional cases. How and to what extent this initial attitude influences one's research is a debatable point. Because of this rather dispassionate motivation for studying new religions, sociologists could easily appear to be cult sympathizers or even cult promoters.

The above approach contrasts sharply with the view of those whose study of the new religions is motivated by theological and/or personal reasons. For religious apologists and evangelizers, the study of the new movements is not an end in itself, an academic activity pursued for the quest of human knowledge and for understanding the variety of human behavior. Rather, the teachings of the cults are studied in order that they might be more easily criticized and refuted. The behavior of the members of new religions is scrutinized so that their allegedly evil intentions and activities and their unorthodox beliefs might be more readily exposed. Many parents, psychologists, and deprogrammers get involved in the study of cults largely to explore ways of extricating their members from organizations they deem antithetical to family life or, more generally, to the fundamental values of Western culture.[27]

While sociologists can at least make an effort at impartiality, many Christian evangelicals and fundamentalists have taken a negative stand that leads them to generalizations on all the new religions. Unlike the majority of social scientists, they are religious crusaders, enthusiastic champions of customary moral values and family unity, and ardent defenders of traditional social norms. They have become so personally involved that their objectivity and impartiality have suffered. Because of their highly charged, emotional stance, those who denounce the cults as evil institutions have been perceived as "cult opponents" or "anti-cultists" with little to offer to the academic study of new religions.

Many sociologists[28] have argued that the anti-cult movement has some of the negative features often ascribed to the new religions themselves. Those involved in the anti-cult movement have retorted by accusing sociologists of having accepted some of the beliefs and values of the new movements and to have sided with their members in the family conflicts that membership has given rise to or aggravated. They have accused scholars of having formed their own "anti-anti-cult movement."[29] In their view, many scholars, especially sociologists, are "misguided academics" or "cult apologists" and, consequently, both their assessments of cults and their recommendations must be summarily dismissed.[30]

Ways of Studying the New Religions

Examining the methods used to investigate the new religions is necessary because the validity and interpretation of the information about them ultimately depends on how researchers go about studying them. What are the procedures one should adopt for finding out exactly what cult members believe, what their goals and practices are, what effects they have on those who join them, what methods they employ to socialize their members, and what demands gurus make of their devotees? How does one reach conclusions about the way new religions operate as distinct subcultures that are at variance or in conflict with the mainline religious groups and culture? Are there suitable methods that can help the researcher not only record the facts faithfully, but also understand their significance?

The methods employed by sociologists to investigate the new religious movements are essentially those that have been applied to the study of traditional religions in various societies and of social processes in general.[31]

Methods

These methods consist of the use of historical materials (when available), comparisons between similar phenomena in the same society and across cultures, controlled experimentation (where possible), sample surveys, intensive interviews, content analysis, and participant observation. Some of these approaches emphasize "fieldwork," which implies the need for an investigation that entails direct contact and interaction with the people under study. The underlying assumption is that those being studied are not only reliable and trustworthy informants, but also that they should have an important, if not determining, say in expounding and explaining their own beliefs and practices. In other words, the sincerity and honesty of the members of new religions are taken for granted unless there are good reasons to believe otherwise.

The method of participant observation is at the heart of the current debate on how new religious movements should be studied. It has been a major source of conflict between the majority of social scientists and those who have taken a negative approach to the cults. Briefly stated, the method of participant observation, which is not new in the social sciences, encourages researchers to study the new movements by establishing direct contact with their members and by taking part, to a limited degree and for some period of time, in their activities and lifestyles. Developed initially by Western anthropologists for the study of non-Western peoples,[32] this method, also known as "fieldwork," is now a well-established method and has been analyzed and discussed for over half a century and has been adopted by most social scientists.[33] The heart of the approach lies in its insistence that the observers should not apply an interpretation or judgment based solely on their own cultural assumptions and points of view. Rather, they should attempt to understand people's behavior from the perspective of the latter's own cultural and religious norms and values. Thus, scholars are urged to avoid being ethnocentric, advice that is being taken seriously by some Christian missionaries in their evaluation of indigenous religions.[34] In their approach to other cultures and religions social scientists favor the adoption of a nonjudgmental attitude and the posture of cultural relativism.[35]

This approach of participant observation with a culturally relativistic attitude is considered problematic also by the scholars who propose it. Sociologists Anthony Giddens and Mitchell Dumeier agree that care must be used in applying this method. "A researcher," they state, "could begin to identify so closely with the group that she becomes too much of an 'insider' and loses the perspective of an outside observer."[36] Conrad Phillip Kottak, an anthropologist, after explaining the need of the researcher's impartiality, remarks: "As human beings living among others, we cannot be totally impartial and detached observers."[37]

Moreover, how does one determine the limits of participation that require more than an outward conformity to some aspects of the behavior and worldview of the members of a new religion under study? Because religion deals with matters of ultimate truth and moral worth, one cannot accept the ideology and lifestyle of a new religion on a temporary and uncommitted basis. Social scientists do not endorse conversion of the researchers to the religions they are studying, but they do insist that they must endeavor to see them from the "inside out" rather than from the "outside in." This implies that sociologists must find some common ground between what they are studying and some of their own religious and/or cultural beliefs, values, practices, and experiences. In so doing, they might be indirectly criticizing some aspects of modern culture and traditional religion and might appear to endorse the beliefs and practices under investigation. Further, participant observation entails not just the detached attendance at religious rituals, but also some kind of personal involvement in the rites themselves. Scholars could easily leave the impression that they are compromising their own religious principles and/or rejecting those of mainline culture.

But participant observation as a method has withstood the test of time. The many monographs on non-Western societies that Western scholars have produced testify that participant observation is, within limitations, a worthwhile venture. The advantages of the method outweigh its disadvantages and can be minimized if the researchers are fully aware of the problems. Participant observation studies people and their religious beliefs and practices directly without any intermediaries. By establishing relationships with those individuals who are being studied, the researcher has a better opportunity of learning about their feelings, experiences, fears, and motivations. Misinformation and misinterpretation that flow from rather casual and indirect studies of other societies and religions can be more easily avoided. Similarly, exaggerations and misunderstandings by disgruntled ex-members and upset family members are not allowed to distort the belief systems and lifestyles of new religious movements.

Some scholars, however, have rejected the methods of participant observation and its accompanying attitude of cultural relativism as useful approaches to understand and evaluate the new religions. They have responded by applying a different method that by and large studies cult life through the eyes of those who have defected, willingly or by force, from the movements.[38] They have further considered the reactions of the relatives and friends of members of new religions as major sources for understanding the effects these movements have on their members. The accounts given by the members themselves and by the scholars who have studied them firsthand are not accepted as honest and reliable portrayers of the new beliefs, values, and practices. Consequently, the literature and activities of the new religious movements are interpreted not in the total context of the members' lifestyles and commitments, but from the cultural presuppositions of those who have embarked on an anti-cult crusade. The goal of these researchers is aimed either at discrediting the beliefs promoted by the cults, persuading the newly converted to return to their previous belief system, and/or suppressing their activities through legal means. Most social scientists think that the criticism of the method of participant observation is a misunderstanding of the whole anthropological and sociological enterprise. They consider the alternative methodological approach as highly inadequate, inaccurate, and misleading. In particular, they maintain that those who rely solely on the testimony of those who left the movements, either through forced deprogramming or exit counseling, have made little effort to understand the apostates' various exit roles and careers.[39]

Moreover, except in a few cases, there is little evidence that social scientists look favorably on the beliefs and practices of the new movements. On the contrary, they are rather viewed as curiosities, anachronisms, or even complete absurdities. Bryan Wilson, for example, holds that charisma, found in many of the leaders of the new religions, is a primitive trait and that its presence in the modern world shows how slowly wish-dreams die out.[40] Not many scholars in their face-to-face approach to the new religions have been remotely attracted, much less converted, to their worldviews and lifestyles. This debate has shown no sign of waning. In fact it has intensified, even though some attempts are being made at bringing both sides together.[41] The labeling of scholars as pro-cultists (cult sympathizers) or anti-cultists (cult detractors) has increased the dichotomy between the two quite different approaches and has not led to the solution to the problem. It has also left little opening for scholars to cooperate in research projects. Recently the debate has centered on three major topics.[42]

The first deals with the objectivity of the scholars who have embarked on the study of a new religious movement and its members. Sociologists have been criticized for not paying serious attention to the pitfalls in the study of cults. Janja Lalich, for instance, has identified four major problems that researchers face when studying new religions.[43] The first problem that scholars face is that they can be easily deceived by the members of the group under study.[44] Group leaders might select both the topics of discussion and stage the events for the benefit of the viewers. Second, the group often makes demands, imposes restrictions, and has recourse to intimidation to influence the research results. Third, cult informants can be trained to give a false impression of what life in the group really is. And fourth, the researchers themselves are susceptible to the charismatic appeal of the cult. Benjamin Beit-Hallahmi is among several scholars who have severely criticized other scholars for conducting research under the auspices and funding of the new religious movements themselves.[45] Sociologists, however, are well aware of the difficulties of fieldwork and whether the funding of their studies has prejudiced their results, which can always be checked by other studies funded by other sources.

The second topic is concerned with the reliability of the information gathered from both cult and ex-cult members. The issue of whether members have been brainwashed to depict the cult in a favorable light or whether they have freely accepted a new ideology and lifestyle is still dividing those who study the new religions. Equally questionable is the reliability of ex-members, especially those who have been pressured to leave by parents or exit counselors. The third topic examines the general impact of the new cults on society. Violence, child-rearing practices, and the position of women are the issues frequently discussed by scholars from both camps.

Studies of new religious movements depict the methodological assumptions of those conducting the research. They also reveal to what extent the researchers have adopted some level of objectivity in their approach. Those who rely solely on reports of ex-cult members have not produced works that are as informative and impartial as those produced by sociologists or as penetrating as those conducted by scholars of religion. One has in mind here the brief cult profiles produced under the direction of the late Jeffrey K. Hadden[46] and theological analyses like that of George D. Chryssides[47] of the Unification Church's belief system.

How Can the New Religions Be Best Classified?

The variety of new religions in Western society leads to another important question. Can they be classified in some coherent fashion? In chapter 1, a major example of a classification based on religious ideologies was presented. Here various kinds of typologies proposed by influential sociologists will be briefly outlined.

Sociological classifications of new religions have tended to focus on the conflicting relationships that they might have with society at large. Roy Wallis divides cults into three categories: (1) world-rejecting, (2) world-affirming, and (3) the world-accommodating.[48] This typology would be applicable to both sects and cults. Its stress is not on the content of belief, but rather on the way each group defines itself vis-à-vis the larger society. Implicit in such a classification is the principle that new religious movements cannot be understood simply as spiritual revivals or resurgences. They are rather envisaged as ways of reacting to society or to some particular sociocultural condition.

A more elaborate proposal has been put forward by Bryan Wilson, who thinks that sects are "deviant responses to the world."[49] Seven types of such responses are then distinguished: (1) conversionist, (2) revolutionist (or transformative), (3) introversionist, (4) manipulationist (or magical), (5) thaumaturgical (or miraculous), (6) reformist, and (7) utopian. Though developed primarily to account for the divisions within traditional Christianity, several of the characteristics that are associated with each division within this typology have been applied to some of the new religions.

A typology tailored specifically for the new religious movements has been proposed by two American sociologists, Rodney Stark and William Sims Bainbridge, who take the degree of organization, or lack of it, as the principal criterion for their distinctions between the various new religious groups.[50] These two scholars classify new religions into three types: "audience cults," "client cults," and "cult movements." The first type (audience cults) is characterized by having virtually no organization; its members remain largely on the consumer level; they do not, as a rule, meet as a group; and they adopt cult beliefs and practices through printed materials, the radio, and television. This kind of cult unites the participants by a mythology and not by a communal structure.

The second type (client cults) is made up of individuals who develop a relationship with their leaders similar to that of patients with their therapists. These cults never become organizations or communities; they have clients, not members, who may retain their formal association with an established church. They make ritual practices available to those who are genuinely interested in the magical and/or healing arts.

The final type (cult movements) consists of organized religious entities that attempt to satisfy all the needs of their adherents. Though the levels of organizational development, the intensity of commitment, and the demands made on the membership may vary, all cult movements look for converts who will break off their attachment to other religious organizations. Cult movements are genuine alternative religions and they alone provoke great hostility from their sociocultural surroundings.

It may be argued that these sociological typologies neglect both the ideological differences between the new religious as well as the experiential dimensions that most of them claim. It may be further objected that none of them would encompass all the new religions. Moreover, most of them seem to have been originally constructed to account for the divisions within Christianity, making their application to a broader religious base somewhat strained. Some sociologists admit that many of the movements do not fit easily in any one particular category. Some would fit comfortably in more than one and several have altered sufficiently enough to merit being placed in a category different from the one they belonged to when they first came into being.

Another weakness of the above classifications is that most of them are highly descriptive and, therefore, fail to deal with the objections raised by those who maintain that new religions require some evaluation. Several social scientists have endeavored to correct this flaw by proposing more normative criteria. Dick Anthony, for example, focuses on differentiating new religions by whether they can be judged to be "authentic" or "inauthentic" paths to transcendence.[51] Frederick Bird takes another approach that centers on moral accountability.[52] He points out that in three types or levels of membership—those of devotee, discipleship, and apprenticeship—new religions provide their own way of mitigating moral accountability. Ken Wilber[53] has proposed an evolutionary scheme of "pre-rational," "rational self-consciousness," and "transrational" levels by which the authenticity and legitimacy of new religious groups can be judged.[54]

Whatever the weaknesses of these sociological divisions, they certainly highlight some crucial questions that must be answered if the new religious movements are to be understood in some depth. When is the sociocultural environment conducive to the emergence and success of new religions? What types of relationships with society do these groups promote? To what extent is knowledge of their organizational structure necessary for understanding them? What factors will lead a new religion to grow or fail or to cultivate a lower or higher tension with society? It would seem that such questions must be attended to before any attempt can be made to evaluate the new religions.

Major Features of the New Movements

It is taken for granted by many scholars that the new religions represent, by and large, a kind of spiritual revival that leads people to abandon traditional churches and denominations. There is little agreement, however, when it comes to specifying those characteristics that are peculiar to alternative religions and setting them apart from traditional religions.

The sociological approach is typified by that of Wilson who carefully avoids making theological judgments on the belief systems of new religions. His catalog of ideal sect characteristics, most of which can, with some modifications, be applied to the new religions, is a good illustration of how a sociologist describes the main features of new religions without denouncing them as destructive entities. Wilson considers sects and new religious movements to be religious entities that live in tension with traditional religion and society.[55] He enumerates eight features of sectarianism: (1) exclusivity, (2) monopoly of truth, (3) a lay organization, (4) rejection of the religious division of labor, (5) voluntariness, (6) the expulsion of members who do not follow the prescribed standards, (7) the demand of total allegiance, and (8) protest against traditional religion and society.[56] Several other features can be easily seen as flowing from those listed by Wilson. Contemporary religious movements tend to set clear boundaries that mark their members as the chosen elite. These members are bound by self-consciousness and conscientious commitments and not by cultural heritage or tradition. Their quests for truth and/or for religious experiences have led them to dedicate themselves to the goals and ideals of a new religion. And they legitimize their claims with reference to a sacred authority, often embedded in a charismatic leader who monopolizes the right to dictate the movement's doctrine and to prescribe its lifestyle.

One of the common characteristics of many cults and sects is their communal dimension. Of the features mentioned by Wilson, most, if not all, indicate that members of these marginal groups form tightly knit communities. Individuals are often first drawn to join a movement by the relationships that exist between members, rather than by the appeal of their ideology. John Saliba has pointed out how new religious groups, such as ISKCON, the Aetherius Society, and Promise Keepers, form religious communities and use various means to maintain them. One common method for this purpose has been the Internet, which is not just a tool for publicizing the organization, but also an effective way to keep members linked by a common bond. Thus, to take one example, the Movement for Spiritual Inner Awareness not only has a Web site[57] full of information about its beliefs and activities. It also routinely sends e-mail to those who want to keep abreast of its activities, which include its radio broadcasts and the travels and talks of its founder John Roger.

Just like all religious organizations, many of the new cults are making extensive use of the Internet, which has become an important feature that no scholar can ignore. Sara Horsfell has pointed out that the Internet is used for internal and external communication and for sharing information.[58] It thus acts as a medium whereby members of a religious group can engage in conversation among themselves and with outsiders. The debate over the cults, their evangelization efforts, and the negative reaction, especially of ex-members, are no longer restricted to the usual media (books, articles, leaflets, radio, and television).[59] Lorne Dawson and Jenna Hennebry have argued that the Internet has so far played a minor role in recruitment efforts of new religions, but as a medium "may be having other largely unanticipated effects on the form and functioning of religion, both old and new, in the future."[60] Debates about the new religions have found an open forum on the Internet, and controversial movements like Scientology have elicited many reactions.[61]

143

The characteristics listed by Wilson do not, by themselves, necessarily imply any positive or negative functions that new religions might fulfill. Some of them, like authoritarianism, monopoly of truth, and exclusivity, can also be found in mainline churches. Most of them can have good and/or bad effects, depending on the social circumstances and the states of mind of both the leaders of the new religions and their followers.

Admittedly, the sociological method of ascribing relatively neutral features to the new religions does not have a great popular appeal. The beliefs and practices of new religions call for an evaluation because (1) they propose different belief systems and lifestyles and (2) they frequently and openly question and/or attack traditional religious and social values. But as an initial approach to the new religions, the sociological method is a safeguard against making hasty judgments about, and wild generalizations on, what members of new religions believe and practice.

Many publicized statements about the violence that is allegedly rampant in the new religions are glaring examples of such overgeneralization.[62] The tragic demise of the People's Temple, in Jonestown, Guyana (where several hundred cult members were either murdered or committed suicide), is taken as the paradigm of a destructive cult, thus implying that all new religious movements might end up like Jonestown.

There are other examples of religious groups that had recourse to murder and self-violence. Aum Shinrikyo in Japan, the Branch Davidian in Waco, Texas, the Order of the Solar Tradition in Switzerland, the UFO Group, "Heaven's Gate," in California, and the Restoration of the Ten Commandments of God, in Uganda, all seem to confirm the view that some cults are prone to criminal and self-destructive behavior. It is doubtful, however, whether any of these groups are typical. It is also questionable whether a general theory of "destructive cultism" or "brainwashing" can account for their suicidal behavior, which might be better explained with reference to sociological[63] and psychological[64] theories of suicide. Lorne Dawson argues that violence in some new religions is better accounted for with reference to social-psychological processes than with the application of the brainwashing theory.[65] Anthony Robbins's attempt to interpret the tragedy of Jonestown under the rubric of "the sociology of martyrdom" is certainly more convincing than the view that attributes its charismatic leader with the uncanny powers of hypnosis and mind control.[66] One must also stress that suicide and murder are types of human aberrant behavior found not exclusively among the members of a handful of new religions.[67]

Gordon Melton has put forward some important considerations for understanding the phenomenon of violence within new religious movements.[68] He first adopts a more inclusive definition of cult-related violence to include not only bodily harm inflicted on cult members but also violent actions perpetrated against these same members by the public. Second, he insists that reports of violence must be carefully investigated. Third, he inculcates the need to adopt the standard sociological approach, namely, to see cult-violence in the broader religious and cultural violence that prevails in many societies. And finally, he proposes that a distinction should be made between the various levels of violence that exist among the new religious movements. Thus the violence that has occurred in a few of the new religious movements must be understood in the larger context of religion and violence and not as an isolated instance that takes place only in marginal religious groups.[69] It should also be borne in mind that violence has its attractive features and pervades many aspects of human life, religion included.[70] Violence is a universal human problem that has elicited numerous debates among scholars from different academic perspectives.[71]

There appears to be agreement on one important point: violence, such as physical child abuse and the unequal treatment of women, exists in some of the new religions. But the corporal punishment of children and the limiting of a woman's social role are social problems and not just religious aberrations. They are present also in many Christian churches that justify their behavior by referring to biblical texts or to tradition. And the kind of violence that is perpetrated and justified varies from group to group. The question can also be raised as to whether the belligerent reaction to the new religions can create or aggravate cult violence.[72] It must be emphasized that violence, such as the mistreatment of children and women, suicide, and murder, is indicative of human social and psychological problems that have existed in Western culture long before the advent of the new religions.

Theories Explaining the Rise of the New Religions

The fifth major debate about the new religions concerns the reason why they have come into being. Their apparently sudden emergence requires an explanation. Why is it that this particular period in the history of

Western culture should witness the rise of so many new religious movements? What factors must be taken into account to understand their dynamics? Most social-scientific literature takes it for granted that the roots of the phenomenon lie in contemporary culture. Several theories have been proposed to show how the Western world since the middle of the twentieth century has become a fertile ground for the successful rise and continued presence of new religions.

The Functional Approach

Probably the most common interpretation of cult formation has been the functional one. Religious revivals are said to emerge to satisfy practical human needs that are not being met, to help people cope with new problems and social conditions that cannot be addressed in other ways, and to act as catalysts for religious change. This view is usually labeled the relative deprivation theory of cult formation, because it starts with the observation that economic distress, lower social status, loneliness, and anomie are at the root of religious movements.[73] Charles Glock discusses five types of deprivation that he maintains are important to explain not only the rise of new religions but also their development and survival.[74] These deprivations are economic, social, organismic (that is, related or linked to mental and physical health), ethical, and psychic (or pertaining to philosophical meaning).

The functional approach is hardly new in the social sciences, especially in sociology and anthropology, where exploring the effects of religious beliefs on both the individual and on society has long been incorporated into their methodology. The following five major functions that religion in general and, by extension, cults and sects serve, have been common in social-scientific literature, particularly in anthropological studies on nonliterate cultures.[75]

Explanatory Functions

Religion is said to offer explanations, interpretations, and rationalizations of the many facets of human existence. It satisfies cognitive and intellectual needs by providing sure and definite answers. Inexplicable problems, which cannot be resolved by any other means, are unraveled by recourse to theological and religious sources of knowledge and arguments.

The new religions have come into being at a time when the mainline churches appear to have retreated, in part, from their dogmatic stance and when scientific progress has brought to the fore new moral and religious questions for which there are no definite answers. New religions, just like fundamentalist churches, are known for providing intellectual security. They counteract contemporary moral ambiguity, providing religiously legitimated answers to human problems.

Emotional Functions

The most common sociopsychological functions assigned to religion are emotional. Religion, by giving the person identity, security, and courage, reduces, relieves, and allays anxiety, fear, tension, and stress. It helps the individual cope with life and face human dilemmas with comfort and confidence. It contributes to emotional integration on both the individual and social levels. The argument, found repeatedly in social-scientific literature, is that when traditional religions cease to fulfill these needs, new religious movements come into being. This view hypothesizes that the rise of the new religions is a response to human psychological needs that the major religious traditions are not fully satisfying. More precisely, the new religions could be offering a holistic self-conception in a culture where the diffusion of personal identity has left many people lost, confused, and afraid.

Social Functions

Many social scientists agree that religious beliefs and practices are instrumental in maintaining, if not creating, social solidarity. Religion is judged to be a force of integration, a unifying bond contributing to social stability and social control and to the preservation of knowledge.

Recent developments in the West have created some doubt as to whether the established religions are fulfilling this important function. To what degree the new religions take the place of the traditional ones is not clear. From one point of view, they stress community living in an age when religious, social, and kinship ties have become rather tenuous and diffuse. Many offer the opportunity for a shared lifestyle in a culture where dislocation of communal patterns has become the norm. They create novel systems of extended kinship in a society where even the nuclear family is showing signs of weakening or breaking down. They further propound, and at times eagerly await, an ideal future situation when the relationship between religion and society will be more harmonious. Yet, from another perspective, they foster conflict with society and between family members and can be judged to be dysfunctional.

Validating Functions

Another function of religion, closely allied with the social one, is that of validating cultural values. Religious beliefs and practices support, at times with moral and spiritual sanctions, the basic institutions, values, and aspirations of a society. Religion inculcates social and ethical norms; it justifies, enforces, and implements a people's ideological assumptions and way of life.

Again, the applicability of these functions to the new religious movements is not obvious. Joining a new religious movement indicates a break with traditional religious and cultural values. The cults, directly or indirectly, pass a condemnatory judgment on their members' previous lifestyles. Yet, at the same time, they give the new ideology and ritual behavior the endorsement of charismatic and revelatory authority and validate the members' abandonment of their previous religion.

Adaptive Functions

Several anthropologists have emphasized the adaptive functions of religious beliefs and rituals. The study of how religious beliefs and membership in a religious group can have repercussions on the individual's chances of survival falls under sociobiology.[76] Observing that there is a definite relationship between religion and both the physical and social environments, some scholars have suggested that, through the use of religion, human beings have been able to adjust and utilize the environment to cater to their own needs. Religion, in this view, is seen as a tool for survival and can be better understood in terms of recurrent adaptive processes.

This approach has been applied to show how many of the rituals (like divination and totemism) found in the religions of nonliterate peoples could, originally, have had ecologically relevant results. It has also been used to explain beliefs and values in some of the great religions. For instance, the Hindu ritual attitude and treatment of the cow has been interpreted as an ecologically beneficial development that has contributed to the adaptation and survival of society in India.[77]

The new religions may serve as ways through which human beings adapt to the current sociocultural environment. One of the more telling criticisms of traditional religion is that, in a modern technological and computerized society, it is rapidly becoming irrelevant to daily experiences. An excellent example would be the observance of Sunday as a day of rest and prayer. In pluralistic societies the ritual practices of just one religion cannot be adopted as the cultural norm. Further, modern industrial society has made the universal ritual observance of Sunday (or any other holy day) virtually impossible. New religions may be attempts to create an ideology and work ethic that fits in more comfortably with the developing lifestyles in the West.

While it would be difficult to outline any direct relationship between the new religions and ecology, it is feasible to build a case for their adaptive function. Many of the new movements, particularly those that align themselves with the New Age movement, are very ecologically minded.[78] The relationship between religion and ecology has been discussed also with reference to the traditional religious groups.[79] In a time in history when the human race is overusing, polluting, and destroying the natural environment, theological and moral views that bestow a divine quality to nature or see it as an expression of divine creativity that must be preserved at all costs may have a survival value.

Further, since membership in the new movements is largely transient, it may be indirectly seen, as explained in chapter 3, as a stage in an individual's psychological development and/or reentry into the larger society. It can also be maintained that some new religions play the role of mental health care and counseling agencies. Occult movements, for instance, promote astrology, a form of divination, which is clearly a process of self-reflection leading to a decision under the guidance of experts, whose role is similar to that of counseling psychologists.[80] Alternative forms of marriage, like the prearranged mass marriages carried out in the Unification Church, are a contrasting substitute for the current precarious married state embodied, for example, in the custom of "serial monogamy" that has become widespread in Western culture.[81] There are different ways through which a person learns how to cope with the stress of intrafamilial relationships, one of which is to adopt a well-defined family lifestyle in a new religion where communal living is encouraged, if not prescribed.

Current Theories of New Religions

The tendency among social scientists, particularly anthropologists and sociologists, to highlight the positive functions of religion is also reflected in their writings on the new religions. If the new religious movements gratify some of the needs of those individuals who join them, then it is easy to conclude that they are beneficial institutions. And if they offer genuine alternatives in an age of social and religious turmoil, then one can readily be led to the view that contemporary religious options perform a necessary and useful service for humanity. It is not surprising, therefore, that anti-cultists have been inclined to see social scientists as supporters or sympathizers of the cults. The functional viewpoint is in direct conflict with the conception of a cult as a spurious religious organization that can have few, if any, beneficial effects both on individuals and society.

It is necessary to bear in mind, however, that the functional explanation of religion and cults has come under heavy attack by several social scientists, even though it has not completely lost its appeal.[82] Besides the admission that religious beliefs and practices may not always have positive results, there are some social scientists who are questioning the whole approach that treats the cults as remedies for deprivation. Because this approach often neglects the religious functions that new religions might fulfill, it could easily be perceived as reductionistic, ignoring the fact that the human religious quest might be responsible for the success of the cults that may function, in part, as vehicles for mystical experiences. Moreover, deprivation theories do not quite explain the causes of deprivation or the reason why individuals join particular religious movements. Several explanatory theories, some of which overlap, have been devised either to bypass the question of deprivation or else to reformulate it more cogently.

One approach, which has been forcefully articulated by Rodney Stark and William Sims Bainbridge,[83] considers the new cults as genuine religious and spiritual revivals, a position that some theologians[84] have found attractive. Since religious awakenings have occurred throughout the history of the West, it can be argued that such revivals appear in cycles and/or take place whenever traditional religions appear to have lost some of their original vitality. The advent of the new religions in the past few decades has coincided with a period in history when the mainline churches may have so accommodated themselves to a secular society that their ability to satisfy the religious needs of their adherents has been diminished. In sociological terms, when religion becomes too secularized one can expect new religious groups to come into being. In other words, secularization and cult formation go hand in hand. Most of those novel religions that survive will, in time, be swept away by the secularization process, thus recreating the conditions that give rise to new ones.

A second approach, proposed by Bryan Wilson, contradicts the above hypothesis and speculates that the presence of the new religions is a confirmation of the secularization hypothesis.[85] The new religions are an indication of the trivialization of religion and not a genuine religious resurgence. They may be considered to be the final gasp of religion, a last but futile attempt to restore the importance that religion used to have in social life. In this view, secularization is an inevitable process because modern technological society leaves no room for religion, ritual, and spirituality. The new religions could be seen as a reaction to the process of secularization, but a reaction that will have little impact on that process.

Marvin Harris, an anthropologist, advances a third position.[86] Dismissing the religious revival theory as unrealistic, he argues that new religions are movements in search of material wealth and power, rather than transcendental and spiritual values. In other words, Harris, in typical Marxist fashion, seeks an economic explanation for the rise of new religions. His position echoes in sociological literature that holds that theology and ideology should not be treated as independent variables in the formation of new religious movements, and that economic factors deserve equal consideration.[87]

A fourth hypothesis, developed by Robert Wuthnow, interprets the new religions as a form of experimental religion.[88] Contemporary society is marked by a system of communication and mobility that increases one's knowledge of different religious options and makes available several spiritual opportunities. In a society that values individual experience and stresses freedom of choice, young adults, who form the bulk of people attracted by alternative religions, become prone to experiment even with religious forms. This experimental outlook may also be a result, in part at least, of the loosening of family ties. Unlike members of tribal societies, people in contemporary Western culture may be less attached to their cultural, family, and religious roots and more prepared and willing to embark on their own personal quest than to accept unquestionably the religion of their parents. Other scholars would stress the prevailing narcissism in Western culture and maintain that the new movements are an expression of this growing trend.[89]

Another theory focuses on the current political scene and speculates that the new religions have sprung from political disenchantment.[90] Antagonism toward, and rebellion against, the economic and sociopolitical system in the West, especially in the United States, was common in the late 1960s. Material success has become to many an all-embracing value that neglects, undervalues, or denies the spiritual dimension of life. It may also have created or aggravated more problems (such as rivalry and intense competition) than it has solved. Joining a new religious movement is a way of opting out of the system, a form of escapism. One can expand this theory to include rebellion against Western culture as a whole and against one's parental authority and religious upbringing. The values and lifestyles that have been passed on by the family and society are rejected as inadequate and unsatisfying.

Related to the aforementioned theory is the view that contemporary change has been too rapid and has, consequently, uprooted people from their parental and cultural moorings.[91] The Western world is in a state of cultural crisis. People feel lost and insecure in a world that questions all absolute values and norms and has become highly impersonal and utilitarian. New religions provide encouragement and certainty to people who are beset by moral and religious confusion and who are in a state of anomie. They fulfill needs that traditional religions have ceased to take care of. This is one form of the deprivation theory of religion tailored to suit the emergence of the new movements.

Another hypothesis speculates that the new religions are indicators of the emergence of new humanism.[92] It starts with the assumption that religion is an evolving phenomenon and attempts to determine specific universal religious trends for the future. It speculates that religion, in its present form, is on the decline and that a new worldview is coming into being, a worldview that has been influenced by Eastern traditions and stresses the immanent, rather than the transcendent, nature of the divine. This new humanism is this-worldly oriented. Although such a perspective has been present in the West for centuries, it now shows signs of becoming the dominant feature in contemporary spiritual life. This theory does not necessarily maintain that a new worldview is replacing that of traditional religions. But it does suggest that traditional religion might be undergoing some radical changes and might not remain the only dominant force in human spirituality in the Western world.

Finally, the rise of the new religious movements has also been related to the breakdown of the "American Civil Religion."[93] In many societies, there has been a religious or quasi-religious regard for civic values and traditions. The complexity of special festivals, rituals, creeds, and dogmas that flow from this nationalist attitude has been given the label "Civil Religion." The United States offers a modern, vivid example of such a religion, which began with the divine mission ascribed to America by the Puritan settlers in New England. The cultural developments and turbulence of the 1960s are related to the incipient breakdown of Civil Religion in the United States. The new religions may be considered attempts to fill the void left by the decline of Civil Religion. Two contemporary religious groups are particularly amenable to this interpretation: the Mormon Church, which came into being in the past century and which is currently experiencing growth in different parts of the world; and the Unification Church that migrated from South Korea to the West in the late 1960s. Both churches exalt the place of America in the divine plan and may be offering a substitute Civil Religion that permeates cultural values and every aspect of life. The principal difficulty with this theory is that it fails to account for the majority of the new religious movements. It is also not clear whether it is applicable to other Western societies outside the United States.

Social-Scientific Critique of Popular Theories

The main sociological critique has been directed toward popular views of new religions, particularly the brainwashing theory discussed in the previous chapter. Sociological researchers share one thing in common: they see the emergence of the new movements as a complex sociocultural phenomenon that cannot be explained simply in terms of individual psychology or as a result of external forces that are destined to bring about the downfall of Western culture.

The brainwashing theory is judged deficient precisely because it fails to take due notice of the sociocultural conditions of Western society and, therefore, ignores some of the main issues that must play a central role in any explanation of the cult phenomenon.[94] Thus, to uphold the view that new religious movements attract people who are mentally ill or psychologically weak does not answer the questions of why they have arisen in a certain period of history and why it is that so many young adults join them. To claim that their leaders are power-seeking individuals who use their charismatic powers to entice naive youngsters into their folds by skillful mind control methods reveals nothing about the reasons why such leaders actually emerge and little about the causes of the alleged vulnerability of those attracted to them. To explain their success by stating that they use carefully planned, deceptive, and brainwashing techniques to gain and maintain members is an outright rejection of any initiative that young adults might take in joining them. Most of those individuals who join new religions, however, have already embarked on a spiritual or religious quest before they ever came in contact with them. They are, therefore, not just passive bystanders who have been unwittingly lured into a new religious movement. Similarly, claims that continuous heavy socialization or indoctrination into cult beliefs and values practically destroys the free wills and minds of cult-members contradict the available evidence. Many of those who join disengage themselves from the new movements on their own initiative, and some of them have reflected critically on the movements to which they belong.

Another popular theory that is not supported by sociological studies is the view that interprets the emergence of the new religions as the result of some kind of well-orchestrated attack on Western culture from outside sources. This position is hardly original and was expressed in the early twentieth century to explain the influx of Eastern religious and philosophical ideas after the 1893 World Parliament of Religions in Chicago.[95] As shown in chapter 2, many of the ideals, values, and lifestyles adhered to by new religions are hardly novel and have existed in marginal groups that have been part of the Western cultural tradition for centuries. New religions are not just an external problem, a kind of missionary invasion from outside that can be stopped by the introduction of social and legal restrictions. They are primarily an internal problem and, hence, direct attacks against them will not succeed in exterminating them. The evidence suggests that Western culture is being influenced and not overrun by Eastern traditions, which are in the process of accommodating themselves to the Western civilization into which they have been transplanted.

It is certainly not difficult to see why sociological views on the new religions have not been very popular. Those who hold that membership in their ranks implies pathology have at their disposal a simple, professional answer to the unusual involvement in a cult, namely, optional or forced therapy for its members. Those who maintain that the new religions are responsible for enticing and brainwashing young adults against their wills propound the equally straightforward solution, namely, that their members should be deprogrammed and subjected to traditional therapy. And lastly, those who are afraid that the influence from the East is bound to lead to the eclipse of Western culture have a strong rationale for insisting that legal and social restrictions should be imposed on the new movements.

Sociologists think that these reactions are based on assumptions that do not fit the facts and that offer superficial and simplistic explanations that neglect consideration of the many problems caused by modern industrialized society and by evolutionary forces that may not be easily identified or controlled by human endeavors. Consequently, they seem to offer little comfort to the worried parents of cult members and to agitated evangelizers. The sociological theories of cult formation and development offer no quick resolutions to the personal problems that plague those who have been personally affected by the presence of the new religions. But they provide the necessary background to understand and deal with issues brought by the rise of the cults. They draw attention to the sociocultural matrix suitable for the emergence of these movements. They focus on the problems of Western society in a period of rapid social change. They emphasize that it is precisely these problems that explain why new religions succeed and that, consequently, they must be addressed. They make people reflect not only on the inevitability of the new religions, but also on their manifold functions. While sociological studies could lead to the conclusion that the problems that alternative movements have brought in their wake may not be easily solved, they also provide information and reflection for ways of coping with them.

Responses to the New Religions

The sixth and final issue in contemporary sociology has to do with the response that society should make to the new religions. Two opposing positions have gradually emerged and solidified since the early 1970s. The first has been identified largely with the activity of the anti-cult movement and has attracted the support of many psychiatrists, lawyers, ministers of religion, and the general public. Its main concerns are the effects of cult life on family members, the well-being of the individuals who become cult members, and the perceived negative results on society and/or religion as a whole. Its methods are mostly confrontational. Besides the dissemination of literature that discredits the cults and the foundation of counseling centers that assist parents in their efforts to remove their offspring from their milieu, those who oppose the new religions have had recourse to the courts to counteract their practices.

A second response, to which many social scientists subscribe, is aimed more at diagnosing the activities of the anti-cult movement itself and analyzing the various anti-cult and counter-cult reactions than dealing directly with the personal problems brought into being by the presence and influence of the new religions.[96] James Beckford, for example, has shown that reactions to the new religions are shaped by the cultural and legal frameworks of the different countries in which they thrive.[97] Thus, whether the cults are considered to be a form of religious deviance, an expression of totalitarianism, or a threat to social order, moral norms, and traditional values depends on the sociocultural contexts in which they thrive.

Further, instead of concentrating largely on the psychological and personal aspects of involvement, many sociologists have drawn attention to the grave social implications that might follow a legally sanctioned anti-cult stand. They have stressed the importance of religious freedom in a pluralistic society and have contended that any legal curtailment of the new religious movements threatens the very fabric of Western culture. Their defense of religious freedom and pluralism has regrettably been interpreted as a pro-cult stance.[98]

The Relevance of Sociology for Understanding the New Religions

The issues discussed in this chapter are expressive of a deep division between two incompatible approaches to, and interpretations of, the new religious movements. The debates have assumed a crusading spirit that has intensified the split between the two groups of scholars studying the new religions. Rarely do members of each camp participate in joint conferences or discussions. Consequently, it would be unrealistic at this stage to hope for a quick and easy resolution to the problems discussed in this chapter.

The sociological approach to the new religions is based on well-established academic principles and, in spite of some weaknesses, has many advantages. The impartial stance of sociologists and their refusal to pass theological judgments should, in fact, be recommended as a necessary initial step to understand the new religions. The neglect of sociological studies by those who have embarked on an anti-cult campaign has contributed to the hysteria that so frequently characterizes the public responses to the new religious movements. An example of such violent denunciation of all cults is the selection of Jim Jones's People's Temple as a paradigm of all new religions. The responsibility of making theological evaluations belongs to theologians, who are called upon to interpret and evaluate the beliefs and practices of the new religious movements in the context of their respective faiths. Similarly, the responsibility of helping those who have been affected by cults' recruitment drives and activities falls on psychologists and counselors. Both responsibilities can be better attended to if sociological studies of the new religions were given their rightful place in the study of contemporary religious change and development.

The sociological approach to the new religious movements provides, first of all, a solid and reliable method for determining and accurately recording their beliefs, rituals, and activities. Second, it places their emergence in a wider religious and cultural context, thus broadening understanding of the phenomenon. Third, it draws attention to some of their social functions, thus showing how entrance into a new religion can have positive consequences. Finally, sociology draws attention to two larger problems that believers of all religions must come to terms with, namely, the increase in the varieties of religious options over the past few decades and, most of all, the changing face of religion at the beginning of the third millennium.

Notes

1. Thomas Robbins, *Cults, Converts, and Charisma* (Newbury Park, CA: Sage, 1988), p. 190ff; and William Sims Bainbridge, *The Sociology of New Religious Movements* (New

York: Routledge, 1997), esp. p. 1ff. See also the many essays on new religious movements published especially in the following journals: *Journal for the Scientific Study of Religion*, *Sociology of Religion* (formerly *Sociological Analysis*), and *Journal of Contemporary Religion*.

2. See, for example, Eugene J. Weber, *Prophecies, Cults, and Millennial Beliefs through the Ages* (Cambridge, MA: Harvard University Press, 1999); and Philip Jenkins, *Mystics and Messiahs: Cults and New Religions in American History* (New York: Oxford University Press, 2002).

3. For standard sociological approaches to religion, confer H. Paul Chalfant, Robert E. Beckley, and C. Eddie Palmer, *Religion in Contemporary Society* (Sherman Oaks, CA: Alfred Publishing, 1981); Keith A. Roberts, *Religion in Sociological Perspective* (Homewood, IL: Dorsey Press, 1984); and Ronald L. Johnstone, *Religion in Society: A Sociology of Religion* (Upper Saddle River, NJ: Prentice-Hall, 6th ed., 2001).

4. Confer Alan Aldridge, *Religion in the Contemporary World: A Sociological Introduction* (Cambridge, UK: Polity Press, 2000), pp. 22–32.

5. See Arthur L. Greil, "Sacred Claims: The 'Cult Controversy' as a Struggle Over the Right to the Religious Label," in *The Issue of Authenticity in the Study of Religion*, ed. Lewis F. Carter (Greenwich, CT: JAI Press, 1996), pp. 47–63.

6. Lewis Carter, "The Problem of Authenticity in the Study of Religious Traditions," in *Between Sacred and Secular: Research and Theory on Quasi-Religion*, ed. Arthur L Greil and Thomas Robbins (Greenwich, CT: JAI Press, 1994), p. 249.

7. Aldridge, *Religion in the Contemporary World*, pp. 17–22.

8. S. Carey, "The Indianization of the Hare Krishna Movement," in *Hinduism in Great Britain*, ed. R. Burghart (London: Tavistock, 1987), pp. 81–91.

9. For a typical example, see David G. Bromley and Anson D. Shupe, *Strange Gods: The Great American Cult Scare* (Boston: Beacon Press, 1981).

10. A. L. Greil, "Secular Religion," in *International Encyclopedia of the Social and Behavioral Sciences*, ed. Neil J. Smelser and Paul B. Baltes (New York: Elsevier, 2001), pp. 13077–82.

11. Bryan Wilson, "Scientology: A Secularized Religion," in *The Social Dimensions of Sectarianism: Sects and New Religious Movements in Contemporary Society*, ed. Bryan R. Wilson (Oxford: Clarendon Press, 1990), pp. 267–88.

12. Ninian Smart, "Implicit Religion across Culture," *Implicit Religion* 1 (November 1998): 23–26. See also Edward Bailey, "'Implicit Religion': What Might that Be," *Implicit Religion* 1 (November 1988): 9–22.

13. Malcolm Hamilton, "Implicit Religion and Related Concepts: Seeking Precision," *Implicit Religion* 4 (May 2001): 5–13.

14. L. C. Young and S. R. Ford, "God Is Society: The Religious Dimension of Maoism," *Sociological Inquiry* 47.2 (1997): 89–97.

15. Richard Fenn, "The Quasi-Sacred: A Theoretical Consideration," in *Between Sacred and Secular*, p. 257.

16. John Steadman Rice, "The Therapeutic God: Transcendence and Identity in Two Twelve-Step Quasi-Religions," in *Between Sacred and Secular*, pp. 157–64.

17. John E. Smith, *Quasi-Religions: Humanism, Marxism, and Nationalism* (New York: St. Martin's Press, 1994).

18. David G. Bromley, "Transformative Movements and Quasi-Religious Corporations: The Case of Amway," in *Sacred Canopies: Organizational Aspects of Religion and Religious Aspects of Organizations*, ed. N. J. Demerath III, Peter Donkin Hall, Terry Schmidt, and Rhys H. Williams (New York: Oxford University Press, 1998), pp. 249–63.

19. Mary Jo Neitz, "Quasi-Religious Movements: Contemporary Witchcraft as a Churchless Religion," in *Between Sacred and Secular*, p. 129.

20. A. Greil and D. Rudy, "On the Margins of the Sacred," in *In Gods We Trust*, ed. T. Robbins and D. Anthony (New Brunswick, NJ: Transaction, 2nd ed., 1990), p. 221.

21. David Bromley and Mitchell Bracey, "The Church of Scientology: A Quasi-Religion," in *Sects, Cults, and Spiritual Communities*, ed. William W. Zellner and Marc Petrowsky (Westport, CT: Praeger, 1998), p. 142.

22. Bromley and Bracey, "The Church of Scientology," pp. 142–43.

23. James C. Livingston, *The Anatomy of the Sacred: An Introduction to Religion* (Upper Saddle River, NJ: Prentice-Hall, 4th ed., 2001), pp. 13–16; and Gary E. Kessler, *Studying Religion: An Introduction through Cases* (Boston: McGraw-Hill, 2003), pp. 12–14.

24. Reflections on what effects the new religions might have are plentiful. Consult, for example, Françoise Champion, "New Religious Movements as Indicators of the De-Structuring of Religion and of Mutations in the Symbolic Field," *Sociologia Internationalis* 38, no. 1 (2000): 47–61; and Toby Lester, "Oh, Gods," *Atlantic Monthly* (February 2002): 37–45.

25. See, for instance, Dave Breese, *The Marks of a Cult* (Eugene, OR: Harvest House, 1998).

26. This is usually the case with organizations such as Family Action, Information and Rescue (FAIR) in Great Britain, and the American Family Foundation (AFF) in the United States.

27. Michael D. Langone, for instance, in his essay "Cultism and American Culture," *Cultic Studies Journal* 3 (1986): 157–72, contends that cults reject the major fundamental values on which American culture rests.

28. See Anson D. Shupe and David G. Bromley, *The New Vigilantes: Deprogrammers, Anti-Cultists, and the New Religions* (Beverly Hills, CA: Sage, 1980).

29. Johannes Aagaard, "Conversion, Religious Change, and the Challenge of New Religious Movements," *Cultic Studies Journal* 8 (1991): 102–3.

30. See, for example, David J. Bardin, "Psychological Coercion and Human Rights: Mind Control ('Brainwashing') Exists" (1994), a privately circulated paper written in response to Nancy T. Ammerman's *Recommendations of Experts for Improvements in Federal Law Enforcement After Waco* (Washington, DC: U.S. Department of Justice and U.S. Department of the Treasury, n.d.; released on October 8, 1993).

31. Neil Smelser, *Sociology* (Cambridge, MA: UNESCO, 1994), pp. 39–55; and Anthony Giddens and Mitchell Dumeier, *Introduction to Sociology* (New York: W. W. Norton, 3rd ed., 2000), pp. 35–42.

32. Conrad Phillip Kottak, in his textbook, *Anthropology: The Exploration of Human Diversity* (New York: McGraw-Hill, 8th ed., 2000), pp. 19–23, lists "observation and participant observation" as the first ethnographic technique. For a study of this method and its

advantages and difficulties, consult Danny L. Jorgensen, *Participant Observation: A Methodology for Human Studies* (Beverly Hills, CA: Sage, 1989); Kathleen Musante De Walt and Billie E. De Walt, *Participant Observation: A Fieldworker's Guide* (Walnut Creek, CA: AltaMira Press, 2002); and Stanley R. Barrett, *Anthropology: A Student's Guide to Theory and Method* (Toronto: University of Toronto Press, 1996).

33. The use of this method is listed in sociology and anthropology textbooks as one of the standard methods used by sociologists and anthropologists. Confer for instance, John E. Farley, *Sociology* (Englewood Cliffs, NJ: Prentice-Hall, 1990), pp. 46–48; and Conrad Phillip Kottak, *Cultural Anthropology* (New York: McGraw-Hill, 6th ed., 1994), p. 21ff.

34. See Eugene Hillman, "Religious Ethnocentrism," *America* (March 23, 1993): 317–19.

35. David Bidney, "Cultural Relativism," in *International Dictionary of the Social Sciences*, ed. David L. Sills (New York: Macmillan, 1968), vol. 3, pp. 543–47.

36. Giddens and Dumeier, *Introduction to Sociology* (New York: W. W. Norton, 2nd ed., 1996), p. 23.

37. Kottak, *Cultural Anthropology*, p. 23.

38. This is typical of many studies published in, for example, the *Journal of Cultic Studies*.

39. See David G. Bromley, ed., *The Politics of Religious Apostasy: The Role of Apostates in the Transformation of Religious Movements* (Westport, CT: Praeger, 1998).

40. Bryan Wilson, *The Noble Savages: The Primitive Origins of Charisma and Its Contemporary Survival* (Berkeley: University of California Press, 1975).

41. See Michael D. Langone, "The 'Two Camps' of Cultic Studies: Time for a Dialogue," *Cultic Studies Journal* 17 (2000): 79–100.

42. Consult, for instance, the various views expressed in Benjamin Zablocki and Thomas Robbins, eds., *Misunderstanding Cults: Searching for Objectivity in a Controversial Field* (Toronto: University of Toronto Press, 2001).

43. Janja Lalich, "Pitfalls in the Sociological Study of Cults," in *Misunderstanding Cults*, p. 126ff.

44. See also Steve K. Dubrow Wilson, "Can Scholars Be Deceived?: Empirical Evidence from Social Psychology and History," *Cultic Studies Review* 1 (2002): 51–64. The author suggests that Bryan Wilson and Karel Dobbelaere, in their book, *A Time to Chant: The Soka Gakkai Buddhism in Britain* (New York: Oxford University Press, 1994), and Phillip Hammond and David Machacek, in their study, *Soka Gakkai in American: Accommodation and Conversion* (New York: Oxford University Press, 1999), have been misled by the people they were studying.

45. Benjamin Beit-Hallahmi, "'O Truant Muse': Collaboration and Research Integrity," in *Misunderstanding Cults*, pp. 35–70.

46. See Jeffrey Hadden's Web page at http://religiousmovements.lib.virginia.edu/.

47. George D. Chryssides, *The Advent of Sun Myung Moon: The Origins, Beliefs and Practices of the Unification Church* (New York: St. Martin's Press, 1991).

48. Roy Wallis, *The Elementary Forms of Religious Life* (London: Routledge and Kegan Paul, 1982).

49. Bryan Wilson, *Religious Sects: A Sociological Study* (New York: McGraw Hill, 1970). See also his *The Social Dimensions of Sectarianism*.

50. Rodney Stark and William Sims Bainbridge, "Concepts for a Theory of Religious Movements," in *Alternatives to American Mainline Churches*, ed. Joseph Fichter (New York: Rose of Sharon Press, 1983), pp. 12–21. Confer also Rodney Stark and William Sims Bainbridge, "Client and Audience Cults in America," in *The Future of Religion: Secularization, Revival, and Cult Formation*, ed. Rodney Stark and William Sims Bainbridge (Berkeley: University of California Press, 1985), pp. 208–31.

51. For a lengthy formulation of this typology, confer Dick Anthony and Bruce Ecker, "The Anthony Typology: A Framework for Assessing Spiritual and Consciousness Groups," in *Spiritual Choices: The Problem of Recognizing Authentic Paths to Inner Transformation*, ed. Dick Anthony, Bruce Ecker, and Ken Wilber (New York: Paragon, 1987), pp. 35–106.

52. Frederick Bird, "The Pursuit of Innocence: New Religious Movements and Moral Accountability," *Sociological Analysis* 40 (1979): 335–46.

53. Ken Wilber, "The Spectrum-Model," in *Spiritual Choices*, pp. 237–60.

54. For a lengthy discussion of these typologies see Robbins, *Cults, Converts, and Charisma*, p. 135ff.

55. Wilson, *The Social Dimensions of Sectarianism*, especially part 1, p. 23ff.

56. Ken Wilber, *Religion in Sociological Perspective* (Oxford: Oxford University Press, 1982), pp. 91–92.

57. Movement for Spiritual Inner Awareness Web site, http://www.msia.org. This Web site is in four languages—English, French, Spanish, and Portuguese.

58. Sara Horsfell, "How Religious Organizations Use the Internet: A Preliminary Study," in *The Promised Land or Electronic Chaos?: Toward Understanding Religion on the Internet. Religion and the Social Order*, ed. Jeffrey K Hadden and Douglas E. Cowen (Greenwich, CT: JAI Press, 2000), vol. 8, pp. 153–82.

59. Jean-Francois Mayer, "Religious Movements and the Internet: The New Frontier of Cult Controversies," in *The Promised Land or Electronic Chaos?*, pp. 249–76; and Massimo Introvigne, "'So Many Evil Things': Anti-Cult Terrorism on the Internet," in *The Promised Land or Electronic Chaos?*, pp. 277–306.

60. Lorne Dawson and Jenna Hennebry, "New Religions and the Internet: Recruiting in a New Public Space," *Journal of Contemporary Religion* 14 (1999): 17.

61. See, for instance, Michael Peckham. "New Dimensions of Social Movement/ Countermovement Interaction: The Case of Scientology and its Critics," *Canadian Journal of Sociology/Cahiers Canadiens de Sociologie* 23 (1998): 317–38. See, for example, "Operation Clambake: The Fight against the Church of Scientology on the Net," http://www.xenu.net (accessed December 12, 2002), a Web page devoted to the negative aspects of Scientology.

62. Marcia Rudin, in her essay, "Women, Elderly, and Children in Religious Cults," *Cultic Studies Journal* 1, no. 1 (1984): 8–26, presents a typical example.

63. See Ronald W. Maris, "Suicide," in the *Encyclopedia of Sociology*, ed. Edgar R. Borgatta and Marie L. Borgatta (New York: Macmillan, 1992), vol. 4, pp. 2111–19.

64. Confer E. S. Schneiderman, "Suicide," in *Encyclopedia of Psychology*, ed. Raymond J. Corsini (New York: John Wiley and Sons, 1994), vol. 3, p. 488–90; David Lester, "Suicide," in *Encyclopedia of Human Behavior*, ed. V. S. Ramachandran (New York: Academic Press, 1994), vol. 4, pp. 347–52.

65. Lorne Dawson, *Comprehending Cults: The Sociology of New Religious Movements* (New York: Oxford University Press, 1998), pp. 128ff.

66. Anthony Robbins, "The Historical Antecedents of Jonestown: The Sociology of Martyrdom," in *New Religious Movements, Mass Suicide, and Peoples Temple: Scholarly Perspectives on a Tragedy*, ed. Rebecca Moore and Fielding McGehee III (Lewiston, NY: Edwin Mellen Press, 1989), pp. 51–76.

67. For a discussion on this issue see Ken Levi, ed., *Violence and Religious Commitment: Implications of Jim Jones's People's Temple Movement* (University Park: Pennsylvania State University Press, 1982).

68. Gordon Melton, "Violence and the Cults," in *Encyclopedic Handbook of Cults in America* (New York: Garland Publishing, 1992), pp. 361–93.

69. There is a growing literature on the topic of religion and violence. See, for example, Mark Jurgensmeyer, *Terror in the Mind of God* (Berkeley: University of California Press, 2002); R. Scott Appleby, *The Ambivalence of the Sacred: Religion, Violence, and Reconciliation* (Lanham, MD: Rowman & Littlefield, 2000); and David G. Bromley and J. Gordon Melton, *Cults, Religion, and Violence* (New York: Cambridge University Press, 2002).

70. Jeffrey H. Goldstein, ed., *Why We Watch: The Attraction of Violence* (New York: Oxford University Press, 1998). See, especially Maurice Bloch's essay in this volume, "The Presence of Violence in Religion," pp. 163–78, where violence in religious rituals is examined.

71. Tamara L. Roleff and Helen Cothran, eds., *Extremist Groups: Opposing Viewpoints* (San Diego, CA: Greenhaven Press, 2001).

72. See Robert D. Hicks, "Cult Label Made Waco Violence Inevitable," in *From the Ashes: Making Sense out of Waco*, ed. James R. Lewis (Lanham, MD: Rowman & Littlefield, 1989), pp. 63–65.

73. See, for example, Charles Y. Glock, "On the Origin and Evolution of Religious Groups," in *Religion in Sociological Perspective*, ed. Charles Y. Glock (Belmont, CA: Wadsworth, 1973), pp. 207–20; and Newton B. Fowler, "Religion Beyond the Churches," *Lexington Theological Quarterly* 16 (April 1981): 78–84. Rodney Stark and William Sims Bainbridge, in their book *A Theory of Religion* (New York: P. Lang, 1987), adopt a theory of deprivation to explain religious commitment and the rise of new religious movements.

74. "The Role of Deprivation in the Origin and Evolution of Religious Groups," in *Cults in Context: Readings in the Study of New Religious Movements*, ed. Lorne L. Dawson (New Brunswick, NJ: Transaction Publishers, 1998), pp. 47–58.

75. For an elaboration of these various functions in the context of the anthropological study of religion, see John A. Saliba, "Religion and the Anthropologists, 1960–1976, Part II," *Anthropologica* 19 (1977): 181–85.

76. V. Reynolds and R. E. S. Tanner, *The Biology of Religion* (London: Longman, 1983), especially chap. 1, "Religion and Sociobiology," pp. 2–17. Confer Brant Wenegrat, *The Di-*

vine Archetype: The Sociobiology and Psychology of Religion (Lexington, MA: Lexington Books, 1990), p. 31ff.

77. Marvin Harris, "The Cultural Ecology of India's Sacred Cow," *Current Anthropology* 6 (1966): 51–59.

78. The *New Age Journal* sometimes dedicates an issue to home and planet ecology. See, for instance, "Sourcebook 1994," *New Age Journal* 10, no. 7 (1993); and "The Annual Sourcebook for '95," *New Age Journal* 11, no. 8 (1995).

79. Consult, for instance, David E. Cooper and Joy Palmer, eds., *Spirit of the Environment: Religion, Value, and Environmental Concern* (New York: Routledge, 1998); and David L. Barnhill and Roger S. Gottlieb, eds., *Deep Ecology and World Religions: New Essays on Sacred Ground* (Albany: State University of New York Press, 2001).

80. David Lester, "Astrologers and Psychics as Therapists," *American Journal of Psychotherapy* 36 (1981): 56–66.

81. See, for instance, Shawn Haley, "The Future of the Family in North America," *Futures* 32 (2000): 777–82.

82. For a summary of such critiques see Robert Wuthnow, "Sociology of Religion," in *Handbook of Sociology*, ed. Neil J. Smelser (Newbury Park, CA: Sage, 1988), pp. 477–79.

83. Rodney Stark and William Sims Bainbridge, *The Future of Religion: Secularization, Revival, and Cult Formation* (Berkeley: University of California Press, 1985).

84. See, for example, Harvey Cox, *Religion in the Secular City* (New York: Simon, 1984).

85. Bryan Wilson, *Contemporary Transformations of Religion* (London: Oxford University Press, 1976).

86. Marvin Harris, *American Now* (New York: Simon, 1981).

87. See, for example, James T. Richardson, ed., *Money and Power in the New Religions* (Lewiston, NY: Edwin Mellen Press, 1988).

88. Robert Wuthnow, *Experimentation in American Religion: The New Mysticisms and Their Implications for the Churches* (Berkeley: University of California Press, 1978).

89. Confer Christopher Lasch, *The Culture of Narcissism* (New York: Norton, 1978). For some critical reflections on Lasch's theory consult Jesse F. Battan, "The 'New Narcissism' in 20th-Century America: The Shadow and Substance of Social Change," *Journal of Social History* 17 (1983): 199–220.

90. See, for example, James T. Richardson, "Studies of Conversion: Secularization or Reenchantment," in *The Sacred in a Secular Age*, ed. Phillip E. Hammond (Berkeley: University of California Press, 1985), pp. 104–21; and Robert Wuthnow and Charles Y. Glock, "Religious Loyalty, Defection, and Experimentation among College Youth," *Journal for the Scientific Study of Religion* 12 (1973): 157–80.

91. Robert N. Bellah, "New Religious Movements and the Crisis of Modernity," in *The New Religious Consciousness*, ed. Charles Y. Glock and Robert N. Bellah (Berkeley: University of California Press, 1976), pp. 333–52; Dick Anthony and Thomas Robbins, "Culture Crisis and Contemporary Religions," in *In Gods We Trust: New Patterns of Religious Pluralism in America*, ed. by Thomas Robbins and Dick Anthony (New Brunswick, NJ: Transaction Books, 1st ed., 1981), pp. 9–31; and Allan W. Eister, "Culture Crisis and the New Religious Movements: A Paradigmatic Statement of a Theory of Cults," in *Religious*

Movements in Contemporary America, ed. Irving I. Zaretsky and Mark P. Leone (Princeton, NJ: Princeton University Press, 1974), pp. 612–27.

92. Robert Wuthnow, *The Restructuring of American Religion: Society and Faith since World War II* (Princeton, NJ: Princeton University Press, 1988).

93. Phillip E. Hammond, "Civility and Civil Religion: The Emergence of Cults," in *Varieties of Civil Religion*, ed. Robert E. Bellah and Phillip E. Hammond (New York: Harper and Row, 1980), pp. 188–99.

94. See John A. Saliba, *Social Science and the Cults* (New York: Garland, 1990), xxxvi–xxxvii. See also James T. Richardson, "A Critique of 'Brainwashing' Claims about New Religious Movements," in *Cults in Context: Readings in the Study of New Religious Movements*, ed. Lorne L. Dawson, pp. 217–27.

95. Wendell Thomas, *Hinduism Invades America* (New York: Beacon, 1930).

96. For literature dealing with sociological studies of responses to the new religious movements, see Saliba, *Social Science and the Cults*, p. 618ff.

97. James Beckford, "The 'Cult Problem' in Five Countries: The Social Construction of Religious Controversy," in *Of Gods and Men: New Religious Movements in the West*, ed. Eileen Barker (Macon, GA: Mercer University Press, 1983), pp. 195–214.

98. There are some notable exceptions to this almost universal stance of sociologists. See, for instance, Edward M. Levine, who, in his essay "Are Religious Cults Religious?" *Cultic Studies Journal* 1, no. 1 (1984): 4–7, argues that the cults do not have a claim to religious legitimacy and, consequently, one cannot apply to them the principle of religious freedom.

THE NEW RELIGIOUS MOVEMENTS IN THE LAW COURTS

The litigation of religious matters in the courts has increased dramatically over the past twenty-five years due, in part, to the problems brought about by the presence and activities of the new religious movements or cults. The arguments presented during court hearings and the statements and decisions of many judges have brought to the fore both ideological and practical issues. The relationship between the civil authorities and the various new religious organizations has, at times, been strained. The occasions when the former have the right to interfere in church matters and to curtail the activities of new religious groups have been among the overriding concerns of those who have followed the court procedures or participated in the legal processes in which new religions have been involved.

The Relationship between Church and State

Basic to any debate on the manner in which cult-related questions are handled in the courtrooms is the autonomy of religious organizations and the degree to which they are subject to the laws of particular societies. The type of relationship between church and state varies in different countries in the West. And so does the legal status of the new religious movements.[1] There is, however, a general agreement on the need to protect religious freedom, especially since most Western countries are religiously pluralistic. It is an accepted principle that one has the right to belong to the religion of one's choice, even though some religious practices may be restricted, if they are held to hinder the common good or infringe on the rights of others. In Western culture undue interference in religious matters is usually avoided both in those countries where the state sponsors or favors one particular religion and in those, like the United States, where a separation between church and state has been constitutionally established.[2]

The central principles of religious freedom were affirmed in the European Convention of Human Rights (1951) and in a resolution adopted by the General Assembly of the United Nations (1981). The European Parliament took up the issue of new religious movements in 1984 and expressed the concern that the new religious movements themselves might be infringing upon human rights. Even though specific criteria for investigating the activities of new religions were recommended, the Parliament strongly endorsed the principle of religious freedom.[3] In 1992, the Council of Europe issued a report on sects and new religious movements that, while admitting that their presence and activities can create social problems, stressed the freedom of conscience and religion.[4]

Bryan Wilson[5] has identified the following four main areas of conflict between marginal religious groups and state authorities. The first is when the new religions directly challenge the state. The second occurs when the teachings of these religions are contrary to public policy. The third takes place when membership in the fringe religions is said to endanger the rights of its members. And the fourth is when the civil authorities are constrained to defend public morality and to protect the public. In practice two types of controversies involving new religious movements have dominated the debates in the law courts. The first deals with the illegal behavior of members of new religions. Cases of child neglect and abuse are typical examples. The second consists of suits that attempt to resolve debates between new religions and individuals. Examples of this are the court cases initiated by ex-members against the sects or cults to which they previously belonged.

This chapter first presents a brief outline of seven, often-interrelated areas of contention: (1) suits brought by ex-cult members and their families, (2) criminal cases, (3) custody cases, (4) tax cases, (5) solicitation cases, (6) zoning/community relations issues, and (7) suits that deal with the legality of deprogramming.[6] Examples are provided to illustrate the nature of each problem and the kind of decisions that civil courts and authorities are called upon to make. Several major thorny issues will then be discussed in order to bring into focus the religious nature of some of the cases. Finally, the quality of the testimony of court witnesses will be dealt with.

Areas of Conflict

Court suits involving the new religious movements have covered a variety of human problems that have been litigated in one form or another long before the new religions arrived on the scene. Although there are some issues brought up in court cases, like that of brainwashing or mind control, that seem to pertain largely to the new religions, the majority of legal problems in which some of them have been enmeshed are hardly novel. It is important to keep this perspective in mind; otherwise one runs the risk of presenting these issues as being peculiar to the new religions, when in fact they are not. Rather, the number of criminal and civil cases in which their members are involved are relatively small compared with the load that most courts routinely carry in the exercise of justice. For instance, family conflicts that revolve around the custody of children and cases of child abuse or neglect are not peculiar to the new religions. They are human problems widespread in Western culture.

Suits Brought by Ex-Members and Their Families

Two of the common accusations against the new religions are that (1) they have harmed both their adherents and their families, and that (2) their activities have inflicted pain and hardship on many members of the community.[7] New religions have been taken to court for a variety of reasons. They have been accused of (1) causing mental distress and psychological damage; (2) kidnapping and brainwashing young adults, thus forcing them to become members; (3) corruption of minors; (4) sexually abusing their members; (5) defamation; (6) alienation of affections; (7) wanton misconduct and outrageous acts; (8) harassment; and (9) wrongful death. Court decisions have varied so much that it is difficult to draw any general conclusions about the legal implications of such processes.

By far the most disputed cases have been those in which the new religions have been charged with recruiting young adults under false pretenses and brainwashing them into new belief systems and lifestyles. Although the theory of mind control or brainwashing has been found wanting by the majority of social scientists, many lawyers still appeal to it[8] and some psychologists and psychiatrists continue to defend it vigorously both as a general theory[9] and as applied to individual groups.[10]

One of the most publicized cases that dragged on for several years in the U.S. courts involved the Unification Church.[11] David Molko and Tracey Leal had been members of the Church for about six months when they were forcibly abducted and deprogrammed. Shortly after their disaffiliation, they brought a lawsuit against the Church claiming that they were misled into joining it and accusing it of fraud, intentional infliction of emotional distress, and false imprisonment. The suit sought the restitution of donations (totaling about $6,000) and compensation for work performed in the Church's service. The Church counteracted with its own charge that the harm brought on the two ex-members was caused by the deprogramming procedures rather than by any of its activities or training programs. In 1986 a judge dismissed the charges against the Church. Three years later and after several appeals, the lawsuit charging the Unification Church with fraudulent recruitment was finally cleared for trial by the California Supreme Court. The matter was eventually settled out of court in November 1989.

The accusation that new religious movements practice brainwashing or mind-control techniques has fared unevenly in the U.S. courtrooms.[12] John Young and Ezra Griffith, in an evaluation of the brainwashing or "coercive persuasion" charge, write that "the concept of coercive persuasion as a means of controlling another's thinking and behavior appears quite far from receiving general professional acceptance as a working model."[13] The courts have not always accepted the testimonies of expert witnesses, who have defended it both in professional writings and in public lectures. An interesting case involved a member of a paramilitary group who was accused of having committed three murders in 2000. A psychologist, hired by the defense, testified that the individual was brainwashed by his two elder codefendants. The court rejected the brainwashing plea and, as part of a plea bargain, the accused received a two-year jail sentence.[14]

Although charges of brainwashing seem to be less common than they were fifteen years ago, they are still sometimes used in court cases. Thus, for instance, the mother of John Walker Lindh, the American who fought with the Taliban, has claimed that her son must have been "brainwashed," a position that might be used in his defense. Jack Hitt, reporting in the *New York Times*, refers to several cases where similar accusations have been made and then remarks:

The few scholars who clung to the brainwashing concept were forced to downsize the idea. Although they admitted a person couldn't be motivated to, say, commit violence simply because of psychological pressure, they pointed out that coercion could have a more subtle effect. Cult members considering quitting the group, for example, could be pressured into staying. The Courts have followed the following reasoning. A former Moonie suing to get his trust fund back would most likely be able to claim that he was coerced. But courts so far have not generally embraced the argument that people can be programmed to commit crimes.[15]

It is possible that brainwashing will eventually cease to be an overriding element in lawsuits against the new religions, not only because mind control is hard to prove, but also because many new religions are taking steps to protect themselves against such an accusation. Thus, for example, some groups (like The Family/The Children of God) are requiring a six-month waiting period from all those who apply to join them. And reform movements within some new religious groups, like the Hare Krishna movement, may lead to initiation programs that are less demanding. New religious movements are influenced by the culture and the legal system in which they thrive, and this could result in the relinquishing of practices that are judged to be antithetical to religious freedom.

Criminal Cases

The tragedy of the People's Temple in Jonestown was a landmark in the history of new religious movements and also in the formation of the public's attitudes to new religions in general. It failed, however, "to provide the anticipated catalyst in the ACM's [anti-cult movement's] war against 'destructive cultism.'"[16] It was an atypical example of how suicide and murder can occur in religious groups. It raised the question of whether such violence can be prevented. More recent events, like the suicides of the members of Heaven's Gate and the Solar Temple, and the murders committed in Uganda by the Restoration of the Ten Commandments of God, have tended to confirm the view of those who maintain that all religious movements are prone to violence and criminal behavior. Robert Hicks, who has written extensively on the allegedly criminal activities of new religions, has remarked that, in the United States, law enforcement agencies tend to treat cult members as criminals.[17] Sociological attempts, such as those of Thomas Robbins, to interpret suicidal acts as forms of martyrdom for a religious cause[18] have had practically no impact on the way these cases are handled by the legal authorities and depicted in the media.

The accusations that many new religions neglect their members and/or treat them with violence have appeared repeatedly in anti-cult literature. The abuse and mistreatment of children tops the list of allegations.[19] Accounts of ritual abuse have a long history.[20] Stories of Satanic worship that include child abuse and sacrifice have become popular news items in newspapers and magazines. Sexual abuse of children, child pornography, and bizarre murders are easily interpreted as being ritual in character and linked to Satanic groups. The case of the drug smuggling and ritual murder cult in an isolated ranch near Matamoros, Mexico, not far from the Texas border, made news headlines in early 1989.[21] It was immediately linked with Satanic worship, even though the evidence for such a connection was not very substantial. Stories of organized Satanic cults have been circulating in the United States since the mid-1980s and in Europe since the late 1980s.[22] Reports of Satanic crimes seem to have subsided, but some cases and accusations still surface occasionally.[23] Thus, for example, in 1999, it was reported that an "Indiana drifter with a history of dabbling in Satanic rituals was charged in dual Federal indictments . . . with setting church fires in Indiana and Georgia."[24] The case against Procter and Gamble, which was accused of having ties to Satanism and making financial contributions to the Church of Satan, has not yet been resolved.[25] Vandalism of graves in cemeteries, the frequency of which seems to have declined, are usually linked with Satanic worship.[26] The books about Harry Potter by J. K. Rowling[27] received negative reactions from many Christian evangelicals[28] who argued that they promoted Witchcraft and Satanism, which are believed by some to be widespread in the West. In some cases, as in the schools in Durham, Ontario (Canada), parents have succeeded in forbidding teachers to read Rowling's books to their students in class.[29]

Whether and to what extent accounts of Satanic rituals and crime are factual or not is debatable. A 1994 survey of psychiatrists in the United States "found no substantiated reports of well-organized Satanic rings of people who sexually abuse children."[30] This does not mean that sexual abuse, sometimes in the context of a Satanic rite, never occurs. But it does suggest that the number of such abuses may have been greatly exaggerated, and it stresses the need to verify any allegations with care. Reports of Satanic sexual abuse are by themselves not legal proof of criminal behavior. Several alleged cases of ritual abuse have led some states to define mutilation and abuse done in a ritual context and to distinguish them from other forms of child abuse.[31]

One of the more notorious cases of criminal behavior by members of a new religious movement is the case of Aum Shinrikyo in Japan in the mid-1990s.[32] Asahara, the founder and leader of the group, and over one hundred of his followers were indicted for releasing sarin gas in a Tokyo subway, for kidnapping, and for producing illegal drugs. Some convictions have already been reached and the remaining members of the group, though they are trying to distance themselves from their leader and his activities, are still under surveillance.[33] In spite of its violent and criminal elements, Aum Shinrikyo has its appeal, because, as one commentator said, cults offer "refuge to disillusioned youth in a Japan that, owing to a pervasive sense of economic doom, is searching for its soul."[34] Although Aum Shinrikyo[35] is an exception, the case tends to corroborate the view that some new religions might be dangerous and that attempts to pinpoint their dangerous features, as described in chapter 1, are necessary in a pluralistic society that values religious freedom.

Custody Cases

Litigation about child custody takes place routinely in the courtrooms, and people of different faiths have often become enmeshed in complicated cases. Generally speaking, the courts are called upon to decide whether one of the parents should be given custody of their children or whether the state itself should take over the care of the children. Problems dealing with child custody are not new, and many of the current court cases are not related to the new religious movements.

A typical case appeared before the Minnesota Court of Appeals in 1987.[36] The divorced parents of two children had agreed to raise their two children in the Lutheran Church (the faith of the mother) and to expose them to the Catholic Church (the faith of their father). The father, however, changed his religious affiliation and wanted to raise his children in his new church. The trial court had contended that exposure to a third religion would be "confusing and detrimental" to the young children, a conclusion with which the Appeals Court concurred. Members of new religious movements sometimes get involved in similar cases when one of the parents joins or leaves a new religion.

Another example comes from an established sect, the Church of God. In 2001, a couple who belonged to the branch of this Church in Aylmer, Ontario, lost custody of their seven children to the state because of their fundamentalist Christian belief in corporal punishment. The parents, supported by their pastor, defied the court order. An agreement was reached by which the parents were barred from taking their kids out of the province and which obliged the parents to accept counseling and to explore other methods of disciplining their children.[37]

One of the new religious movements that have been involved in lengthy court hearings regarding child custody cases is The Family (The Children of God).[38] Since the mid-1970s the sexual practices of this group have aroused a lot of criticism and antagonism. Although The Family claims that it has reformed its practices regarding sex, which is now restricted only to adults, several ex-members have accused its members of exposing their youngsters to unhealthy sexual behavior.[39] In many countries, including the United Kingdom, Norway, Italy, France, Argentina, Peru, Venezuela, and the United States, state agencies have conducted investigations of accusations of child abuse.[40] In some instances, the children of The Family were removed from their communal home and put into state-run homes. In June 1993, for instance, forty children from The Family's commune in Aix-en-Provence, France, were put under state protection, and twelve adult members were accused of "inciting children to debauchery."[41] A few months later, several of The Family's homes were raided, and many adults were arrested and the children taken into protective custody. It was believed that the children had been physically and psychologically abused. In those cases where judgment has been made, no evidence of child abuse and neglect have been found, and all the children were eventually returned to their parents.

Tax Cases

The tax-exempt status of religious and/or charitable institutions has been taken for granted in many countries, even though objections have been raised to some financial practices pursued by a few individual organizations.[42] In the United States such exemption is seen as flowing from the First Amendment of the Constitution that stipulates that Congress "should make no law respecting the establishment of religion or forbidding the free exercise thereof."[43] In the United Kingdom, many religious groups have been granted exemption from paying taxes by establishing charitable trusts.[44] Thomas Robbins observes that there are both legitimate and illegitimate financial practices among the new religions.[45] He discusses several financial misdealings allegedly perpetrated by the new religions, such as the royalty payments made by the Church of Scientology to its founder L. Ron Hubbard, and concludes that some new religions may be more prone to abuse tax laws than the established institutions and churches.

Several high-profile cases of alleged tax evasion by new religions have highlighted the need to examine their financial operations. The publicized trial and conviction of Reverend Sun Myung Moon, the founder and leader of the Unification Church, is a case in point.[46] In the early 1970s, before his Church was formally instituted as a religious organization according to U.S. law, Moon was convicted of tax evasion. Many established Christian churches came to the defense of the Unification Church because they saw in Moon's prosecution and conviction a threat to their own financial status. This case showed how inextricably linked the legal issues involving the new religious movements are with those of the more established religions.

The resurfacing of Paganism and Witchcraft and the request of their adherents for tax-exempt status has been a source of confusion. In Western tradition Witchcraft has been, and still is, routinely linked with Satanism and hence thought to be the antithesis of religious belief and practice. It should not come as a surprise if requests for tax exemption by Witchcraft covens and Satanic churches are challenged in court. While the tendency of the U.S. courts has been to grant Pagan groups the same preferential treatment granted to regular churches, there are some noteworthy exceptions. Thus, in 1986, the Supreme Court of Rhode Island found that the Church of Pan was not, strictly speaking, a religious organization and revoked the tax-exempt status granted to it by a lower court. The Church's motives and activities, rather than its stated purpose, were judged to be the determining factors. Since its monthly meetings consisted of nothing else but discussions on environmental issues, the court concluded that the Church of Pan was not a religion and, therefore, did not deserve to be given the status of an established religious organization.[47]

Solicitation Cases

A number of the new religions are known for their public campaigns to attract members and to collect funds. On several occasions, the management of airports, bus and train stations, and other public facilities have sought to ban or regulate solicitation practices on the grounds that they are a public nuisance and/or use deceptive means to attract new members and gain support and money.

Members of new religious movements have run into trouble with the law because they publicly sought monetary donations for various projects. In 1987, for instance, several Hare Krishna devotees were arrested in West Virginia for collecting donations allegedly under the false pretense of funding their program to feed poor people.[48] In France, several of the new religions appear to be on the brink of bankruptcy and have been accused of "trying anything to generate income" in ways judged to be a public nuisance.[49]

These attempts at devising ways of soliciting donations result, in part, from the very conditions in which new religious movements exist. Unlike the established churches, new religions do not have a strong base for generating the funds needed for any institution to survive, much less to grow and prosper. Besides soliciting funds from the general public, several new religions have embarked on projects that are run like businesses with cheap labor willingly provided by the devotees. It is the new religions' inherent economic instability that underlies their more questionable economic endeavors.[50] Moreover, new religions cannot grow unless they attract people from the general public and, therefore, membership drives are necessary for the movement's growth.

Recruitment and fund-solicitation tactics of new religions have come under attack because of their alleged "deceitfulness." This accusation implies either that the members of the new religions intentionally do not identify themselves clearly when evangelizing or that they do not specify to prospective donors how the funds will be used. In Great Britain some new religions have been so active in recruiting that there is a campaign to ban sects, like the London Church of Christ, from using university facilities.[51] Fears that vulnerable students might be easy targets underlie such concern. The Los Angeles Church of Christ has encountered similar reactions with regard to its activities on the campus of the University of Southern California. Some have accused it of not making recruits sufficiently aware of what membership involves.[52] The concern that new religions are dedicating many of their resources to recruiting university students is widespread. Hence, the need is felt to take legal action to protect these students exposed to cult recruitment practices.[53] To what extent would restrictions on the evangelizing activities of new religions conflict with religious freedom is questionable.

The criteria for deciding whether solicitation is intentionally deceptive are not always clear. Similarly, whether and to what degree public solicitation by members of new religions constitutes a public nuisance is debatable. There are cases that, though not typical, can be cited as examples of undue harassment. In Aberdeen, Scotland, for instance, recruiters for the Word of Life International elicited a negative and quite justifiable response when they started knocking on the doors inside university halls of residence at nighttime.[54]

Many people, however, seem to have found the right formula for brushing aside the enthusiastic distributors of religious literature and for ignoring the evangelizing sermons and enthusiastic witnessing of devotees. Solicitation, even if persistent and obnoxious, does not necessarily consist of undue pressure. Few solicitors persist if the initial reaction is negative. Rather than enact laws that restrict public speech or discriminate against a few marginal religious groups, it would be better, and certainly less conflicting, to educate people on how to deal with solicitors and how to avoid harassment.

Zoning/Community Relations Issues

Many new religions consist of relatively small groups of individuals that can be compared to extended families that may be large enough to have an impact on residential areas, particularly when their homes serve also as places for religious worship, social gatherings, and seminars. Further, the kind of relationships that members of the new religions establish with the community at large can lead to conflicts.

A clear example of zoning regulations that conflict with the activities of new religions is the attempt by the Hare Krishna movement to maintain their Bhaktivedanta Manor near Watford, some twenty miles northwest of London, England, as a place of worship. The district council argued that the manor was originally planned as a college and not a temple. Its continued use as a temple violated planning regulations and, because of the traffic it attracted, was a nuisance to the residents of the area.[55] The issue was finally solved and the Manor is now a center for the celebration of many traditional Hindu festivals and houses the College of Vedic Studies.[56]

The issue of community relations can be illustrated by the action the government of Singapore took in response to the activities of the Unification Church.[57] In July 1990, this Church was officially banned from the island when one of its organizations, known as the Moral Home Society, was legally dissolved. The government maintained that the Unification Church's continued existence "was prejudicial to public welfare and good order." Foremost among the reasons brought forth to support this claim were the activities of Church members to attract people to abandon their homes and families in order to become full-time members of the Church. The Moral Home Society's teachings and methods were judged to be harmful to religious harmony, family life, and social cohesion. The question that comes to mind in reviewing this case regards the nature of religious discipleship. Religious motives have always played a key role in people's decisions to abandon their lifestyles, family attachments, and economic advantages. In the New Testament Jesus demands that his followers make a complete and radical dedication to God's kingdom.[58] Some Christians today make decisions to join a monastic community where they sever their ties with their families, relatives, and friends and live in relative seclusion. Can the Christian Church be accused of disrupting family ties and members of monastic institutions forced by a civil court to abandon their commitment?

Another much-publicized cult activity that strained community relations was the reported statement (in October 1989) by Elizabeth Clare Prophet, leader of the Church Universal and Triumphant, that a nuclear war with the Soviet Union was imminent. The one thousand residents of the Church's ranch in Corwin Springs, Montana, took the prophecy seriously.[59] Believing that famine, pestilence, and economic collapse would follow the nuclear attacks, they began building shelters and storing food and water. Tensions between the Church and the surrounding communities increased when the rumor was spread that Church members were stockpiling weapons for civil defense purposes. The anxieties and apprehensions were somewhat diffused when the Church officials explained that what their leader had predicted was the beginning, on April 23, 1990, of a twelve-year cycle that would bring an increase of negative karma, leading to possible disasters and catastrophes. Charges, which never materialized in court suits, that the Church is ignoring laws aimed at protecting the environment have been repeatedly refuted by its members.

Libel Law Suits

Many of the new religions, dismayed by the wave of propaganda against them and by the constant threat of deprogramming, have gone on the offensive. Some cult members who survived unsuccessful deprogramming efforts have sued both their parents and their hired deprogrammers for violation of civil rights, abduction, false imprisonment, and psychological harm.

Because the word "cult" has acquired such a negative connotation, the simple accusation that a group is a new cult can have considerable repercussions both on its recruitment efforts and finances. Some religious groups have sued the offending parties for libel. An excellent example of a Christian group that reacted to this kind of labeling by initiating a lawsuit is the Local Church of Witness Lee (1905–1997), a church that originated in China in the 1920s and was then exported to the West.[60] Witness Lee moved to Southern California in 1962 and until his death was its most prominent leader, providing theological and spiritual direction to the movement by his teachings. While in sociological terms the Local Church is best described as a Christian sect, some of its practices, such as the reliance on their leader, could easily fall under the label of cult.

Since the mid-1970s the Local Church has been in conflict with portions of the evangelical anti-cult community that disagreed with some major theological doctrines that the Local Church taught and with certain expressions of piety in its worship. Taking the lead in the increasing campaign against the Local Church was the Spiritual Counterfeits

Project,[61] an evangelical organization in Berkeley, California, that specializes in studying the new religions and denouncing them as cults because of their unorthodox Christian beliefs and practices.

Two major books that have their source in the Spiritual Counterfeit Project accused Witness Lee of heresy. One, written by Jack Sparks,[62] covered several of the new religious movements and contained a chapter on the Local Church that suggested that, among other things, Witness Lee denied the traditional doctrine of the Trinity. The other, coauthored by Neil Duddy[63] and the Spiritual Counterfeits Project, was dedicated to a technical theological debate regarding Lee's alleged doctrinal errors. The authors, however, went beyond theological debates and accused the Local Church of being a destructive cult that used mind control to keep their members in line and of creating unnecessary social and psychological problems for those who joined it. These insinuations led to considerable opposition to the group and to some loss of membership. When attempts to resolve the issues by theological exchanges and to seek retractions and apologies by the authors or their publishers failed to restore harmony, the Local Church decided to file suit for libel. A settlement with the publisher of Sparks's book was reached out of court and brought an apology, the withdrawal of the book from circulation, and a financial settlement. The charges against the authors of the other book were heard in an uncontested trial, held in San Francisco in May 1985, after years of deliberation during which thousands of pages of depositions were accumulated.[64] The Local Church won a moral victory when an $11 million judgment was passed against the book's authors.

Lawsuits like the one described above can be easily dismissed as petty religious debates that should have no place in civil courts. The charges brought by the Local Church, however, deal with matters that pertain to any society that values religious freedom and that assumes that one is entitled to practice the religion of one's choice without harassment and intimidation. Besides, the accusations against the Local Church went beyond those of heresy and suggested that the authority system and lifestyle of the Church were harmful to its members. Civil courts are not interested in whether a particular Church's teachings are heretical or not. But they are concerned with any practices that endanger the mental and psychological welfare of Church members.

Some Reflections on the Religious Issues in the Court Rooms

Many accounts of, and reports on, court cases omit the intricate argumentation that takes place during the trial proceedings and the reasoned court decisions on the issues under discussion. Few efforts have been made to understand the religious and spiritual reasons that are adduced to justify the behavior under dispute. Judges, lawyers, and jury have been called on to reflect upon and make judgments on religious and theological matters that are inextricably bound with the practical issues debated in the courtrooms.

When Is a New Cult a Religious Entity?

One of the decisions that a court is frequently called to make regards the religious character of the organization being sued. What makes a group of people, united with a common purpose and lifestyle, a religious or charitable, rather than an educational, political, or economic, entity?

While traditional religions are taken for granted, new ones tend to arouse suspicion and must prove themselves. A new religion's claim to be a genuine spiritual institution is often questioned, if not categorically denied. In like manner, its petition to be accepted as a charitable trust might arouse misgivings regarding its intentions. Consequently "[i]n charity law a religion must have certain characteristics to be acceptable."[65] The legal system must establish criteria to determine the religious nature of a new organization.

Most nation-states in Western culture adopt some form of church-state separation. They distance themselves from any particular religious ideology, reject allegiance to any particular church, allow freedom of religion, and/or adopt a secular worldview. Yet at times they are called upon to decide whether groups like the Unification Church, a Yoga Institute, and Scientology should be treated as religions on par with the mainline traditions. It is quite understandable that the recent growth in religious diversity has created difficulties for the interpreters of the law. Both judges and lawyers, for example, find themselves in situations where they have to define what "religion" is. In a society where the Judeo-Christian tradition forms the basis not only of most people's beliefs and practices but also of public morality, the presence of alien, apparently exotic, belief systems and rituals can be too readily dismissed as something not pertaining to religion at all.

In determining whether a religious organization is a bona fide religion, judges have to ask two basic questions. The first is whether the insistence on the religious character of a group is a subterfuge for illegal activities and the second whether its application to become legally classified as a religious (or charitable) organization is only a convenient way of gaining tax exemption.

A good illustration of the kind of conflict that might arise between the state and some new religions is the custom that incorporates the consumption of illegal drugs in religious rituals. In the United States the problem received widespread publicity in the late 1960s, when Timothy Leary advocated the use of the drug known as LSD as a way of achieving religious ecstasy.[66] Leary, who was convicted on the charge of transporting marijuana illegally, was not original in his claim. But his endorsement and encouragement of the use of drugs highlighted the practices of several religions that have employed drugs in ritual context to achieve a mind-altering state believed to enhance union with the divine.[67]

During the past fifteen years religious seekers have sometimes experimented with drugs in order to achieve the "vision quest," a common goal in Native American religions.[68] The use of drugs, especially peyote, among some U.S. Native Americans is a relatively recent phenomenon in their history.[69] The presence of peyote in religious rituals dates, however, from pre-Columbian times when it was discovered among several Indian tribes in Mexico. It spread into the United States in the eighteenth and nineteenth centuries in part as a reaction to the negative effects of colonialism.

Peyote is a wild cactus that contains mescaline, an alkaloid drug that has hallucinogenic effects similar to those of LSD. During the ritual the tip of the cactus or button is eaten or drunk in the form of tea. Those who ingest the button are said to experience ecstatic visions. The use of peyote became part of the ritual of the Native American Church[70] in 1918 and still remains central to this Church's services.

The immediate public reactions to eating peyote during religious rituals were negative. The members of the Native American Church were involved in legal problems in several states, including Colorado, Utah, Mexico, Arizona, and California. By the late 1950s the courts' attitude toward peyote began to change, and several states passed exemption clauses that permitted its religious use. The California Supreme Court ruled in 1964 that the Native American Church couldn't be deprived of the use of peyote for religious purposes. Federal drug legislation in 1970 threatened the custom that allowed the members of the Native American Church to partake of peyote in their services, but in 1971 their exemption was retained. In 1994 Congress amended the 1978 American Indian Religious Freedom Act "to provide for the traditional use of peyote by Indians for religious purposes, and other purposes."[71]

How does one determine whether church membership is nothing but an excuse for taking hallucinatory drugs? Two factors probably helped the courts decide. The first is the attitude of the American Indians who belong to the Native American Church. They treat "peyote" as a holy object. They do not distribute it indiscriminately nor do they encourage people to join their Church because of the drug's purported spiritual benefits. This attitude became clear during the early 1970s. Many non-Native Americans tried to join this Church, but were refused membership. The Native Americans wanted to keep out those whose main interest was taking drugs and not participating in a religious ritual that they believed was central to their religion.

The second factor is the careful control of the peyote by Church officials. In the Native American Church, the shaman is the central religious or spiritual figure who is thought to possess psychic powers. He keeps and distributes the peyote buttons. The peyote ritual starts with a pilgrimage of the Church members who collect the peyote buttons and hand them over to the shaman. The peyote ceremony[72] is held in the evening in a teepee and lasts through the night. The drug, called "Father-Peyote," is placed on a crescent-shaped mound that is carefully constructed so that it faces west, while the two horns of the crescent face east. After prayer and smoking, the "peyote" is eaten in sacramental fashion. The ritual communion is then followed by singing and drumming and by a long period of contemplation. To the courts, the way the Native Americans treat and use peyote is a clear indication that the partaking of the drug is religious in nature.

The issue of whether illegal drugs can be used in religious services is a continuing problem. Several churches have argued that the use of marijuana and/or other drugs are sacramental in nature and have spiritual healing powers.[73] U.S. courts, however, have been reluctant to accept the argument of freedom of religion brought forth by these churches to seek exemption from federal and state laws. In one particular case, the Church of Marijuana, the court argued that the church's "social and philosophical beliefs do not rise to the level of 'religious beliefs.'" In other words, unlike the use of peyote by the Native American Church, the smoking of marijuana by the members of the Church of Marijuana was not a "religious" act. Hence, it cannot be condoned and no exception can be granted for its use.[74]

The presence of churches that encourage the use of marijuana may have led the courts to reexamine the use of peyote among Native Americans. A 1992 Supreme Court ruling upheld an Oregon law that made it a crime to possess or use peyote even in Native American religious services.[75] Two Native Americans were fired from their state jobs as drug counselors because they had participated in a religious ritual involving the ingestion of peyote. A majority of the judges hearing the appeal argued that the ban did not violate the Native Americans' constitutional right to free exercise of religion. The dissenting judges maintained that the Oregon law was not supported by a compelling government interest and pointed out that Church members consume the drug in a "carefully circumscribed context" that "is far removed from the irresponsible and unrestricted recreational use of unlawful drugs." The ruling against the use of peyote was confirmed when the Supreme Court denied a request, made by several religious organizations, for a new hearing. The State of Oregon's ban against peyote was sustained, even though the members of the Native American Church are technically still exempt from such restrictions by federal law and by the legislations of over twenty other states. To further complicate the legality of peyote, an Idaho law, enacted in 1991, allowed Native Americans to legally transport the drug peyote to their reservations for religious ceremonies and health purposes.[76] The debate about the use of peyote by Native Americans is far from over.[77]

The financial status of the new religions or cults has figured prominently in attacks made against them. Some groups have the unenviable reputation of being wealthy and of running lucrative businesses under the guise of religion.[78] In the United States, Scientology has been involved in so many court cases that deal precisely with this question that it offers an excellent example of the problems courts encounter when they are called to determine whether beliefs and practices are religious in nature. J. Gordon Melton states:

> the history of Scientology has to a large extent been a history of controversy. Since 1958 the Church has been in almost constant litigation with the Internal Revenue Service. It fought a ten-year battle with the Food and Drug Administration, and in Australia it ended over sixteen years of war with the government in 1983.[79]

Scientology's legal battles in the United States have a long history. In June 1989, the U.S. Supreme Court ruled that Church members could not deduct the cost of Scientology courses or services from their federal income taxes. In a 5-to-2 decision the judges maintained that the two main practices of Scientology, auditing and training, are services for which people are charged set fees amounting to several thousand dollars. Scientology students, in the court's opinion, are not making free religious contributions but paying for services and, consequently, they cannot deduct the cost on their federal income tax forms.

Similar court battles have been waged in different European nations. In March 2000 the Italian Supreme Court ruled that Scientology is a religion and hence exempt from taxes, but its drug rehabilitation program (called Narconon) is not tax exempt. On the other hand, the Charity Commission of England and Wales rejected Scientology's application to be registered as a charity, which would have given it tax exemption on par with other religions that are registered as charities. British law defines religion as belief in a Supreme Being, a belief that is expressed in worship. Scientology was judged as not being a religion since it does not include the worship of God in its practices. Scientology has been involved in law cases in many countries including Russia, Spain, Greece, Germany, and Switzerland[80] and is still struggling to assert itself as a bona fide religion on par with the mainline traditions.

The debate centers round the religious nature of the practice of auditing, which is pivotal in the worldview and practice of Scientology.[81] Scientologists believe that the real self (called the "Thetan") is hampered from developing and expressing itself fully by both the body and the mind. Auditing is the main discipline for removing the obstacles to human development and allowing the individual to reach the state of "Clear," a condition in which one's negative reactions have been erased and the individual is "in control over his own mental matter, energy, space and time." The auditor, a spiritual counselor or guide, uses a mechanical device, called the E-Meter, as a "confessional aid" in the process of releasing the Thetan. In the auditing sessions the E-Meter is employed to indicate areas of tension. It consists of a small electrical device, a rectangular or circular box, to which two handles are attached by wires. The person being audited holds the handles while the auditor asks him or her standardized questions. A moving dial on the E-Meter records how those being audited react to these questions. Scientologists, in their catechism, describe the E-Meter as follows:

> The E-Meter is a shortened term for *electropsychometer*. It is a religious artifact used as a spiritual guide in the Church confessional or counseling session. It is for use only by a Scientology minister or a Scientology minister-in-training to help the preclear locate and confront areas of spiritual upset. . . . The E-Meter is used to help the individual who is being audited to uncover truth.[82]

The court was unimpressed by the Scientology claim that auditing is a religious method for reaching the state of spiritual freedom or enlightenment and that the fees charged can be compared to tithing in some Christian churches. It ruled that, because the payment for auditing is commensurate with the type and amount of service rendered, the fees are not charitable gifts. Like tuition for church schools, payment for church-sponsored counseling sessions, and fees for medical care in church-run hospitals, the monetary compensation for auditing sessions is not tax deductible. The court's decision has repercussions and ramifications that go beyond Scientology. The American Jewish Congress was dismayed by the court's ruling because it indirectly questions whether members of any synagogue or church can deduct religious contributions for tickets for religious services on high holy days, Mass stipends, or mandatory tithing. A 1993 decision by the U.S. Internal Revenue Service granted the Church of Scientology and its many corporations tax exemption, thus ending one of the longest legal disputes involving a new religious movement.[83]

What Are the Boundaries of Religious Freedom?

One of the central accusations that have been directed against the new religions is that their deceptive recruitment tactics and strong indoctrination processes deprive people of those intellectual and emotional qualities necessary for making free choices. Entry into a new religious movement is, therefore, not a question of religious conversion, made freely without compulsion, but one of mind control or brainwashing.[84]

The implications of this theory on court trials and decisions have been devastating. For if the cult member is a virtual prisoner or slave in the cult's enclave, hasn't the state the right to interfere and remove him or her by force? And if the individual had been deceived into becoming a member, isn't the institution that forced the commitment liable to the damages inflicted on the unsuspecting individual? If, on the other hand, the cult member made a free choice to join a new religion and if his or her entrance is the result of a genuine religious conversion, what right has the state to intrude? Similarly, if an individual elects to follow an ascetic lifestyle in an Eastern religious movement, one might question the parents' rights to have him or her removed by force. How can the members of the jury in a civil court decide whether the person who joins a new religion has had a genuine religious conversion?

One of the most notorious instances that illustrate the above dilemma is the George case. The main elements of this dramatic story can be summarized as follows. In 1977, Robin George, a high school student and legally a minor, became interested in the Hare Krishna movement. Her parents, worried that she would drop out of school and, hoping that her interest was a passing phase, reached an agreement with her that allowed her to keep her connections with the Hare Krishna Temple in Los Angeles while still attending school. Robin, however, got more involved in this Eastern religion and decided to drop out of school and formally join the movement, in spite of her parents' objections. Afraid that her parents might get a court order to remove her from the temple, Robin traveled from one Hare Krishna temple to another. Eventually, however, her whereabouts were discovered and she was abducted and deprogrammed. She then completely reversed her attitude and joined her parents in suing the Hare Krishna movement for keeping her against her will, forcing her to accept an alien belief system, and inflicting psychological damages upon her. The judgment, which included damages totaling over $30 million (later reduced to $9.7 million), went against this Hindu religious group. The appeals dragged on the case for years. In 1989 a Los Angeles court dismissed Robin George's claim that she had been brainwashed by the Hare Krishna movement.[85] The suit was finally settled in 1993.[86]

The jury in this lawsuit had to pass an implicit judgment on the nature and validity of religious conversion. But doesn't this make the civil court an arbiter in a theological debate? Is there an age when the individual can be judged competent to accept freely a system of belief and ritual, just as there is an age when the young adult is considered mature enough to vote or contract a marriage? There is no doubt that Robin George was technically under age. The reasons for maintaining that her decision to join the Hare Krishna movement was illegal are, however, far from clear. The George case has had one major effect on many new religions. It has made them cautious and more wary of accepting people who are not recognized as adults by the law.

When Does Religion Lead to Child Abuse or Neglect?

It has been a tacitly approved principle in Western culture that the parents have the right to determine the religious upbringing of their children. The religion of the parents can dictate the kind of food their children receive, the strictness of the behavior they are expected to follow, the punishment they receive for not obeying, and the kind of medical treatment they get. This has not been a problem with the majority of Christian churches, where the regulations regarding food are minimal and where the rearing of children and the punishments inflicted for misconduct conform to a large degree to what is culturally and legally accepted as normal. Further, in most Christian churches, prayer for one's health is accompanied by medical attention that is in harmony with modern healthcare standards.

Serious problems begin to surface when, for instance, a religious group insists that corporal punishment should be strictly meted out to recalcitrant children. Among Christian fundamentalists, the Bible has been adduced as a justifiable rationale for such treatment, even when it results in grave bodily harm. The difficulties become more complex when the sect or cult nurtures a deep antagonism toward a society that is labeled unchristian or evil. Refusal to take advantage of modern medical treatments, when these are perceived to conflict with one's religious beliefs, becomes a pattern. When is the refusal to supply one's children with what is considered essential childcare a case of child neglect or abuse? And under what conditions can government regulation or interference be justified?

Cases about children who are severely harmed by physical punishment or neglected by the withholding of medical treatment are becoming all too frequent.[87] Religious reasons given for the rigorous enforcement of parental and group rules and for not applying standard medicine are not very convincing, especially when physical or psychological damage is the outcome. To outsiders, the punishments also appear to be completely out of proportion to the alleged offenses of young children who may not have yet reached the age of reason. The refusal to make use of modern medicine is unintelligible in a society noted for its scientific advancement. A strong case can be made for the argument that the state has the right and duty to intervene and prosecute the offending parties

One of the most notorious cases involved the House of Judah, a fundamentalist Christian communal sect in Michigan that flourished in the early 1980s.[88] A twelve-year-old boy, who was generally reluctant to obey his parents and elders, skipped his assigned chores. After an initial punishment, he reacted by refusing to eat, for which he was exposed to further discipline. He was taken to one of the main buildings of the camp and locked, head and wrists, in the camp's stocks. Hunched over, he received thirty strokes with a thick wooden stick. At least one blow landed on the spine and killed him. Investigations revealed that the House of Judah had a clearly defined rigorous system of corporal punishment that was graded in proportion to the offenses made. The state authorities reacted by removing all children from the camp and by charging the child's mother with manslaughter and William Lewis, the camp leader, and several other members with child cruelty. Although the state's intervention in this case was justified, the incident still raised many legal questions regarding its right to intervene in order to protect children from treatment detrimental to their health.[89]

The problem of supplying underage children with medical treatment becomes more acute in situations involving groups like the Church of Christ, Scientist, which, though not a new religious movement, has at times been lumped with "destructive" cults. Christian Scientists reject most forms of modern medical procedures and have recourse to their own practitioners who are church members trained to handle all kinds of ailments usually treated by medical doctors. These practitioners do not prescribe medication; they "pray" over the matter. They argue that there is plenty of evidence to show that spiritual methods have cured physical illnesses.[90]

Much misunderstanding of Christian Science stems from the fact that its use of the word "prayer" has quite a different meaning from that employed by the majority of Christian churches. Praying over a sick person generally refers to the Christian's petition to God for a special healing intervention and is, therefore, a sign of faith in God's power and concern for human welfare. For the Christian Scientists, however, prayer is a kind of reinforcement of their faith in God who, through Jesus, has already saved and healed human beings from all their miseries. There is consequently no need to ask God for a miraculous curing of the apparently sick person. This being the case, having recourse to a medical doctor can be easily perceived as a sign that one's faith is lacking. The decision to take a sick child to a doctor or a Christian Scientist practitioner is the parents'. But what if the child is not given medical treatment and dies? Who bears responsibility for his or her death?

In the early 1980s Christian Science became embroiled in a legal suit precisely because a young boy died after he was taken to hospital much too late to be given any effective medication. The Swan case was reported in popular magazines throughout the United States.[91] Briefly, in 1977, Matthew Swan, then fifteen months old, began acting in a sickly fashion and his Christian Scientist parents took him to a practitioner. As the child grew worse, they tried another practitioner with little apparent result. Finally, the parents rushed their son to a hospital where he was diagnosed as suffering from advanced meningitis. When the parents were told that the hospital would get a court order to allow the doctors to treat the boy, they acquiesced and gave permission to the doctors. The son, however, did not survive. The disappointed and disillusioned parents left the Christian Science Church and sued it and the practitioners for the death of their son.[92] The Church and the two practitioners were charged with negligence and misrepresentation. There was an implicit accusation that the Church conditioned ("brainwashed") the parents to reject modern medicine and to believe in spiritual healing. Consequently, both the Church and its practitioners who inculcated the Church's teachings were to be blamed for the premature and unnecessary demise of their child. The question as to whether the practitioners were guilty of medical malpractice was also raised.

After lengthy legal depositions, exchanges, and appeals, the case never made it to a trial court. The refusal to have the matter tried in civil court was based on constitutional grounds. The Michigan Supreme Court, in an order dated November 2, 1988, concluded that the behavior of the parents and church practitioners did not subject them "to civil liability to the child's estate for resulting damage as a matter of common law or in implementation of statutory mandate." In November 1989, the U.S. Supreme Court upheld this ruling, thus ending a protracted debate in which experts on both sides participated. The courts have, however, been more successful when Christian Scientist parents have been sued by the state for involuntary manslaughter and child endangerment.[93]

The debate about religious healing and whether the state should intervene has not subsided. The Swans have founded an organization called CHILD (Children's Healthcare Is a Legal Duty), which aims "to protect children from abusive religious practices, especially religion-based medical neglect."[94] Besides filing lawsuits and amicus briefs, the organization supports laws that protect children when medical health is denied them for religious reasons and emotional support for those who suffer from medical neglect.

How Does One Deal with Religious Violence?

In spite of the many reports on cult-related violence, there are very few studies that survey the types and frequency of violence that occur within new religions or are justified by religious ideology. J. Gordon Melton has analyzed the matter with some care and provided some guidelines to understand and deal with it.[95]

Melton begins by proposing a broader definition of violence that includes not only bodily harm but also the destruction of property. One can also widen his definition to include the verbal abuse and slander that are used to attack religious groups. Melton rightly points out that three types of violence related to the new religions must be considered: violence (1) against cults, (2) between the cults themselves, and (3) initiated by cults. He suggests that cult-related violence be placed in the larger context of religious violence and that rumors about such violence should be carefully distinguished from factual occurrences that are subject to proof. There are also different levels of violence. Given the number of new religious groups, it becomes clear that only a handful of them can be suspected of committing or condoning acts of violence. Generalizations about the violence of cults are therefore unwarranted. Judging from the number of reported cases, evangelical and fundamental Christian churches seem more prone to some forms of violence than are those groups that bear the label of cults or new religions.

There is good reason to believe that the roots of cult-related violence are deeply embedded in one's culture and ideology. Robert McAfee Brown points to seven comprehensive areas of concern relating to religion and violence: (1) nuclear weapons; (2) terrorism; (3) the death penalty; (4) sexual violence; (5) the drug culture; (6) disinformation (or violence against truth); and (7) revolution.[96] Brown's discussion indirectly points to the complexity of the violence that has been associated with the new religions. Violence has been, and still is, perpetrated by members of traditional religions and justified by scriptural quotes. Hence, prosecution and punishment of the offenders will, by itself, not solve the problem.

One of the major causes of cult-related violence is the difficulty people have in coping with religious pluralism, a difficulty that will be discussed in some detail in the next two chapters. The inability to deal with the variety of conflicting religious beliefs and practices and to treat people with dignity and respect, no matter what their religious persuasions might be, is a principal cause of religiously motivated violence, which is not, incidentally, restricted to Western culture. Moreover, psychological and social factors might, at times, be responsible for violence. Ritual child abuse, for instance, is probably understood better as a sociopsychological than a religious problem. Jean-François Mayer examines religious violence from an international perspective and concludes:

> The exploration of some common psychological features among the leaders of those groups as well as the examination of the perception that groups have of the relation to their environment might offer other promising perspectives for understanding the dynamics that sometimes transform idealistic truth-seekers into ruthless murderers or terrorists.[97]

Two of the greatest problems for law enforcement agencies are (1) how to recognize when a new religious group is likely to commit violence and (2) how not to overreact if it occurs. Knowing the new movement's ideology and being able to identify those characteristics that might incite or increase violence are the best means to prevent it and to diffuse it. As Catherine Wessinger has pointed out, those millennial groups who believe strongly that the end will come in a catastrophic manner are likely to feel persecuted, especially when any action is taken against them.[98] They can easily respond by violence that is justified by their belief that the final battle against evil is at hand. Wessinger has drawn up a list of eighteen characteristics that are a cause for concern. Interaction, internal, and belief factors can motivate members of new religions to take the initiative and engage in violent behavior (as in the case of Aum Shinrikyo), or to respond in kind to (real or perceived) violence against them (as in the case of the Branch Davidians in Waco). A few examples provided by Wessinger will suffice to illustrate some of the factors that must be taken into consideration.

> As a result of conflict and opposition from mainstream society, the group abandons proselytizing to gain new converts, and turns inward to preserve salvation for its members alone. [Interaction factor]

> Followers are overly dependent on a charismatic leader (who claims authority from an unseen source, such as God) as the sole means to achieve their ultimate concern (salvation). [Internal factor]

> Belief in reincarnation is combined with catastrophic millennialism and belief that the group is being persecuted. [Belief factor][99]

Finally, it should be insisted that Western society has many laws against all kinds of violence and brutality and it is doubtful whether the activities of the new religious movements call for the enactment of more legislation. The problem lies in the fact that laws do not change people's attitudes, nor do they automatically ameliorate social conditions and psychological states. Unless the roots of violence are addressed, it is more than likely that it will continue to mar the religious scene for a long time to come. And unless efforts are made to understand the new religions that are inclined to violence, it will be practically impossible to resolve tense situations peacefully.

Court Testimony and Expert Witnesses

The discussion of cult-related issues in the courtrooms requires witnesses, jury members, lawyers, and judges who are not only impartial but also knowledgeable in religious and theological matters. The fact that cult members belong to out-of-the-mainstream groups renders them more susceptible to be victims of disguised prejudice or sheer ignorance. And because many of the new religions are based on Eastern philosophical traditions, most of those who take part in court cases are less likely to understand them. Experts called to give testimony for or against new religious movements are an essential element in the court proceedings. Knowledge of religious and theological matters is necessary for reaching judgment. Five different types of witnesses have testified for or against the new religions.

Family Members

The parents of cult members take a central part in the legal process involving the new religious movements. Their view of the cult is, understandably, negative. Family members tend to look at new religions as evil organizations that threaten both society and the family. They refuse to listen to different points of view, to consider that new religions might have some attractive features, and that the home situation might have contributed to their children's problems prior to their involvement. Their anguish and frustration, coupled at times with their anger and guilt-feelings, might affect their testimony, making it unreliable.

Ex-Cult Members

Many times ex-cult members have testified against the new religion to which they formerly belonged. They have rarely given a favorable impression of their lives in the cult. Their participation, before the trial, in anticult activities raises disconcerting questions about their impartiality. Forced deprogramming has often led cult members to repudiate their respective ideologies and lifestyles and transformed them from avid cult promoters to vociferous detractors. Their testimony must be carefully sifted and compared to that of more impartial observers of the new religions.

Current Cult Members

Members of new religions have dedicated a lot of time and energy defending themselves against charges brought against them. Some lawyers who are cult members have frequently led the defense of their organizations. Like ex-cult members, they have an important stake in the outcome of the trial, an outcome that might have crippling repercussions on their lifestyles and the success of their missions. The members' testimonies in support of their religious beliefs and activities should certainly not be taken for granted. Their presence in the trial is, however, essential if jury members and judges are to make a fair and just decision.

Experts in Religious Matters

A variety of scholars, especially sociologists,[100] have been called to describe the belief system and lifestyle of the cult in question and to express their opinions on the nature of the problem under discussion. Their testimonies have one principal advantage, namely, that their disciplines have provided them with the tools to study and evaluate religion. Their opinions are not usually marred by anti-cult rhetoric. But there are many self-styled experts who are probably more noteworthy for anti-cult oratory than for understanding the modern religious scene. If experts are to present objective testimony on religious beliefs and practices, they need to be carefully screened.

Psychiatrists

Several psychiatrists and psychologists have become regular expert witnesses against the new religions, even though their training in religious matters and their knowledge of non-Western traditions are minimal.[101] Their opinions have been requested because many of the accusations against the cults have revolved around two major points. At issue have been (1) the psychological state of their members, both before and after commitment, and (2) the emotional and mental effects that a lifestyle of a particular new religion might have on its members.

The competency of psychiatrists and psychologists to testify in religious matters should not, however, be taken for granted. Many of these professionals are noteworthy for their antagonistic disposition toward religion, a disposition that does not render them detached observers of the current religious scene. Judges should realize that trained psychiatrists may have little of worth to reveal about religion, and that some of their negative testimony against the new religions is equally applicable to the major Christian churches.

Conclusion

It would seem that the value of religious freedom in pluralistic societies should remain an overriding criterion when dealing with marginal religious groups. Religious freedom implies that the new religions should not be subjected to unjustifiable harassment because of their unusual beliefs and behaviors. Leo Pfeffer, writing from the perspective of the U.S. Constitution, states that "the purpose of the first amendment's guarantee of freedom of religion was and is the protection of unpopular creeds and faiths."[192] While there is no doubt that the cults have brought or revived many legal and social issues that must be resolved, there is serious doubt whether specific laws designed to curtail them are really necessary. The 1992 Council of Europe's report states explicitly that

> the freedom of conscience and religion guaranteed by Article 9 of the European Convention on Human Rights makes major legislation on sects undesirable, since such legislation might well interfere with this fundamental right and harm traditional religions.[103]

In the West there is enough legislation to handle most, if not all, of the legal issues that the new religious movements have aggravated or brought to the fore.[104] An excellent example is the case of immigration laws that they have often been accused of breaking. In the United Kingdom attempts are being made to use already-existent immigration laws to bar entry for undesirable cult leaders.[105] It must be emphasized, however, that the breaking of these laws is not a new problem brought about by the new religions. In fact, most Western countries are facing serious immigration problems that make the abuses by members of new religions look minuscule. In the United States illegal immigration is a major problem and the number of cult members who have illegally entered the country is negligible. This does not mean that when members of new religions break these laws they should not be prosecuted. Rather, it should draw our attention to two main considerations. First, the efforts to bypass or circumvent immigration laws should be seen in perspective of a much larger issue; and, second, transgressions in this respect by members of the new religions do not warrant the enactment of any special law designed solely for them.

The legal debates brought about by the new religious movements are not likely to subside in the near future. The reason for this is twofold: they are not a passing fad, and conflicts between state and church are endemic to a religiously pluralistic culture and to the very nature of new religions. The lengthy lawsuits brought against the new religions may have had the effect of strengthening, rather than weakening, them and of exacerbating the already existing controversy.

The best way to handle the legal problems pertaining to the activities of the new religious movements is to treat them not as forms of organized crime or pathology hiding under the mantel of religious respectability. Rather, unless there is clear evidence to the contrary, they should be regarded as alternative minority religions struggling to gain a foothold in a hostile environment. It must be stressed that new religions should conform to the law of the country in which they seek to become established. But it must be emphatically stated that any prosecution of new religious movements that resemble a crusade or a persecution might have profound and undesirable repercussions on both society and traditional religions. It is advisable that most of the cases that are not criminal in nature are best heard in a different forum where reconciliation and compromise, rather than costly and protracted litigation, should be the goals of all the parties concerned.[106]

Notes

1. Some of these differences are listed in the "The Council of Europe's Report on Sects and New Religious Movements," *Cultic Studies Journal* 9 (1992): 97. James A. Beckford, in his *Cult Controversies: The Societal Response to the New Religious Movements* (London: Tavistock, 1985), shows how the social and cultural differences between the United Kingdom, Germany, and France have had an impact on how the new religions are conceived as legal problems. For a survey of issues from the point of view of law in the United Kingdom, see Anthony Bradney, "New Religious Movements: The Legal Dimension," in *New Religious Movements: Challenge and Response*, ed. Bryan Wilson and Jamie Cresswell (London: Routledge, 1999), pp. 81–100.

2. For a discussion on the constitutional issues that affect the new religions in the United States, see William C. Shepherd, *To Secure the Blessings of Freedom: American Constitutional Law and the New Religious Movements* (New York: Crossroads Publishing, 1985).

3. See David Wilshire, "Cults and the European Parliament: A Practical Political Response to an International Problem," *Cultic Studies Journal* 7 (1990): 1–14. The text of the 1984 European Parliament's Resolution is given on pp. 11–14.

4. "The Council of Europe's Report on Sects and New Religious Movements," *Cultic Studies Journal* 9 (1992): 89–119.

5. Bryan Wilson, "Sects and the State: Some Issues and Cases," in *The Social Dimensions of Sectarianism: Sects and New Religious Movements in Contemporary Society* (Oxford: Clarendon Press, 1990), p. 31.

6. Probably the best Internet source for original documents of the legal conflicts involving new religions in different countries is the Web page of the Center for Studies on New Religions (located in Turin, Italy). See http://www.cesnur.org/. *The Cult Observer* (now combined with the *Cultic Studies Journal* in a new publication, *Cultic Studies Review*), published by the American Family Foundation, contains news items dealing with court cases in which the new religions are involved.

7. See, for instance, Steven Pressman, "Taking Cults to Court for Psychological Injuries," *New Jersey Law Journal* 130 (March 9, 1992): 4.

8. A good example is Susan Landa's article, "Children and Cults: A Practical Guide," *Journal of Family Law* 29 (1991): 591–622. The author accepts the theory that cults are destructive organizations that recruit new members deceptively and maintain them by well-developed methods of mind control. See also the paper, David Bardin, "Psychological Coercion and Human Rights: Mind Control ('Brainwashing') Exists" (Bonita Springs, FL: American Family Foundation, n.d.).

9. See, for instance, Margaret Thaler Singer and Richard Ofshe, "Thought Reform Programs and the Production of Psychiatric Casualties," *Psychiatric Annals* 20 (1990): 188–93; and Paul R. Martin, Lawrence A. Pile, Ron Burks, and Stephen D. Martin, "Overcoming Bondage of Revictimization: A Rational/Empirical Defense of Thought Reform," *Cultic Studies Journal* 15 (1998): 151–91. Many of the essays published in Michael D. Langone, ed., *Recovery from Cults: Help for Victims of Psychological and Spiritual Abuse* (New York: W. W. Norton, 1993), are based on the assumption that mind control is common in new religious movements.

10. See, for example, Stephen A. Kent, "Brainwashing and Re-Indoctrination Programs in The Children of God/The Family," *Cultic Studies Journal* 17 (2000): 56–78.

11. Confer Stephen G. Post, "The Molko Case: Will Freedom Prevail?" *Journal of Church and State* 31 (1989): 451–64.

12. Thomas Robbins and James A. Beckford, "Religious Movements and Church-State Issues," in *Religion and the Social Order: The Handbook of Cults and Sects in America*, ed. David G. Bromley and Jeffrey K. Hadden (Greenwich, CT: JAI Press, vol. 3A, 1993), p. 202.

13. John Young and Ezra Griffith, "A Critical Evaluation of Coercive Persuasion as Used in the Assessment of Cults," *Behavioral Sciences and the Law* 10 (1992): 96.

14. See "Brainwashing Defense Fails Teen in Alleged Oara Group," *Cultic Studies Review* 1 (2002): 122–23.

15. Jack Hitt, "The Return of the Brainwashing Defense," in *New York Times* (December 15, 2002): 6, 116.

16. Anson Shupe, David G. Bromley, and Edward F. Breschel, "The Peoples Temple, the Apocalypse at Jonestown, and the Anti-Cult Movements," in *New Religious Movements, Mass Suicide, and the Peoples Temple: Scholarly Perspectives on a Tragedy*, ed. Rebecca Moore and Fielding McGehee III (Lewiston, NY: Edwin Mellen Press, 1989), p. 153.

17. Robert Hicks, "Many Law Enforcement Officers Have Been Instructed to Consider Membership in a 'Cult' as Tantamount to a Crime," *Los Angeles Daily Journal* 106 (March 16, 1993): 6.

18. Thomas Robbins, "The Historical Antecedents of Jonestown: The Sociology of Martyrdom," in *New Religious Movements, Mass Suicide, and Peoples Temple*, pp. 51–76.

19. Marcia Rudin, "Women, Elderly, and Children in Religious Cults," *Cultic Studies Journal* 1, no. 1 (1984): 8–36; and Shirley Landa, "Warning Signs: The Effects of Authoritarianism on Children in Cults," *Areopagus* 2, no. 4 (1989): 16–22.

20. James Randall Noblitt and Pamela Sue Perskin, *Cult and Ritual Abuse: Its History, Anthropology, and Recent Discovery in Contemporary America* (Westport, CT: Praeger/Greenwood Publishing Group, 2000).

21. Lengthy reports and commentaries were carried in the *New York Times* (April 13, 1989): I, 1:4; 10:5; 26:5; (April 14, 1989): I, 14:5; and (April 17, 1989): I, 14:1, 3.

22. In London, for example, the *Times* has, since 1990, published many reports of Satanic cases. See *The Times Index 1990–1993* (Reading, UK: Newspapers Archives Development Ltd., 1994) where under "sexual offenses," a section on "satanic practices" is listed.

23. See references to Satanism and ritual abuse in *The New York Times Index 1997–2001* (New York: New York Times Company, 1998–2002) and in *The Times Index 1997–2002* (Reading, UK: Gale, 1998–2002).

24. See Neil MacFarquhar, "Man Is Indicted in 10 Church Fines in Indiana and Georgia, One in which a Firefighter Died," *New York Times* (April 21, 1999): A14.

25. Geanne Rosenberg, "P&G Suit Against Amway Revived," *New York Times* (March 21, 2001): C8.

26. See the report of such a case by Stacey Stowe. "Nothing Scared in Cemetery Vandalism," *New York Times* (October 31, 1999): 14CN, 1.

27. J. K. Rowling, *Harry Potter and the Sorcerer's Stone* (1998), *Harry Potter and the Chamber of Secrets* (1999), *Harry Potter and the Prisoner of Azkaban* (1999), and *Harry Potter and the Goblet of Fire* (2000), all published by Arthur A. Levine, New York. At the time this book was put into publication the first two in the series had already been made into movies.

28. For reactions to the books about Harry Potter see the Web page of the Center for Studies on New Religions, http://www.cesnur.org. For a Christian interpretation that does not equate the magic of Harry Potter with modern Witchcraft and/or Satanism, and consequently with evil, see Connie Neal, *What's a Christian to Do with Harry Potter?* (Colorado Springs, CO: Waterbrook Press, 2001), and *The Gospel According to Harry Potter: Spirituality in the Stories of the World's Most Famous Seeker* (Louisville, KY: Westminster John Knox Press, 2002).

29. Confer "'Harry Potter' Readings Cursed by School Board," *New York Times* (September 11, 2000): A, 41E.

30. Daniel Goleman, "Proof Lacking for Ritual Abuse by Satanists," *New York Times* (October 14, 1994): A13.

31. Consult Ronald R. Bullis, *Sacred Calling, Secular Accountability: Law and Ethics in Complementary and Spiritual Counseling* (Philadelphia: Brunner-Routledge, 2001), pp. 151–52.

32. For a brief profile of this group see Jackie Fowler, "Aum Shinrikyo," (2001), available on Jeffrey K. Hadden's Web page, http://religiousmovements.lib.virginia.edu (accessed December 22, 2002).

33. For up-to-date accounts of the legal proceedings against this cult, see the Web page of the Center for Studies on New Religions, http://www.cesnur.org. Confer several brief reports under the heading "Aum Shinrikyo" *Cultic Studies Review* 1 (2002): 90–94, 190–95.

34. Tim Larimer, "Why Japan's Terror Cult Still Has Appeal," *Time* (June 10, 2002): 8.

35. For studies on this movement, see Mark R. Mullins, "Aum Shinrikyo as an Apocalyptic Movement," in *Millennium, Messiahs, and Mayhem: Contemporary Apocalyptic Movements*, ed. Thomas Robbins and Susan J. Palmer (New York: Routledge, 1997), pp. 313–24; and Robert J. Lifton, *Destroying the World to Save it: Aum Shinrikyo, Apocalyptic Violence, and the New Global Terrorism* (New York: Metropolitan Book–Henry Holt, 1999).

36. Carl H. Esbeck, "1987 Survey of Trends and Developments on Religious Liberty in the Courts," *Journal of Law and Religion* 6 (1988): 184–85.

37. See the report "Aylmen Church of God," in *Cultic Studies Review* 1 (2002): 95–96.

38. For a profile of this religious group see Paul Jones, "The Family (The Children of God)" (2001), available on Jeffrey K. Hadden's Web page, http://religiousmovements.lib.virginia.edu (accessed December 22, 2002). For a short account of some of the controversies that surrounds this groups see J. Gordon Melton, *Encyclopedic Handbook of Cults and Sects* (New York: Garland, 2nd ed., 1992), pp. 229–30.

39. Some are still doubtful whether The Family has made any changes in their libertarian sexual mores. See, for example, Robert B. McFarland, "The Children of God," *Journal of Psychohistory* 21 (1994): 497–99; and Joe Maxwell, "Have The Children of God Cleaned Up Their Act?" *Christianity Today* 36 (December 14, 1992): 42–43.

40. Legal documents from various countries on this issue are reproduced in the Web page of the Center for Studies on New Religions, http://www.cesnur.org.

41. For legal problems The Family has encountered in France see CESNUR's report, "The Children of God/The Family Court Cases in France, 1991–2000," on its Web page http://www.cesnur.org/testi/TheFamily/france.htm (accessed April 28, 2003).

42. Thomas W. John, "Preventing Non-Profit Profiteering: Regulating Cult Employment Practices," *Arizona Law Review* 23 (1981): 1003–32.

43. See James E. Wood, "New Religions and The First Amendment," *Journal of Church and State* 24 (1982): 455–62.

44. Bryan Wilson, "Sects and the State: Some Issues and Cases," in *The Social Dimensions of Sectarianism*, p. 30.

45. Thomas Robbins, "Profits for Prophets: Legitimate and Illegitimate Economic Practices in New Religious Movements," in *Money and Power in the New Religions*, ed. James T. Richardson (Lewiston, NY: Edwin Mellen Press, 1988), pp. 70–116.

46. For a thorough account of this case and its implications, see Carlton Sherwood, *Inquisition: The Persecution and Prosecution of the Reverend Sun Myung Moon* (Washington, DC: Regnery Gateway, 1989).

47. Carl H. Esbeck, "1986 Survey of Trends and Developments in Religious Liberty in the Courts," *Journal of Law and Religion* 4 (1986): 439.

48. *The Cult Observer* (March/April 1988): 9.

49. *The Cult Observer* 8, no. 10 (1991): 9.

50. Frederick B. Bird and Frances Westley, "The Economic Strategies of New Religious Movements," in *Money and Power in the New Religions*, p. 65.

51. Confer the reports in the *Times* (March 12, 1993):1f; (March 12, 1994): 1f; (July 6, 1994): 5h.

52. See the report in *The Cult Observer* 8, no. 2 (1991): 7.

53. Marcia Rudin, ed., *Cults on Campus: Continuing Challenge* (Bonita Springs, FL: American Family Foundation, 1991).

54. *FAIR News* (Spring 1994): 13.

55. This was reported in the *FAIR News* (Spring 1994): 7–8. For more detailed accounts see the *Times* (March 13, 1992): 1c, and (February 27, 1989): 2e.

56. See the Bhaktivedanta Manor's Web page, http://www.krishnatemple.com/index.

57. For a brief report on this case, see *The Cult Observer* (September–October 1990): 12.

58. See, for instance, Matthew 10:34–37 and Luke 9:57–60. David S. Lovejoy discusses this issue at length in his essay, "Shun Thy Father and All That: The Enthusiasts' Threat to the Family," *New England Quarterly* 60 (1987): 71–85.

59. See "Expecting a Nuclear Attack from the USSR," *Areopagus* 3.2 (1990): 53–54. Confer also Jocelyn H. DeHaas, "The Mediation of Ideology and Public Image in the Church Universal and Triumphant," in *Church Universal and Triumphant in Scholarly Perspective*, ed. James R. Lewis and J. Gordon Melton (Stanford, CA: Center for Academic Publications, 1994), pp. 28–29.

60. For a brief description of this religious group and the controversy it has aroused see Melton, *Encyclopedic Handbook of Cults in America*, pp. 249–57. For a more recent profile, see Lisa E. Brooks, "The Local Church" (2001), available at Jeffrey K. Hadden's Web page on new religious movements, http://religiousmovements.lib.virginia.edu (accessed December 22, 2002).

61. The Spiritual Counterfeits Project organization is still operative. See its Web page, http://www.scp-inc.org/body.html (accessed December 22, 2002).

62. Jack Sparks, *The Mind-Benders: A Look at Current Cults* (Nashville, TN: Thomas Nelson, 1977). In this book eight new religions are examined and said to share one thing in common, namely, the use of brainwashing to control the members' minds.

63. Neil Duddy, *The God-Men* (Downers Grove, IL: InterVarsity Press, 1981) was originally published in German a couple of years earlier under the title *Die Sonderlehre des Witness Lee und seiner Ortsgemeinde* (Berneck, Switzerland: Schwengler-Verlag, 1979).

64. John Saliba was one of the expert witnesses called upon to give testimony in the civil trial.

65. Kenneth Dibble, "Cults and New Religious Movements and the Law of Charity," paper presented at the seminar on New Religious Movements and the Law held at the London School of Economics, May 7, 1994, p. 2.

66. For a brief discussion of this case see Richard J. Regan, "Regulating Cult Activity: The Limits of Religious Freedom," *Thought* 61 (1986): 186–87.

67. Confer Thomas Lyttle, "Drug-Based Religions and Contemporary Drug-Taking," *Journal of Drug Issues* 18 (1988): 271–84.

68. See Kevin Krajack, "Vision Quest (Ritual Hallucinogens)," *Newsweek* 119 (June 3, 1992): 62–63.

69. For a study of the peyote religion, see Omar Call Stewart, *Peyote Religion: A History* (Norman: University of Oklahoma Press, 1987); David Friend Aberle, *The Peyote Religion among the Navaho* (Chicago: Aldine Publishing, 1966); and Weston La Barre, *The Peyote Cult* (New York: Schocken Books, 4th ed., 1975).

70. For a study of this church see Jay Fikes, "A Brief History of the Native American Church," in *One Nation Under God: The Triumph of the Native American Church*, compiled and ed. Huston Smith and Reuben Snake (Santa Fe, NM: Clear Light Publishers, 1996), pp. 165–73.

71. Reuben Snake, "Native American Religion," in *One Nation Under God*, p. 149.

72. For one account of this ceremony see Phil Cousineau and Gary Rhine, "The Peyote Ceremony," in Smith and Snake, *One Nation Under God*, pp. 77–101.

73. For information about Churches that promote the use of drugs as a sacramental ritual, see http://www.onlinepot.org/potchurches.htm (accessed January 24, 2003).

74. Bullis, *Sacred Calling, Secular Accountability*, pp. 29–30.

75. See Linda Greenhouse, "Use of Drugs in Religious Rituals Can Be Prosecuted, Justice Rules," *New York Times* (April 18, 1990): A22. Confer also Douglas Laycock, "Peyote, Wine, and the First Amendment," *Christian Century* (October 4, 1989): 876–77; and Richard F. Duncan, "Religious Freedom Denied," *First Things*, no. 5 (1990): 12–13.

76. Confer "Indians May Transport Peyote," *New York Times* (April 1, 1991): A12. The debate about the use of peyote in Oregon has also made the headlines. See, for example, "Oregon Court Finds Peyote Use Is Legal in Indian Ceremony, *New York Times* (October 19, 1988): A25; and "Oregon Peyote Law Leaves 1983 Defendant Unvindicated," *New York Times* (July 9, 1991): A14.5.

77. For the debate that surrounds the use of peyote in the Native American church see, for example, Robert McFadden, "High Court Is Criticized for Striking Down Federal Law Shielding Religious Practices," *New York Times* (June 27, 1997): A22.

78. Richard Behar made this accusation against Scientology in his provocative essay, "The Thriving Cult of Greed and Power," *Time* (May 6, 1991): 50–57.

79. Melton, *Encyclopedic Handbook of Cults in America*, p. 132. See also J. Gordon Melton, *The Church of Scientology* (Salt Lake City, UT: Signature Books, 2000).

80. The documents pertaining to all the lawsuits referred to in this paragraph can be found in the Web page of the Center for Studies of New Religions, http://ww.cernur.org (accessed December 22, 2002).

81. For Scientology's own description of auditing, see Hubbard Dianetics Foundation, *What Is Scientology?: The Comprehensive Textbook of the World's Fastest Growing Religion* (Los Angeles: Bridge Publications, 1992), pp. 156–63.

82. Hubbard Dianetics Foundation, *What Is Scientology?* p. 155.

83. See Stephen Labaton, "Scientologists Granted Tax Exemption by the U.S.," *New York Times* (October 14, 1993): A1.

84. For several essays that discuss this point see Thomas Robbins, William Shepherd, and James McBride, eds., *Cults, Culture, and the Law: Perspectives on New Religious Movements* (Chico, CA: Scholars Press, 1985), especially pp. 59–91.

85. *The Cult Observer* 6, no. 5 (1989): 6–7.

86. *The Cult Observer* 10, no. 5 (1993): 5.

87. See Seth Asser and Rita Swan, "Child Fatalities from Religion-Motivated Medical Neglect," *Pediatrics* 101 (1988): 625–29.

88. This case was widely reported in the news media. See, for instance, *New York Times* (July 9, 1983): I5; (July 14, 1983): I13; (July 15, 1983): I6; (January 13, 1984): I12; (January 14, 1984): I7; (January 21, 1984): I13.

89. See Gregory M. Gochenour, "House of Judah: The Problem of Child Abuse and Neglect in Communes and Cults," *University of Michigan Journal of Law Reform* 18 (1992): 1089–19, where some of the legal issues are discussed.

90. Confer, for instance, Stephen Gottschalk, "Spiritual Healing on Trial: A Christian Scientist Reports," *Christian Century* 105 (June 22–29, 1988): 602–5.

91. See, for example, Rosalind Wright, "A Matter of Life and Death," *Good Housekeeping* 210 (March 1990): 86ff; and Kevin Delaney, "'We Thought Our Faith Could Save our Child'—(Death from Meningitis after Christian Scientist Parents R. and D. Swan Withhold Medical Treatment)," *Redbook* 168 (January 1987): 104–6.

92. The Swans have become very active in promoting medical care for children even when the faith of their parents does not allow it. See Rita Swan, *The Law's Response When Religious Beliefs Against Medical Care Impact on Children* (Sioux City, IA: Child, Inc., 1990). The Swans have, in fact, led a crusade against Christian Science, especially against its teaching regarding medical treatment. See Roger Rosenblatt, "A Woman at Christmas—(Death of Former Christian Scientist R. Swan's Son Due to Withholding Medical Treatment)," *Life* 13 (December 1990): 43; and Lori Miller Kase, "Swan's Way—(R. Swan's Crusade Against Religious-Based Medical Neglect of Children)," *American Health* 11 (July–August 1992): 16ff.

93. See David Margolick, "In Child Deaths, A Test for Christian Science," *New York Times* (August 6, 1990): A1. Many of these reported cases are appealed. In the Twitchell case, the negative judgment against the parents was reversed by a superior court. Confer "Christian Scientists Are Cleared of Manslaughter," *New York Times* (August 12, 1993): A16. For a discussion of these cases see James T. Richardson and John Dewitt, "Christian Science Spiritual Healing, the Law, and Public Opinion," *Journal of Church and State* 34 (1992): 549–61. For reports on various court cases dealing with the withholding of medical care for religious reasons, see Rick Ross's Web page http://www.rickross.com/groups/foc.html (accessed December 22, 2002).

94. See CHILD's Web page http://www.childrenshealthcare.org (accessed December 28, 2002). Confer Rita Swan, "Children, Medicine, Religion, and the Law," *Advances in Pediatrics* 44 (1997): 491–543.

95. Melton, *Encyclopedic Handbooks of Cults*, pp. 361–93.

96. Robert McAfee Brown, *Religion and Violence* (Philadelphia: Westminster Press, 1987).

97. Jean-François Mayer, "Cults, Violence and Religious Terrorism: An International Perspective," *Studies in Conflict and Terrorism* 24 (2002): 373.

98. Catherine Wessinger, *When the Millennium Comes Violently: From Jonestown to Heaven's Gate* (New York: Seven Bridges Press, 2000).

99. Catherine Wessinger, "New Religious Movements and Conflicts with Law Enforcement," in *New Religious Movements and Religious Liberty in America*, ed. Derek H. Davis and Barry Hankins (Waco, TX: J. M. Dawson Institute of Church-States Studies 2002), pp. 130–33.

100. James T. Richardson discusses the role of sociologists in giving court testimony. See his essay "Sociology and the New Religions: 'Brainwashing,' the Courts, and Religious Freedom," in *Witnessing for Sociology: Sociologists in Court*, ed. Pamela Jenkins, J. Steven Kroll-Smith (Westport, CT: Praeger, 1996), pp. 115–34. See also Larry D. Shinn, "Cult Conversions and the Courts: Some Ethical Issues in Academic Expert Testimony," *Sociological Analysis* 53 (1992): 373–85.

101. For a lengthy discussion of their testimony, see Dick Anthony, "Religious Movements and Brainwashing Litigation: Evaluating Key Testimony," in *In Gods We Trust: New Patterns of Religious Pluralism in America*, ed. by Thomas Robbins and Dick Anthony (New Brunswick, NJ: Transaction Books, 2nd ed., 1990), pp. 295–343. Cf. Donald T. Lunde and Henry A. Sigal, "Psychiatric Testimony in 'Cult' Litigation," *Bulletin of the American Academy of Psychiatry and the Law*, 15 (1987): 205–10; and John Young and Ezra Griffith, "Expert Testimony in Cult-Related Litigation," *Bulletin of the American Academy of Psychiatry and the Law* 17 (1989): 257–67.

102. Leo Pfeffer, "Equal Protection for Unpopular Sects," *New York Review of Law and Social Change* 11 (1979–1980): 11.

103. Cited in *Cultic Studies Journal* 9 (1992): 118.

104. Two possible exceptions might be those cases involving (1) child custody litigation and (2) medical treatment of members of religious groups that rely on spiritual healing rather than on modern medicine.

105. Confer "UK Prime Minister to Use Immigration Laws to Keep Undesirable Cult Out of Britian," *Times* (April 21, 1994): 1B.

106. A good example of this is the agreement reached in the mid-1970s between the city of Seaside Heights, New Jersey, and the Hare Krishna movement. Hare Krishna devotees were allowed to continue soliciting on the city's boardwalk, provided they no longer make physical contact with any person or use voice-magnifying devices. Confer George Vecrey, "Problem of Solicitation: Unification Church and the Hare Krishna Lawsuit," *New York Times* (February 5, 1979): 4:8.

CHAPTER SIX

THE NEW RELIGIONS IN CHRISTIAN THEOLOGICAL PERSPECTIVE

As was pointed out in chapter 1, one of the common definitions of a cult or new religion is theological. This approach starts with a faith perspective that cannot appeal to that kind of neutrality or detachment claimed by the social sciences.[1] Its goal is not to describe the beliefs and practices of cults and sects and to assess their sociological import, but primarily to evaluate their truth claims and moral principles. Because Christian theology is the systematic analysis of those religious truths that are accepted as divine revelation, Christians are naturally concerned about religious orthodoxy. And because Christianity is a way of life with a sacramental or ritual system as well as a moral code, Christians must be attentive to orthopraxis, "correct behavior" (including ritual). The new religions offer systems of belief and practice that need to be appraised in the light of Christian revelation.

Several issues about the new religions must, therefore, be dealt with. The first regards the religious or spiritual nature of these new movements. In what sense can they be called religious entities? The second deals with their relationship with Christianity. How do the teachings and practices of the new religions differ from those of Christianity, and can they be harmonized with Christian doctrine and morality? The third is concerned with the various kinds of theological reactions to the new religions. In other words, what should the Christian believer's response to their presence be? And finally, one must take into account the pastoral problems that have followed in their wake. What can pastors say and do to help those worried parents of cult members who have come to them for help? Are there any educational means by which young adults can be so grounded in their faith that they would never consider joining a new religion? And how does one treat those who have left the faith of their upbringing and joined a new religious movement?

Are the Cults "Religious" Entities?

In some Christian circles, many of the new religions are too readily dismissed as nonreligious or pseudo-religious groups. Evangelical and fundamentalist Christians have reacted negatively to the new religions because they see them as spurious religious entities that have no relation to genuine spirituality. They have formed counter-cult organizations to attack the new religions that propound unorthodox doctrines and foster many practices that conflict with Christian morality. On the other hand, those individuals who are involved in the anti-cult movements are largely secular movements that consider new religions as evil institutions because they manipulate individuals by using methods of brainwashing or mind-control.[2] Christian responses to the new religions, however, have often incorporated in their refutation of cults many accusations commonly found in the anti-cult movement. They have accused the new movements of being preoccupied with the accumulation of wealth and of making heavy psychological demands on their members. Many of the negative features ascribed to the new religions and discussed in chapter 1 have been used to buttress the Christian response.[3] But they have ignored those positive religious or spiritual features that attract new members in the first place. These writers fail to distinguish clearly between orthodoxy on the one hand, and religiosity or spirituality on the other. Orthodoxy refers to correct belief and is narrow in scope. Religiosity and spirituality are much broader concepts and connote the type of belief system, experience, and ritual practice irrespective of whether these are true or false, real or imaginary, or morally right or wrong.

There can be little doubt that the majority of new religions easily fall under the broad definition of religion that has become standard in the academic study of religion.[4] They promote classical religious ideologies and use rituals that are similar to those of other religious traditions. They profess belief in God or in some supernatural reality that directs human life. They insist that life has a spiritual or nonmaterial aspect and that there is an afterlife. And they endorse the practice of a spirituality that leads to ultimate and transcendent goals. These are all religious in nature, no matter how different they are from Christian teachings and practices. One cannot understand the attractive qualities of the new religions or formulate a response to their presence, unless one recognizes and treats them as religious entities.

It would seem that many of the new religions are offering genuine spiritual options to those who join them. Those that are based on Eastern religions and philosophies are more correctly categorized under, for instance, Hinduism or Buddhism. Many groups, such as those that align themselves with the New Age movement, are rather syncretistic in their ideology, uniting aspects from Eastern and Western traditions and/or from the occult tradition. They differ too radically from mainline Christianity to be rightfully called Christian. There are some borderline organizations, such as the Way International and the Local Church of Witness Lee,[5] that could be unacceptable deviations from the major currents of Christian theology and practice. Such groups, however, take their main inspiration from Christian sources and consider themselves genuine expressions of the Christian faith.

Scientology, for example, can be considered a new religious group, even though for a long time the U.S. Internal Revenue Service questioned its religious nature.[6] Some observers have commented that its main practices look more like a form of psychological counseling than a spiritual discipline. Yet the members of Scientology insist that they are religious and call their organization the "Church of Scientology."[7] Scientologists believe in a Supreme Being, even though they do not define this being as a personal saving God with whom they are personally related. And though there is no formal worship service to God, there are other basic rituals, such as sermons at church meetings, christenings, weddings, and funerals. One of their central practices, that of "auditing," has, in spite of its psychological overtones, some similarities to the Christian custom of the confession of sins.

Another model of a religious group is Transcendental Meditation (TM), which is advertised as an effective tool for achieving individual health and world peace.[8] Unlike Scientology, the leaders of this new movement insist that their organization is not a religious entity. They argue that the meditation they teach is simply a well-developed technique that automatically leads to happiness in this life, improves its practitioners' physical, mental, and psychological conditions, enhances the quality of their activities, and has positive repercussions on the social environment. Offering no official creed or moral code and shunning the labels of "church" and "religion," the leaders of Transcendental Meditation promote its presumed benefits as a psychotherapeutic practice. TM is thus a method for human growth and development, a way both of enhancing human potential and of leading to peace and happiness.

The religious character of Transcendental Meditation, however, was upheld in court when the organization was sued, in the mid-1970s, for using the public school system of New Jersey to teach their basic course on "The Science of Creative Intelligence."[9] Two major reasons were advanced to show that Transcendental Meditation is a religion. First, it has an underlying philosophical and religious system that includes "God-realization" as the individual's ultimate goal. Second, membership in the movement is achieved through an initiation rite, known as "puja" (worship), which has obvious religious connotations, including the recitation of prayers to Hindu deities and the veneration of a long line of gurus.[10]

Many Eastern religious movements promote practices like meditation and yoga that have a well-established basis in the history of Indian traditions and are founded on Hindu or Buddhist spiritual ideas and exercises. The Hare Krishna movement (ISKCON) has been a recognized Hindu devotional branch of Hinduism in India since the sixteenth century.[11] Its members maintain that several of their standard practices, like celibacy among some of its members and vegetarianism, are justifiable on religious grounds. In like manner, the Unification Church can be considered a new religion, since it includes a belief system and carries out ritual practices that traditionally fit into the concept of religion.[12] Thus, for example, its mass marriage ceremonies, which have attracted the attention of the media, have a sacramental quality about them. In the mid-1970s a commission of the World Council of Churches examined the theology of the Unification Church and found it defective from a Christian standpoint, but it never questioned its claim to be a bona fide religious organization.[13] Even though the Unification Church and some other new religious movements might have a political and economic agenda, their explicitly religious thrust nevertheless leaves no other option but to classify them as religions.

Are the New Religions Compatible with Christianity?

The new religions, therefore, could be offering alternative religious and spiritual beliefs, goals, and practices. If so, they raise the question whether they are formidable competitors to traditional religion or whether they are complementary to Christian belief and practice. In other words, are the teachings and activities of the cults so opposed to Christian tenets and moral standards that they should be totally rejected? Or do they contain some elements of truth and some commendable ethical and spiritual practices that can stimulate Christian theological discourse and nurture or revive the Christian spirit? And can some practices of the new movements be incorporated into Christianity?

The study of comparative religion leaves no doubt that, in spite of their many differences, all world religions share many beliefs, values, and ritual practices. A nonmaterialistic attitude and the quest for religious or mystical experiences of union with the holy seem to be at the core of the majority of religions.[14] The common bonds that unite different religions were highlighted by the bishops at the Second Vatican Council in an unprecedented document titled "Declaration on the Relationship of the Church to Non-Christian Religions." This document affirms that many of the world's great religions recognize, directly or indirectly, the existence of a Supreme Being on whom all creation depends. On Hinduism, for instance, the Fathers of the Council state that those who belong to this ancient religion "contemplate the divine mystery and express it through an unspent fruitfulness of myths and through searching philosophical inquiry." Hindus, further, "seek release from the anguish of our condition through ascetical practices or deep meditation or a loving, trusting flight toward God."[15] The stress on the similarities between world religions has enabled believers from different religions (including such leaders as the pope, the archbishop of Canterbury, and the Dalai Lama) to join together in worship or prayer services.

The common features that religions often share can be concretely demonstrated by considering one form of prayer, namely, the Roman Catholic practice of reciting the rosary.[16] The rosary developed as various Christian devotions coalesced over a period of four centuries. Its origins lie in the practice of counting the 150 psalms sung during the divine office and can probably be traced to Irish monks.[17] By the twelfth century the recitation of 150 Hail Marys, which was always linked with the practice of meditating on the mysteries of Christ, was a regular prayer among some laity. The rosary was simplified into the form known today by the early fifteenth century and was made popular by the Dominicans through their preaching, writings of rosary books, and promotion of the Rosary Confraternity. In 1569, Pope Pius V officially approved the custom of praying the rosary, stressing the meditation of the mysteries was as an essential part of it. Many popes, in particular by Pope Leo XIII who issued several short encyclicals on the subject, have encouraged it.[18] And, quite recently, Pope Paul John II has added another set of Christian mysteries for meditation while reciting it.[19] The popularity of the rosary may have waned over the past few decades, but it has certainly not died down and attempts to revive it are common.[20] A different version of the rosary can also be found in the monastic institutions of the Eastern Orthodox Church.[21]

The custom of using beads as an aid to vocal and mental prayer has, moreover, a history that probably predates the Christian era. It most likely arose in India where both Hindus and Buddhists have long used the counting of beads to record the number of prayers muttered.[22] Muslims also took up the custom and developed a rosary "that normally consists of thirty-three beads with a tassel, and is run through the fingers three times to complete the ninety-nine names of Allah."[23] Whether Christians borrowed the idea from the East is a debatable point. What is certain is that the counting of prayers on beads was given a Christian meaning and adapted into the theology and devotional practice of the Catholic Church.

The above discussion is relevant because it raises the question whether, and to what extent, some new religious practices can be incorporated into Christianity and transformed into Christian forms of prayer and meditation. Yoga and Zen are two common Eastern practices that have become known through the activities and publications of several of the new religious movements. What is not generally known is that, before the onset of the new religions, Christian missionaries in Asia had been considering the possibility of incorporating these practices into Christianity. Many Christians, both in the East and in the West, have in fact been practicing Christianized versions of Zen and Yoga for several decades.[24] One must note that some Christian writers have advised caution in taking up such Eastern methods without proper guidance.[25] Further, a recent letter to the Catholic bishops from the Vatican's Congregation for the Doctrine of the Faith has warned Catholics of some of the dangers of Eastern methods of meditation.[26] The fact remains, however, that a blanket condemnation of Yoga and Zen does not hold up to contemporary scholarship.[27] Moreover, many Christians have found these techniques useful and have succeeded in bestowing upon them a genuine Christian spirit. Christian Zen and Christian Yoga have become topics of discussion in Catholic periodical literature and tools to enhance spiritual practices in retreat houses.

The emergence of Christian Yoga and Christian Zen leads one to ask whether certain practices of the new religions can help Christians in their spiritual lives. New religions could, for example, lead to the rediscovery of forms of Christian prayer that have been abandoned or ignored. And they raise the question whether some Eastern meditative and spiritual practices could be transformed and incorporated into Christian spirituality. Transcendental Meditation can be taken as an excellent illustration. Statements by officials of the TM foundation have insisted that TM does not imply adherence to a particular religious doctrine or philosophy. Moreover, some Christians, who have taken up the habit of reciting the TM mantra, have remained loyal members of the Christian Church. While the incorporation of TM into Christian spirituality and devotion might be premature, the possibility of a Christian TM should not be ruled out. The initiation to TM (with its reference to Hindu gods) and the various TM mantras (which are allegedly unintelligible, though possibly names of various Hindu gods and/or goddesses) contain elements that make them inappropriate for Christian use. Yet the mode of prayer used in TM is hardly novel to Christian spirituality. The praying of the rosary, for example, can function like a mantra, when the quiet slow recital of the Hail Marys, without too much reflection, prevails.

In the first few centuries of the Christian era, the Desert Fathers used to repeat the Jesus prayer, "Lord Jesus Christ, Son of God, have mercy on me" (confer Luke 18:38), in mantra fashion. These early Christians stressed the need for the "prayer of the heart," a prayer without images and concepts and without imagination and discursive reason.[28] In order to maintain a continuous remembrance of God, they used to spend hours reciting the Jesus Prayer, while at the same time maintaining a certain physical posture and using a technique to control their breathing. This custom was developed in Eastern Christianity and was known as hesychasm, which means "quiet," "tranquility," and "stillness." It was devised as a means of reaching contemplative prayer.[29] In the West, a similar form of prayer was used by Christian mystics and proposed by the fourteenth-century author of the mystical work called *The Cloud of Unknowing*.[30] Known as "centering prayer," it has been rediscovered by several Catholic writers, such as Basil Pennington.[31] And attempts have been made to revive it, especially in retreat houses.

Such a comparative approach may present problems for the believer. One of its dangers is that of syncretism, whereby non-Christian elements are absorbed recklessly and without much reflection into Christian practice and spirit. Applied with understanding and discrimination, however, one can overcome these problems and enrich Christian devotional life. The comparative method can have three major beneficial results. It makes religious life a living reality, opening it up to growth and improvement. Further, it encourages believers to delve deeper into the intellectual and devotional richness of the Christian faith itself. And, finally, it facilitates the development of more effective evangelization programs.

Theological Approaches to the New Religions

Christian reactions to the presence of the new religions have been sporadic and at times vociferous. There is no consensus among Christian writers about the theological meaning of the new movements. Nor is there agreement about the proper pastoral response to their successful missionary activities in the West. Though the new religions may have not recruited a sizable percentage of the population, they have made themselves felt through the public media and/or their proselytizing activities. That they call for a response can hardly be doubted. Three general types of response to the new religions can be observed and are discussed in the following sections.

Neglect of the New Religions

The most common reaction to the new religions has been to ignore them. The mainline Christian Churches have been slow in addressing themselves to the questions raised by the presence of the new religions. They have been unable to offer guidelines and assistance to those Christians whose children have joined cults. One of the more prevalent complaints of parents of cult members has been that the pastors of their churches are unable to help them because of their lack of knowledge about the new religions.

This neglect, whether it is intended or not, is indirectly based on both practical and theoretical grounds. The contemporary alternative religions, it can be argued, form a small minority of the population, so small that they are unlikely to have lasting impact on traditional religions. The majority of them, even when they give the impression that they are attracting many young adults, do not have large memberships. The Unification Church, for instance, which has at times conducted forceful evangelical campaigns, has never succeeded in recruiting large numbers of followers in the West.[32] Many cults have fewer than a few hundred fully committed members. Paying too much attention to the new religions might indirectly be doing them a service by drawing attention to their beliefs and practices and by presenting them as a viable alternative to traditional faiths.

Television and newspaper reporters are prone to depict the new religions in sensational fashion. They rarely, if ever, point out that relatively few individuals join them and that many of those who join do not persevere in their newly found faith. This excessive public exposure of the new religions becomes clear when one reflects on the publicity that Satanism has received in the news media. The media attention to Satanism, particularly in the 1980s and early 1990s, gave the impression that many people are getting involved in the most bizarre forms of ritual that include wanton orgies and infant sacrifice. J. Gordon Melton distinguished between two forms of Satanism. The first consists of those he labels "sickies." He writes:

> These are disconnected groups of occultists who employ Satan worship to cover a variety of sexual, sado-masochistic, clandestine, psychopathic, and illegal activities. These groups typically engage in grave-robberies, sexual assaults and bloodletting (both animal and human). These groups are characterized by a lack of theology, an informality of gatherings, ephemeral life, and disconnectedness from other similar groups.[33]

A second group consists of public rather than secret organizations. Here Satanism is a religion with a sophisticated theology and Satan a powerful symbol. Participation in structured ritual is followed. Membership in the former group is not easy to determine. It cannot, however, be large, otherwise their criminal activities would surface frequently. Reports of tens of thousands of children being sacrificed in Satanic Black Masses are, however, nothing but a form of irresponsible sensationalism.[34] Not a single case of human sacrifice in a Satanic ritual has ever been conclusively proven to have actually taken place. There is simply not enough evidence to build a case for a Satanic scare.[35] Of those groups that are publicly known Melton mentions ten, six of which are defunct.[36]

This attitude that neglects the presence of the new religious movements, however, has its disadvantages. It fails to recognize that a major religious shift might be occurring in Western culture, and that the ideas that the new religions propagate might influence Christianity, even if they do not survive. There are, for instance, many Hindu and Buddhist religious movements that seem to have established a foothold in the West. Their presence is, to some degree, responsible for the renewed interest in reincarnation in some Christian circles. The New Age movement, which is a diffuse movement with no central organization or commonly accepted set of dogmatic beliefs and ritual practices, is also spreading a variety of religious and philosophical ideas and magical practices that cannot be easily, if at all, reconciled with Christianity.[37] Books dealing with New Age topics occupy many shelves in libraries and bookstores. Many traditional Christian values and beliefs are being challenged and sometimes openly attacked by New Age speakers who claim novel revelations. Neglecting the study of new movements might be a form of escapism from the issues that Christians are facing at the beginning of the third millennium.

A more positive and insightful approach to the new religions is thus required. Not only must Christianity clarify its own position and defend itself against outside interference; it must also develop a theological framework that makes some sense of the presence of other religions, including those that have emerged since the late 1960s.

The Apologetic Approach

Probably the most popular response to the rise of contemporary movements has been the apologetic approach, even though, nowadays, its place among major Christian denominations doesn't seem to be as prominent as it used to be.[38] Apologetics is concerned with the proofs advanced in favor of the Christian faith and with its defense against the claims of other religions. It can take two distinct, though obviously related, forms. The first, which one can label positive apologetics, expounds and clarifies the tenets of Christianity, pointing out how they differ and excel, morally and philosophically, over all other religious claims. The second form, which can be called negative apologetics, attacks other religious beliefs, pointing out their weaknesses and inconsistencies.

Though apologetics, as a branch of Christian theology, is a relatively recent development, attempts to argue in favor of the Christian faith date from the very beginning of the Church. St. Paul's sermon on the Areopagus, recorded in the Acts of the Apostles (17:22–31), is an example of apologetics used by the first Christians to preach the Good News to the pagans of the Roman Empire. The form positive apologetics has taken over the centuries has changed. By the Protestant Reformation apologetics had become a controversial theology about disputed matters within Christianity itself. Protagonists of the various Christian churches strove to prove that their theological views and religious practices were the correct ones and dedicated many of their efforts to attack or ridicule the positions of their adversaries. Negative apologetics expressed itself in the mutual misunderstandings, accusations, and condemnations that often ruled the relationships between the majority of Christian churches that proliferated in the post-Reformation period.

Positive Apologetics

Both positive and negative apologetics have been employed in the Christian response to the new religious movements. Because so many of the new religions propound religious beliefs and practices that differ from and contradict basic Christian tenets, the need is felt to explain clearly what the Church teaches. Some members of new religious movements have explicitly stated that their views are in fact in harmony with Christianity. This has led many Christians to become aware of the necessity and urgency to clarify the major Christians doctrines and to demonstrate how they differ from the beliefs that the new movements espouse. This type of response is dogmatic, in the sense that it specifies and stresses the orthodox beliefs, values, and practices of the Church and refuses to compromise on matters that are judged to be essential to Christian doctrine.

A typical specimen of positive apologetics is the work of the late Walter Martin, whose life was dedicated to expounding and refuting the teachings of various sects and cults. In one of his more popular books,[39] Martin deals principally with several nineteenth and early to mid-twentieth-century religious groups, such as the Jehovah's Witnesses, Christian Science, Mormonism, Armstrong's Worldwide Church of God, the Baha'i Faith, the Theosophical Society, and Zen Buddhism. He follows a similar pattern in the treatment of these groups: a brief history, an outline of their teachings, and a lengthy refutation of those beliefs that contradict the Bible. In dealing with the Jehovah's Witnesses, for instance, Martin list biblical passages and refutes the theological stance of basic Christian doctrines as the Trinity, the Deity of Christ, the Atonement, the existence of hell and eternal punishment, and the spiritual nature and destiny of the human person.

By the late 1960s and early 1970s, Martin began directing his apologetic approach to the new religious movements. These included such groups as the Way International, the Children of God (later known as The Family), the Foundation of Human Understanding (of Roy Masters), Nichiren Shoshu Buddhism, Silva Mind Control, and Hindu groups like the Hare Krishna movement and Transcendental Meditation. He follows a pattern used in his previous work and examines the ideology of new religious movements with respect to the major Christian tenets contained in the Bible and expounded in creedal statements.

Some of his conclusions are worth mentioning, since they illustrate both his method and the kind of theological judgment he passes on the new religious movements. On the founder of Children of God (COG), he writes:

> David Berg is a false prophet: his prophecies do not come to pass, and he preaches doctrine contrary to the Bible. Berg claims to be God's prophet and the chosen dictator over the Children of God. He has held his own writings above the authority of the Bible. He rejects those portions of the Old and New Testaments which contradict his own beliefs and practices. The sexual aberrations of the COG completely divorce his followers from the rank of obedient Christians.[40]

On Hindu religious movements he makes a sweeping theological analysis that allows for little hope of rapprochement between Christianity and Hinduism. He states:

The religion of Hinduism, for all its diversity, cannot expand to include Christianity as one of its sects. There is no harmony between Christianity and Hinduism/ISKCON/TM. Hinduism denies the biblical Trinity, the biblical Jesus Christ, the biblical salvation. While the Hindu works out his own salvation and has no future other than becoming one with impersonal mind, the Christian looks forward to eternity with the Creator of the Universe.[41]

Because Martin aims at refuting the cults from the standpoint of the Bible, the correct interpretation of Scripture is highlighted in his study of those religious movements that distort the Christian message. His *Cults Reference Bible*[42] is a meticulous attempt to demonstrate how the sects and cults misquote and misinterpret the Christian Scriptures. It includes short essays that treat schematically and comparatively the following ten major groups: the Baha'i, Christian Science, the Hare Krishna movement, Jehovah's Witnesses, Mormonism, Transcendental Meditation, the Unification Church, the United School of Christianity, the Way International, and the Worldwide Church of God. After a brief description of each, he compares their beliefs with five main Christian teachings: those on God, Christ, the Holy Spirit, sin, and salvation. By so doing he draws attention to his overriding conviction that all new religions, whether they are variations of Christianity or of some Eastern religion, are at odds with the major doctrines of the orthodox Christian faith and hence should be totally rejected. Biblical passages that show where the cults interpret Scripture passages erroneously and where Scripture disproves their favorite beliefs and practices are carefully footnoted.

Martin's typical evangelical approach has many positive elements. It relies heavily on the Bible. It concentrates on the essentials of Christian doctrine. It indirectly stresses the need that Christians should be solidly grounded in their faith and be intellectually prepared to defend it. It warns of the danger of stressing superficial similarities between Christianity and other religions. Underlying his method is the assumption that the evangelization efforts of new religions have a positive impact on those individuals whose knowledge and understanding of their faith leave much to be desired.

One of the major problems with Martin's response to the new movements is that it lacks understanding of Eastern religions and, consequently, of those movements that base their ideology on them. To dismiss

Hinduism and the Hare Krishna movement as religions that aim "at becoming one with impersonal mind" neglects the theistic element found in
Hinduism as well as the personal devotional to God among Hare Krishna
members. Many Hindus describe themselves as "monotheists."[43]

Moreover, Martin's approach can easily degenerate into an attack
against both the new religions in general and the honesty and intentions
of cult leaders and members. Martin does not engage in diatribes against
their leaders, yet he sometimes leaves the impression that greed for money
regularly motivates the leaders of the new religions, that their members
are gullible individuals, and that their leaders often run a racket and not a
religious movement. Though he dwells more on the theological differences between Christianity and the new religions, he still accuses the later
of using deceptive techniques to gain members. Cult leaders, he states,
"have one primary purpose: they take biblical Christianity and change it
into a clever counterfeit of the real thing."[44] Further, he thinks that many
immature Christians are lured into joining quasi-Christian churches. On
the religious state of those who join new religious movements, Martin expresses an unmistakably clear opinion that ignores the religious and spiritual satisfaction that some people find in their new commitments. He
writes, for instance, in connection with the organization of Roy Masters:

> Those who are involved with the Foundation of Human Understanding
> are in double jeopardy. Not only are they being robbed of the opportu-
> nity for true salvation in Christ, but they are also being robbed of the op-
> portunity for abundant life in Christ.[45]

Martin's response to the new religions stresses the uniqueness of
Christianity to such a degree that the similarities between different religions are completely ignored. By failing to see that non-Christian religions, including the new ones, might contain some truth and goodness, he
leaves unanswered the central question about why people ever consider
joining them. By doubting the motivations of all cult leaders and the sincerity of many cult members, he has no other option but to draw a rather
unrealistic picture of cult life and spirituality. And by indirectly denying
that holiness can be found outside Christianity, he closes his eyes to the
exemplary life and work of many people of other faiths. Moreover, he is
unable to assign to the new religions a coherent theological role, except

perhaps the negative one, namely, that of providing some kind of test to orthodox Christians who continue to maintain their faith against all odds.

Negative Apologetics

The deficiencies of apologetics in providing, by itself, a theological Christian encounter with the new movements is confirmed even by a brief survey of Christian books and magazine articles that address the cult issue. The necessary defense of Christianity has frequently degenerated into a shouting match between members of different religious groups. In such encounters, participants are inclined to engage in monologues rather than dialogues. Their efforts are directed at hurling abuse against one another, rather than building bridges of understanding. This is the heart of the confrontational approach of negative apologetics. The most forceful line of argumentation has been an attempt to show that the new religions are the work of Satan himself. This attack is not novel in the history of Christianity and has for many centuries been also directed toward non-Christian religions in general.

Some Evangelical and fundamentalist writers have developed this particular form of negative apologetics almost into an art. *Larson's New Book of Cults*[46] provides a case in point. Its author, Bob Larson, admits that new religions must be understood in the framework of the various religions from which they derive their belief systems. He, consequently, dedicates several chapters to outline the teachings of Hinduism, Buddhism, Taoism, and Islam. Besides the many factual inaccuracies and misunderstandings that occur throughout his presentation, Larson exhibits a distinct talent in relating all these religions to Satanic powers. Thus, for instance, he states that "the polytheistic and idolatrous practices of Hinduism are pagan forms of worship which constitute collusion with demonic forces."[47] Summing up the errors of Buddhism he asserts: "Idolatrous sects [of Buddhism] that advocate demonic ceremonialism and the propitiation of spirits constitute a form of witchcraft that is scripturally forbidden."[48] He finds classical Taoism atheistic and bordering on pantheism, while modern Taoism is "polytheistic and idolatrous and involves consultation with familiar spirits."[49] Though he does not ascribe the same connection to demonic forces to Islam, he sees nothing positive in the mystical experiences of the Sufis. For him the "Dervish trance-states exhibit the characteristics of biblically defined demonic possession."[50] Showing no knowledge of the rich tradition of Christian mysticism and of the deep spirituality that the practice of Christian contemplation entails, he brushes aside all kinds of meditative and mystical experiences as dangerous conditions that leave the individual open to the influence of, and possession by, evil spirits.

With this theology of religions as a background, the new movements are readily judged to be modern expressions of dangerous, sinister organizations that draw us away from the one true God of the Bible. Larson briefly outlines the beliefs and practices of about ninety contemporary cults, pointing out their major errors in the light of the Bible. He carefully notices the various appeals that each group might have to possible members, but he fails to see anything positive or constructive in the new religions. And he makes no distinction between the evaluation of their teachings and practices from a Christian theological standpoint and the accusation that their members are agents of Satan himself. He seems to make the blanket judgment that everybody who does not accept the Good News of the Gospel is necessarily an evil person in league with the devil.

Larson's approach is not only cynical but also unproductive. It directly contradicts the one sanctioned both by the Catholic Church and the World Council of Churches. It further hampers understanding of the phenomenon of new religions as a whole and raises too many insoluble scriptural, theological, and pastoral problems. The implication that the contemporary world is dominated by diabolical interference requires more analysis than the citing of a few biblical passages. The New Testament, after all, brings a message of "Good News" and announces that Christ has conquered evil and the devil by his passion, death, and resurrection. Many Christians will find it hard to harmonize the encompassing, subtle success of Satan with the infinite goodness and providence of God. Besides, the "Satanic principle," used as a weapon against the new religions, is not a very practical evangelical tool. Several cults, particularly those with Christian roots, have used the same argument to their advantage.

This approach has at times reached the state of hysteria as, for example, has happened in the case of the New Age movement.[51] In fact, many of the reactions to this movement are more concerned with denouncing its theological errors and delineating its carefully concealed Satanic connections than with attempting a constructive understanding and evaluation of its beliefs and practices.[52] Many Christian commentators see nothing positive in the movement and leave unanswered the question of why it has become popular.[53] Some responses to New Age teachings and rituals encourage Christians to embark on a crusade. Peter Jones, for example, writing from an evangelical perspective, maintains that the New Age is a return to the Gnosticism of the first three centuries of the Christian era. He connects it with what he thinks are many contemporary problems, including homosexuality, witchcraft, feminist spirituality, concern for ecology, and spiritual healing techniques, all of which are indiscriminately lumped together as modern deviations from the truth. He outlines the aims of his study as follows:

To *clarify* the true nature of the forces opposing Christians today and to demonstrate their interconnectedness;

To *warn* the Church of the battle that lies ahead in order that Christians might be prepared;

To *encourage* believers to "fight the good fight" using the weapons of faith, particularly the sword of God's Word, by which pagan Gnosticism was once already put to flight from the early Church, and by which it will be put to flight again.[54]

The Deficiencies of the Apologetic Approach

Without denying the fact that the apologetic approach, especially the positive one, is sometimes useful and necessary, it must be stressed that one can enumerate at least six main obstacles that render its use in responding to contemporary religious movements very limited, and often unsuitable and ineffective.

First, apologetic beliefs are not conducive to empathetic understanding. Particularly in the hands of evangelical and fundamentalist Christians, they become a vehicle for expressing and generating antagonism and animosity that render mutual understanding impossible. Because of their belligerent character, apologetic debates elicit negative reactions and intensify conflicts. When those defending Christianity openly question the sincerity of all cult leaders and members, their arguments lose most of their effectiveness. Any value of apologetics is squandered when the parties involved do not listen to one another.

Second, the apologetic approach stresses, largely or solely, the differences between the various religious affiliations. Similarities, which are the basis for understanding both Christianity and other religions, are bypassed or ignored. As was pointed out above, apologetical works have frequently attacked the new religions for their mystical tendencies. There are, however, many points of contact between the various types of mystical experiences found in Christianity and in the new religions. Religious and mystical experiences could become avenues of communication between the various religions, rather than walls dividing them.

Third, the apologetical approach ignores real theological problems within Christianity as a whole. Those who cite select biblical passages to refute other religious beliefs seem unaware of the difficulties involved in biblical interpretation. The Bible has been subjected to different interpretations within Christianity itself.[55] Besides, quoting Bible passages to buttress dogmatic views might be convincing to those who already adhere to those opinions. But it is doubtful whether the technique will have any impact on those who have abandoned their Christian upbringing and taken a different stance on doctrine or on those whose ideology is based on different religious premises.

Fourth, apologetics, especially of the negative variety, has little evangelical value. In sociological terms, attacks against the new religious movements perform the function of "boundary maintenance." In other words, all that the heated denunciations of the new religions do is to reinforce the attitudes and beliefs of both their members and detractors. Apologetic debates rarely lead unbelievers or apostates to convert; they do not succeed in persuading renegade Christians to abandon their new beliefs to return to the faith of their birth. Harangues against the new religions do not lead their members to listen attentively to the arguments of zealous evangelizers. On the contrary, they drive them further away and elicit similar belligerent responses.

Fifth, the insistence on the apologetic argument could easily convey the idea that people can be persuaded by some rational argument to have faith in God or to accept the Christian faith. But faith is a free gift of God and not something that can be acquired or bestowed by the power of human reasoning and logic. St. Paul must have had this theological truth in mind when he wrote to the Corinthians:

> As for me, brothers, when I came to you, it was not with any show of oratory or philosophy, but simply to tell you what God had guaranteed.

During my stay with you, the only knowledge I claimed to have was about Jesus, and only about him as the crucified Christ. Far from relying on any power of my own, I came among you in fear and trembling and in my speeches and sermons that I gave, there were none of the arguments that belong to philosophy; only a demonstration of the power of the Spirit. And I did this so that your faith should not depend on human philosophy but on the power of God. (1 Corinthians 2:1–5)

And lastly, apologetics, especially when it is negatively oriented, is not easily harmonized with Christian charity. Diatribes give a bad image of Christianity. They serve to confirm the cult members' decision to abandon the faith of their youth for a more inclusive, more peace-loving, and less belligerent faith.

Johnson's Analyses of the Evangelical Approach

Probably the most insightful, carefully articulated, and detailed analysis of a Christian approach to the new religious movements is that of Phillip Johnson, who aligns himself with the evangelical branch of contemporary Christianity.[56] He amplifies the apologetic model mentioned above and divides it into six major branches. These he describes and evaluates in some depth. The first model, which he labels "the pre-eminent apologetic method," or "the heresy-rationalist apologia," is aimed at exposing the heretical views of the new religions and also proposing arguments to prove that their doctrines are false. After examining some of its positive features and the main literary works that expound it, Johnson suggests that this approach is deficient in many ways. He describes those who engage in this kind of refutation of the cults as "armchair" apologists[57] who denounce the doctrines and practices of the new religions without ever having visited their places of worship and who condemn their members without having conversed with them. He, therefore, encourages fieldwork for those evangelists and apologists who target the new religions. He writes:

Before we do that [that is, develop a ministry strategy] we must leave our armchairs and as a matter of ministry routine set aside time for proper field research. Field research involves meeting devotees at their festival, ashrams, retreat centers and places of worship, to ascertain not just what they believe but also to observe the dynamics of their faith, how they apply and live by their faith.[58]

Johnson gives a lengthy evaluation of this model, particularly as it is applied to the Church of Jesus Christ of Latter-day Saints. He insists that one must understand other faiths in their own categories and not in the frame of Christian thought. He compares Buddhist apologists who try to understand Evangelicalism from a Buddhist standpoint to those evangelicals who attempt to understand other religions in terms of Christian theological concepts. He observes:

> Suppose a Buddhist apologist sought to analyze evangelical beliefs, and charted our doctrines according to the categories of Buddhist belief: dukkha [sorrow; suffering], tanha [desire; thirst], nirodha [cessation of suffering], magga [The Eightfold Path], anicca [impermanence], anatta [no-self], nirvana [rebirth; release from suffering; enlightenment] etc. The resulting portrait would be a strange one indeed precisely because the principle [sic] teachings of Buddhism address different questions, conceive of reality in a vastly different way, and operates [sic] under a different "cultural logic" from those we find in, say, the Westminster Confession or the Lausanne Covenant.[59]

Johnston also thinks that we might learn something from the new religions. In this respect he agrees with the reflections on the new religious movement made in the Vatican report and in the consultation of the World Council of Churches/World Lutheran Front. He writes:

> If we start seriously exploring the reasons why people are delving into new age spirituality rather than the church, we might start squirming in our seats. . . . It might be very disturbing for us to discover that new age spirituality is tackling issues and meeting needs where the Bible speaks but the church is largely silent. Perhaps instead of seeing "sewage" we might find ourselves humbled and chastened for our spiritual neglect.[60]

Johnson examines five other models. The first is the end-times prophecy and conspiracies, which are viewed by the new religions as either an immediate precursor of the second coming of Christ or an indication of Satanic activity. The second examines the apostate testimonies, which are used as arguments against the beliefs and practices of the new cults. The third is spiritual warfare, which looks on the universe as a battleground between the forces of good and evil and encourages Christians to play their part in the defeat of the enemy. The fourth is "cultural apologetics," which concerns itself with the Western movement away from its Christian heritage. And finally, Johnson describes the "behavioralist apologetics," which adopts the brainwashing theory as part of the apologetic response to the cults. In each case Johnson points out their strong points and weaknesses.

The Dialogical Approach

Johnson's approach represents an innovative evangelical approach to the theological understanding of the new religions and to the application of a more productive pastoral program. In the last part of his work,[61] he proposes a holistic method, which takes into account the twenty-first century with the movement toward globalization, the rise of religious pluralism, and the cultural changes that are its hallmarks. His goal is evangelical and appears to aim toward conversion, even though this is never explicitly dealt with.[62] There is no mention, much less an exploration of, dialogue.

Since the early 1960s a new theological approach began to take hold of the Christian world through the efforts of the World Council of Churches and of the Second Vatican Council. Known as the dialogue approach, this method of understanding non-Christian theologies and of relating to non-Christians has become the official position of the majority of the mainline Christian Churches. At first used to improve the relationship between the divided Christian churches, the dialogue method has been adopted to include the relationship between different religions. The Catholic Church, with its Pontifical Council for Inter-Religious Dialogue, continues to make valuable contributions to the sympathetic understanding of the many diverse and complex religious traditions. The World Council of Churches has a department dedicated to the task of fomenting dialogue between Christianity and other religions.

In its statement on non-Christian religions, Vatican II admits that the world's great religions have long spiritual traditions. Though the differences between Christianity and other faiths seem at times overwhelming, the Council Fathers opted for giving consideration to what human beings share in common and to what promotes fellowship. They state that as members of the human race all people share the same origin and ask the same basic questions about the meaning and purpose of life. All human beings are searching for God, the divine mystery in their lives. They aim at a common goal and are guided by one divine providence. "We cannot in truthfulness call upon God who is Father of all if we refuse to act in a brotherly way toward certain men, created though they be in God's image."[63] Instead of, for instance, criticizing and ridiculing Hinduism for its pagan beliefs and accusing it of Satanic practices, the Council openly declares that Christians and Hindus share some important religious beliefs and aspirations that makes mutual conversation between them possible and fruitful. The bishops gathered at the Council recommend that, instead of talking disparagingly of people of other faiths, Catholics should not only esteem them for their good qualities but, above all, manifest genuine Christian love in their relationships with them. This approach is in sharp contrast to the apologetic approach described above. Though the Council does not deal with, much less solve, the many problems that have to be overcome in relating to people of other faiths, it does chart a very clear path, namely, that of dialogue.

In another document, the "Declaration on Human Freedom," the council stresses the need to respect individual consciences even when these affirm unorthodox religious truths.[64] In this declaration, the use of psychological and/or social pressures to convert other people is denounced as an infringement of the religious rights of individuals that include the freedom to abandon their Christian faith, even though such a decision cannot be sanctioned. It further calls upon Catholics to abandon the attitudes of suspicion, prejudice, and hostility that have often marked their relationships with those who profess different religious convictions.

Without abandoning the missionary nature of the Christian faith, the Council changes the focus of its evangelizing efforts. A more recent document issued by two pontifical bodies actually harmonizes dialogue with the church's evangelizing mission.[65] Knowledge of one's faith, a deep commitment to Christian values, and an expression of one's beliefs in daily living are judged to be more effective and convincing forms of spreading the Good News of the Gospel. The use of forceful proselytizing methods or of rational arguments meant to show the weaknesses in other faiths are not regarded as effective evangelizing methods.

In 1986 the Vatican issued a preliminary report that discussed the recent emergence of religious movements and their impact on the Christian faith.[66] One of the chief features of this report was that it adopted attitudes expressed by the bishops at the Second Vatican Council in their "Declaration on Non-Christian Religions." Although concerned that some Catholics are joining new religious groups, the writers of the 1986 report take seriously into account the "Declaration on Religious Freedom," which stressed the dignity and inviolable rights of the human person.

While admitting that dialogue with the new religions may not always be possible, the 1986 Vatican report still recommends that efforts be made to engage in genuine and meaningful communication with their members.[67] The report does not indulge in accusations against, and condemnations of, sects or cults. It does not suggest ways in which their beliefs can be refuted by arguments and their practices curtailed by legal and/or social means. Moreover, it does not advance apologetic arguments to defend the doctrinal position of the Catholic Church. Rather, it focuses on the lessons that can be learned from the successes of the new religious movements and on the continuous need for improving Christian life and behavior.

Concern with the relationship between the various Christian churches and between Christianity and other religions has been the major focus of many exchanges held under the auspices of the World Council of Churches. The relationship between mission, evangelization, and dialogue are central themes that recur in the deliberations and conversations between representatives of different religious traditions. Although a variety of views have been expressed regarding the possibility of reconciling mission with dialogue, there seems to be agreement on the principle that the pursuit of dialogue should not be identified with the Church's mission of evangelization. The Christian mission to preach the Good News, though a necessary part of Christian life, is not to be directed to lead non-Christians to abandon their religious traditions and commitment.[68] Pressures to do so, be they political, economic, psychological, or religious, are frowned upon as infringements of religious freedom.

The documents of the World Council of Churches also discuss the final goal of dialogue that, among Christians Churches, is unity. It appears to be an unstated principle, however, that such a goal is not to be achieved by forcing any Christian Church to give up its identity nor by creating one new Church to replace all denominations.

The goal of dialogue between representatives of the world religions are less pretentious and directed more to mutual understanding and cooperation in areas of agreement. Several documents warn against the dangers of compromising the authenticity of the Christian faith and of creating a kind of syncretistic religion.[69] This latter approach is mirrored in a much less detailed statement prepared jointly by the World Council of Churches and the Lutheran World Federation at a consultation, held in 1986,[70] which dealt specifically with the new religions. The statement, issued at the culmination of a long series of discussions, focuses on the need to understand the new religious movements with their distinct ideologies and missionary enterprises. It makes it clear that we must "protect the rights of the new religious movements to go about their activities, even though we may radically disagree with their beliefs and world-views."[71] Explicit suggestions are made for a response to the new religions that covers four main areas of church life—education, dialogue, ministry and renewal of the church, and ecumenical collaboration.

Pastoral Issues in Dealing with the New Religions

The aforementioned documents on sects and cults cannot be interpreted as an anti-cult statement that aims at combating the new movements by legal, social, and religious efforts. They are rather pastoral (meaning related to ministry) documents, pastoral in the sense that their writers had primarily in mind the spiritual welfare of members of the Christian Churches. The Vatican report, in conclusion, states that "The 'challenge' of the new religious movements is to stimulate our own renewal for a greater pastoral efficacy."[72] Pastoral programs, however, cannot be effectively developed unless the issues facing the Christian Church in the third millennium are first identified. Failure to do so could easily result in poor and quite useless suggestions. Thus, for example, Paul Garden, after describing the inroads made by the new movements as a serious threat, gives three strategies and solutions. The first is that pastoral training should include instructions as to how to protect congregations from cultic groups. The second is that "organizations which emphasize evangelism and discipleship should take special care to specifically inoculate new converts and young believers against cult recruitment."[73] And third, Western missionaries who are knowledgeable should be enlisted to help in other continents. Because the author failed to identify the real reasons behind the rise of new religions and the current cultural conditions that favor their success, he could only make suggestions that are practically impossible to execute. For how does one "protect" congregations from cults or "inoculate" young people to make them immune to their recruitment efforts?

Those who are involved in religious teaching and counseling must, therefore, face several pastoral issues that the new religions have made somewhat more pressing. Briefly, the first of these issues is religious pluralism. The second is the spiritual state of the person who has joined a new religion. The third deals with the ways and means that might prevent people from abandoning their traditional religion to enter a new movement. The fourth grapples with the questions of whether and how cult members can be returned to their original faith.

Religious Pluralism and the New Religions

One of the major problems that confront those who are consulted in their capacity as priests or ministers of religion is the question of religious pluralism. This question, which has theological, intellectual, and psychological dimensions, is explored in some detail in chapter 7. Here it suffices to say that religious counselors themselves must first come to terms with theological diversity before they can be of help to those Christians whose lives have been directly affected by their relatives' decision to join a new religion.

It should be emphasized that knowledge of one's faith, together with involvement in the life of the believing community, are the necessary requirements for a discriminating approach to the prevalence of religious pluralism that has been accentuated by the presence of the new religions. One positive way of dealing with the status of cult members is for individuals to be educated further in their religious traditions. Pastors need to be acquainted with the theology of religions, an area often neglected even in seminaries. Parents and relatives of cult members could enroll with profit in those adult education programs that address the issue of religious pluralism and which explore ways members of different faiths can treat and relate to one another. Catholics, in particular, could start with the various documents of Vatican II, especially those that deal with non-Christian religions and religious freedom.

Christians of other major denominations will find that the World Council of Churches has drafted many useful documents that deal with the relationship among various religions. Continuing education in one's traditional faith is one of the more effective ways in preventing young adults from joining a new religion and in giving their parents the grounding in their faith necessary to help them cope with the success the cults might have had in recruiting their children.

Religious pluralism has become a reality in much of the Western world. Any Christian response to the new religions is bound to fail if Christians are not prepared to exist in harmony with people whose religious beliefs and spiritual practices are different from theirs. Gordon Melton draws attention to the need to carefully look into the social and historical background of the new religions, to accurately survey their variety and numbers, which are often exaggerated, and to question some of the common assumptions people make about them. He concludes by stating that the

> facts suggest that we should develop some structures within the Christian community whose goal is assisting Christians to exist in peace in a religiously pluralistic culture. Thus, while our primary aim might be evangelistic, we should also be loving and understanding neighbors, able to interact with people on the multitudinous issues we face in common, and should contribute to the building of the social order in which we and our families participate.[74]

The Spiritual Status of Those Who Join New Religions

One of the most difficult theological questions that the parents of cult members raise deals with their children's spiritual state. Those who join a new religious movement appear to be making an ultimate rejection of the faith of their upbringing. To Christians, this appears to be sheer apostasy, a formal, conscious rejection of God's grace and the church. Consequently, one has every reason to be worried about the spiritual well-being of the members of the new religions.

While becoming a member of an alternative religious group involves, as a rule, the acceptance of a belief system that cannot be harmonized with the traditional Christian faith, it is interesting to note that few of the new religions demand a formal rejection of the convert's previous faith.[75] In fact, it is Christian fundamentalist groups that often require such renunciation and encourage converts to relinquish completely their past religious affiliation as a period during which they were dominated by Satan. Most of the new religions never attack the Christian faith. Some, on the contrary, insist that becoming a member of a new religion does not necessarily mean that one has to abandon one's religious heritage. Scientologists, for instance, argue that "Scientology does not conflict with other religions and other religious practices. Quite often Scientology church members rekindle a greater interest than ever in the subject of religion—including the one of their birth."[76]

It would seem, however, that the majority of those who join new religions have broken their ties with the Christian Church to which they had belonged. Yet the break may not be as absolute as it first appears. Those who join new religions are, more often than not, not fully committed to the church of their parents. Involvement in a new religion is hardly an act of apostasy in the strict meaning of the term. Conversion to a new religious perspective and lifestyle could represent a turning to genuine religion for the first time in one's life, the first conscious, free religious decision or fundamental option.[77] When one hears the personal accounts of conversions or reads scholarly descriptions of them, one is led to the conclusion that some converts might be spiritually better off than they were before. In other words, although joining a new religious movement cannot be, theologically speaking, the correct answer to whatever difficulties converts might have been facing, conversion may have spiritually benefited the convert. To many, membership in a new religion is the initial step in their spiritual journey to God, rather than an explicit rejection of a faith they never quite had.

Moreover, there are several psychological and social factors that play a part in the conversion process. Many young adults have to face cultural pressures that they never learned how to cope with, much less resist. Although there is little doubt that free will plays a role in the conversion process, the joining of a new religion is not a simple response to a direct call from heaven, no matter how willing cult members may be to ascribe their decision to divine intervention. Neither is it the result of a well-executed theological debate or philosophical assessment. Further, it is not the product of some irresistible and cunning recruitment technique. The spiritual state of the individual, the various adolescent problems that confront young people, and the timing of the evangelizing efforts all play a part in a person's decision to join a new religion.

Preventive Measures to Involvement in a New Religion

If the churches are serious about responding to the new religions, they have to begin by taking steps to prevent their members from opting out of their traditional churches in search of an alternative religious experience and sense of belonging. New religions succeed because they appear to offer what other churches do not have. They recruit both young and adult men and women because church members are dissatisfied with their current church experience and have decided to look elsewhere for their spiritual nourishment. Responding to the new religions requires some soul searching on the part of the mainline churches. This is precisely what the Vatican document on sects and cults has done. By reflecting on what might be attracting young adults to the new movements, the document draws attention to what the churches must do to counteract the appeal of the new religions.

This Vatican document outlines nine main reasons why the new religious movements have spread in contemporary Western culture: (1) the quest for belonging, (2) the search for answers, (3) the search for wholeness, (4) the search for cultural identity, (5) the need to be recognized as special, (6) the search for transcendence, (7) the need for spiritual guidance, (8) the need of vision, and (9) the need of participation and involvement. According to the document these are genuine needs and aspirations of the human spirit. There is an implicit suggestion that the Church has been rather remiss in addressing the above-mentioned needs, since the Vatican document urges the Church to strive to provide its members with the necessary opportunities for fulfilling their needs and aspirations. Although the document maintains that recruitment practices play a part in a cult's success, it admits that the new movements have something positive to offer, irrespective of whether their offer materializes or not.

Reclaiming Cult Members

Another major question asked by parents and ministers of religion is whether cult members can be talked into abandoning their new commitment and be reconciled to the faith of their upbringing. In other words, are there any methods that can be effectively used to lead a cult member to "reconvert" to Christianity? This issue is foremost in evangelical literature, though it pertains to all churches that have lost members to the new religions.

Unfortunately, the above question has no easy answer. Parents have frequently endeavored to convince their children, who had joined a new religion, to pay one final (desperate) visit to the pastor of their church or some other priest, elder, or minister of religion in order to discuss religious matters. By this time, however, members of new religions are already entrenched in their commitment, which is constantly being reinforced by their new lifestyles, religious practices, and communal activities. Those counselors and ministers of religion who have talked to cult members are aware of how difficult it is to persuade them that they have taken the wrong path and should return to their original religious traditions.

Several things must be considered when dealing with attempts to persuade cult members to return to their original churches. From a religious point of view it should be insisted that faith cannot and shouldn't be forced on anyone. Religious commitment is a free act and no amount of pressure can make an individual a genuine Christian. Deprogramming or coercive exit counseling can never be justified from a theological standpoint. The two recent religious documents discussed above have no place for it in their theological assessment. One pastoral letter issued by a Catholic bishop in Italy stated categorically that deprogramming that includes physical coercion cannot be reconciled with Catholic morality.[78] Besides there are so many legal and psychological ramifications to the practice of deprogramming that it would be much wiser if parents were categorically advised not to try it. A further observation is that deprogramming, which might be rather expensive, does not necessarily succeed in extracting the individual from the new religion and could create new problems both for the cult members and their parents. Exit counseling, though less forceful, can be extremely argumentative and it is basically an attempt to pressure the individual to abandon his or her new faith.

More positively, parents should maintain a good relationship with their children who are cult members. Christian charity and patient understanding are more likely to influence these members than are diatribes, subterfuge efforts, and insistent arguments to make them abandon their new faith. The parents' own commitment to their religious faith might be one of the factors that could lead cult members to reexamine their decision. Parents who manifest their faith by the way they live and relate to others are bound to influence their children more than the arguments of counselors, pastors, or deprogrammers.

J. Gordon Melton and Robert L. Moore provide a set of guidelines for helping families to cope with the problems that membership of their children in new religions often create. Their suggestions are based not only on good counseling principles, but also on sound theological grounds. They advise parents not to pressure their children to reconsider and abandon their new commitments. They stress that honesty, respect, and trust, not hostility, should dominate their relationships with their children. They conclude by advising parents that, in some cases, they must learn to "accept the fact that a normal healthy child of a normal healthy family may spend his or her life as a member of an alternative religion."[79] While this might appear to be a somewhat fatalistic statement, it does alert people to the fact that there are certain situations in life that cannot be altered. Many devout religious parents have learned to maintain a healthy relationship with their children who have totally abandoned their faith and have become hedonistic, materialistic, or atheistic in their outlooks. It is often just as hard to reconvert members of new religious movements to their former religious affiliation as it is to convince atheists or agnostics to return to their previous church membership.

It is part and parcel of the leadership duty of the church to help people come to terms with, and make sense of, conditions that cannot be altered or are by their very nature unchangeable. Believers learn to cope with the disappointments of life, with human suffering, and with death. Membership in a new religion could, in some cases, be compared to these similar situations which have no remedy or cure. There is, however, faith in a merciful and loving God that will enable parents of cult members not to despair of their children's new commitment. Parents must, at times, learn to accept their sons' and daughters' new status without approving of it. Conversions to new religions can, in fact, be an occasion for the parents and relatives to develop and renew their own spiritual lives.

New Religions as Signs of the Times

Current theological assessments of the new religions are in agreement on at least two major issues. The first is that the new religious movements cannot be harmonized with traditional Christianity. The second is that they present a challenge that cannot be ignored. Theologians, however, are sharply divided with regard to the practical measures that should be taken to meet the new challenge. One approach seeks confrontation, the other prefers dialogue and reconciliation. Neither of the two gives a quick remedy to counteract the success of the new religions. While the attacks of the fundamentalist approach may be emotionally satisfying, they aggravate the situation by increasing hostilities. Dialogue has the advantage of laying the grounds for a fruitful exchange between members of new religious movements and their relatives, but its rather low emotional key doesn't make it popular. The confrontational approach, especially if it endorses forceful means to suppress the new religions, may promise quick results, while the dialogue approach requires more patience and understanding. In the long run, however, dialogue has a better chance of producing positive results, since it keeps members of new religions in touch with the faith of their upbringing and maintains a healthy conversion and exchange of views.

About forty years ago the bishops gathered at Vatican II argued that, in order to fulfill the missionary task of the Church and to serve the needs of humankind, Christians must be alert to the "signs of the times."[80] In a report to the 1990 cardinals' Consistory, Cardinal Ernesto Corripio Ahumada interpreted the new religious movements as signs of the times.[81] New religious movements are indicators of genuine religious needs and aspirations at a time in history when spiritual yearnings are being downplayed or ignored. They offer an excellent opportunity for the Christian Church to better understand its mission, to adapt and react more meaningfully and relevantly to the changing needs, problems, and conditions of modern times, and to reform and renew itself in the spirit of the Gospel.

Notes

1. For a discussion on the difference between the theological and academic approaches to religion, see, for example, James C. Livingston, *Anatomy of the Sacred: An Introduction to Religion* (Upper Saddle River, NJ: Prentice-Hall, 4th ed., 2001), p. 24ff. Confer also Gary E. Kessler, *Studying Religion: An Introduction through Cases* (Boston: McGraw-Hill, 2003), pp. 18–22.

2. See Jeffrey K. Hadden, "Conceptualizing 'Anti-Cult' and 'Counter-Cult,'" available on his Web page http://religiousmovements.lib.virginia.edu/cultsect/anticounter.htm (accessed December 12, 2002). Hadden gives several examples of countercult and anti-cult organizations.

3. This is particularly true of some critics of fundamentalist churches. Ronald Enroth, for example, in his book, *Churches that Abuse* (Grand Rapids, MI: Zondervan, 1992), finds fault with some Christian churches on both theological and psychological grounds.

4. Many studies on world religions follow this approach. See, for example, Theodore M. Ludwig, *The Sacred Paths: Understanding the Religions of the World* (New York: Macmillan, 3rd ed., 2001); Lewis M. Hopfe, *Religions of the World* (New York: Macmillan, 6th ed., 1994); and Michael Molloy, *Experiencing the World's Religions: Tradition, Challenge, and Change* (Mountain View, CA: Mayfield Publishing, 2nd ed., 2002). The new or alternative religions are being included in many books on world religions.

5. For some information on these groups and the controversies surrounding them see J. Gordon Melton, *Encyclopedic Handbooks of Cults in America* (New York: Garland, 2nd ed., 1992), pp. 249–58 and 315–22, respectively. For more recent profiles on these two movements see Lisa E. Brooks, "The Local Church," (1998) and Maria J. Whitmore, "The Way International," (1998), both available at Jeffrey K. Hadden's Web page http://religiousmovements.lib.virginia.edu/nrms (accessed December 12, 2002).

6. See, for instance, the case reported in "Religious Organization/Ministries: Taking Power: Federal," *Religious Freedom Reporter* 7 (1987): 719–24. In this suit the Ninth District Court of Appeals of California upheld a previous decision that the Church of Scientology did not qualify for tax exemption for religious reasons between the years 1970 and 1972. As was pointed out in chapter 5, Scientology has since been granted such exception and hence is recognized as a religious entity.

7. See Hubbard Dianetics Foundation, *What Is Scientology?: The Comprehensive Textbook of the World's Fastest Growing Religion* (Los Angeles: Bridge Publications, 1992), especially part 9, "A Scientology Catechism," p. 541ff.

8. See, for instance, A. H. Chapman, *What TM Can and Cannot Do for You* (New York: Berkeley Publishing, 1976).

9. The complete text of the federal court's opinion has been published under the title *TM in Court* (Berkeley, CA: Spiritual Counterfeits Project, 1978). For commentaries on the court's decision, consult Peter Maabjerg, "TM Is a Religious Practice, Court Rules," *Update: A Quarterly Journal of New Religious Movements* 2, no. 1 (1978): 27–30; Robert D. Baird, "Religious or Non-Religious: TM in American Courts," *Journal of Dharma* 7 (1982): 391–407; and John E. Patton, *The Case Against TM in the Schools* (Grand Rapids, MI: Baker Book House, 1976).

10. A short description of this rite is provided by Robert S. Ellwood and Harry S. Partin, *Religious and Spiritual Groups in Modern America* (Englewood Cliffs, NJ: Prentice-Hall, 2nd ed., 1988), pp. 194–97. Though the TM initiation ceremony is both private and secret, it has been unofficially published in, for example, *Update: A Quarterly Journal of New Religious Movements* 3, nos. 3–4 (1979): 20–45. One must add that there is no way of checking whether this published version accurately represents the one officially used.

11. Kim Knott, *My Sweet Lord: The Hare Krishna Movement* (Wellingborough, UK: Aquarian Press, 1986); and Charles R. Brooks, *The Hare Krishna in India* (Princeton, NJ: Princeton University Press, 1989).

12. See George D. Chryssides, *The Advent of Sun Myung Moon: The Origins, Beliefs, and Practices of the Unification Church* (New York: St. Martin's Press, 1991), p. 19ff, where he describes the doctrines of the church.

13. Agnes Cunningham, J. Robert Nelson, William L. Hendricks, and Jorge Lara-Braud, "Critique of the Theology of the Unification Church as Set Forth in the *Divine Principle*," in *Science, Sin, and Scholarship: The Politics of Reverend Moon and the Unification Church*, ed. Irving Louis Horowitz (Cambridge, MA: MIT Press, 1978), pp. 103–8. See also the negative assessment of the British Council of Churches (Youth Unit), "The Unification Church: A Paper for Those Who Wish to Know More," unpublished paper (c. 1978).

14. See John Carmody, *Mysticism: Holiness, East and West* (New York: Oxford University Press, 1996); and Robert S. Ellwood, *Mysticism and Religion* (New York: Seven Bridges Press, 2nd ed., 1999).

15. Walter M. Abbott, ed., *The Documents of Vatican II* (London: Chapman, 1966), pp. 661–62.

16. See J. G. Shaw, *Story of the Rosary* (Milwaukee: Bruce, 1954); and Franz Michel William, *The Rosary: Its History and Meaning* (New York: Benzinger Brothers, 1952). Herbert Thurston had made, in the early twentieth century, a thorough historical study that was published in six installments in the British periodical *The Month* (1900–1910). For Thurston's own summary of his work see, "Rosary, The," in *The Catholic Encyclopedia* (New York: Encyclopedia Press/London: Caxton Publishing, 1912), vol. 13, pp. 184–87.

17. F. J. Kelly, "Rosary," *The New Dictionary of Theology*, ed. Joseph A. Komonchak, Mary Collins, and Dermot A. Lane (Wilmington, DE: Michael Glazier, 1987), pp. 908–9; W. A. Hinnebusch, "Rosary," in the *New Catholic Encyclopedia* (New York: McGraw-Hill, 1966), vol. 13, pp. 667–70; and John D. Miller, *Beads and Prayers: The Rosary in History and Devotion* (London: Burns and Oates, 2002).

18. All these encyclicals are reproduced on the Vatican Web page, http://www.vatican.va/holy_father/leo-xiii (accessed January 10, 2002).

19. *Apostolic Letter Rosarium Virginis Mariae of the Supreme Pontiff John Paul II to the Bishops, Clergy and Faithful on the Most Holy Rosary* (Washington, DC: United States Conference of Catholic Bishops, 2002).

20. See, for example, Basil Pennington, *Praying by Hand: Rediscovering the Rosary as a Way of Prayer* (San Francisco: HarperSanFranciso, 1991); Liz Kelly, *The Seeker's Guide to the Rosary* (Chicago: Loyola Press, 2001); Teresa Rhodes McGheee, *Ordinary Mysteries: Rediscovering the Rosary* (Maryknoll, NY: Orbis Books, 2001); and Anne Vail and Caryll Houselander, *Joy of the Rosary: A Way to Meditative Prayer* (Liguori, MO: Liguori Publications, 1998).

21. Donald Attwater, "Rosary," in *A Catholic Dictionary* (New York: Macmillan, 1985), p. 438.

22. Shawn Madigan, "Rosary," in *The New Dictionary of Catholic Spirituality*, ed. Michael Downey (Collegeville, MN: Liturgical Press, 1993), p. 833.

23. Arthur Jeffrey, *Islam: Muhammad and His Religion* (New York: Bobs-Merrill, 1958), p. 93.

24. Confer Swami Abhisiktananda (Henri Le Saux), "Yoga and Christian Prayer," *Clergy Review* 35 (1971): 473–77; Marie Hamelin, "Yoga—Yes or No?" *Review for Religious* 33 (1974): 817–27; Nancy Roth, *An Invitation to Yoga* (Cambridge, MA: Cowley Publications, 2001); John Kind, *Christ Mind, Zen Mind* (Toronto: Anglican Book Club, 1998); and Robert E. Kennedy, *Zen Spirit, Christian Spirit* (New York: Continuum, 1996).

25. For, example, William Johnston, "Zen—The Present Situation," *East Asia Pastoral Review* 20 (1983): 344.

26. An English translation of the letter can be found in *Origins* 19 (December 28, 1989): 344.

27. See, for example, John A. Saliba, "Learning from the New Religious Movements," *Thought* 61 (1986): 232–36.

28. For the difference between these two forms of prayer, see Harvey Egan, "Christian Apophatic and Kataphatic Mysticism," *Theological Studies* 39 (1978): 399–426.

29. See Kallitos Ware, "Hesychasm," in *The Westminster Dictionary of Spirituality*, ed. Gordon S. Wakefield (Philadelphia: Westminster Press, 1983), pp. 189–90.

30. *The Cloud of Unknowing and the Book of Privy Counseling*, translated by William Johnston (Garden City, NY: Doubleday, 1990).

31. See Basil Pennington's two books, *Centering Prayer* (Garden City, NY: Doubleday, 1980) and *Call to the Center* (Garden City, NY: Doubleday, 1990).

32. J. Gordon Melton states that at its peak in the mid-1970s, the Unification Church had some six thousand members in the United States. By 1980 the number went down to below five thousand and has remained stable. See his *Encyclopedia of American Religions* (Detroit: Gale Research, 1996), pp. 702–3. Eileen Barker in her book, *New Religious Movements: A Practical Introduction* (London: Her Majesty's Stationary Office, 1989), p. 216, thinks that the church has never had more than ten thousand full-time members in the West.

33. Melton, *Encyclopedia of American Religions*, p. 165.

34. For a balanced assessment, see Chas S. Clifton, "The Three Faces of Satan: A Close Look at the Satanism Scare," *Gnosis*, no. 12 (Summer 1989): 9–18.

35. Robert D. Hicks, *In Pursuit of Satan: The Police and the Occult* (Buffalo, NY: Prometheus Books, 1991). Confer Melton, *Encyclopedia of American Religions*, p. 165.

36. Melton, *Encyclopedia of American Religions*, pp. 798–800.

37. See James R. Lewis and J. Gordon Melton, eds., *Perspectives on the New Age* (Albany: State University of New York Press, 1992). For a study of Christian reactions to the presence of the New Age, see John A. Saliba, *Christian Responses to the New Age Movement: A Critical Assessment* (London: Geoffrey Chapman, 1999). A recent (February 3, 2003) Vatican document on the New Age movement, "Jesus Christ, The Bearer of the Water of Life: A Christian Reflection on the 'New Age,'" dwells on the incompatibility between Christian faith and the New Age. The document can be found in the Web page of the Center for Studies of New Religions, http://www.cesnur.org/2003/vat_na_en.htm (accessed January 10, 2002).

38. See Francis Schüssler, "Apologetics," in *The New Dictionary of Theology*, pp. 44–48.

39. Walter Martin, *The Kingdom of the Cults* (Minneapolis: Bethany Fellowship, 1965).

40. Walter Martin, *The New Cults* (Santa Ana, CA: Vision House, 1980), p. 196.

41. Martin, *The New Cults*, p. 101.

42. Walter Martin, *Cults Reference Bible* (Santa Ana, CA: Vision House, 1981).

43. See, for example, B. Kali Turner, ed., *Multifaith Information Manual* (Toronto, Canada: Ontario Multifaith Council on Spiritual and Religious Care, 1995), p.125.

44. Martin, *The New Cults*, p. 11.

45. Martin, *The New Cults*, p. 317.

46. Bob Larson, *Larson's New Book of Cults* (Wheaton, IL: Tyndale House, rev. ed., 1989).

47. Larson, *Larson's New Book of Cults*, p. 70.

48. Larson, *Larson's New Book of Cults*, p. 82.

49. Larson, *Larson's New Book of Cults*, p. 88.

50. Larson, *Larson's New Book of Cults*, p. 99.

51. One of the best examples of this is Constance Cumbey, *The Hidden Dangers of the Rainbow: The New Age and Our Coming Age of Barbarism* (Shreveport, LA: Huntington House, 1983).

52. Saliba, *Christian Responses to the New Age Movement*, pp. 54–56.

53. Mitch Pacwa's book on the subject, *Catholics and the New Age* (Ann Arbor: Servant Publications, 1982) is an excellent example of this totally negative approach.

54. Peter Jones, *The Gnostic Empire Strikes Back: An Old Heresy for the New Age* (Phillipsburg, NJ: P & R Publishing, 1992), p. x.

55. Confer, for instance, Kenneth Hagen, Daniel J. Harrington, Grant R. Osborne, and Joseph A. Burgess, *The Bible in the Churches: How Different Christians Interpret the Scriptures* (Mahwah, NY: Paulist Press, 1985).

56. See Phillip Johnson's lengthy four-part essay, "Apologetics, Mission & New Religious Movements: A Holistic Approach," *Sacred Tribes: Journal of Christian Missions to New Religious Movements* 1, no. 1 (2002). This is an electronic journal and can be accessed at http://www.estonenet.com/cm/tribes/issue1 (accessed January 10, 2002).

57. This is the same criticism that E. E. Evan-Pritchard, in his book *Theories of Primitive Religion* (Oxford: Clarendon Press, 1965), p. 5, made of those "armchair anthropologists" who wrote volumes on the lives and religions of nonliterate societies without ever having been present at one of their rituals or talked to their members.

58. Johnson, "Apologetics, Mission & New Religious Movements," part 1, p. 25.

59. Johnson, "Apologetics, Mission & New Religious Movements," part 2, p. 28. For a brief outline of Buddhism see, for example, Roy C. Amore and Julia Ching, "The Buddhist Tradition," in *World Religions: Eastern Traditions*, ed. Willard G. Oxtoby (Don Mills, Ontario: Oxford University Press, 2nd. ed., 2002), pp. 198–315.

60. Johnson, "Apologetics, Mission & New Religious Movements," part 2, p. 39.

61. Johnson, "Apologetics, Mission & New Religious Movements," part 4, pp. 1–88.

62. See also J. Gordon Melton, "New Religious Movements," ed. John W. Morehead and Everett Shrophire, *International Review of Frontier Missions* 15 (1998): 113–62.

63. "Declaration on the Relationship of the Church to Non-Christian Religions," in *The Documents of Vatican II*, p. 667.

64. "Declaration on the Relationship of the Church to Non-Christian Religions," in *The Documents of Vatican II*, pp. 675–76.

65. Pontifical Council for Inter-Religious Dialogue and Congregation for the Evangelization of Peoples, "Dialogue and Proclamation: Reflections and Orientations on Interreligious Dialogue and the Proclamation of the Gospel of Jesus Christ," in *Redemption and Dialogue*, ed. William R. Burrows (Marknoll, NY: Orbis, 1994), pp. 93–118.

66. The English version of this document can be found in *Origins* 16 (May 22, 1986): 1–10, and also in *New Religious Movements and the Churches*, ed. Allan R. Brockaway and J Paul Rajashekar (Geneva: WCC Publications, 1987), pp. 180–97. For an analysis of, and commentary on, the document see John A. Saliba, "Vatican Response to the New Religious Movements," *Theological Studies* 53 (1992): 3–39. For further discussions on the new religions in the wake of this document see Michael A. Fuss, ed., *Rethinking New Religious Movements* (Rome: Pontifical Gregorian University, 1998).

67. For a discussion of the difficulties involved in this dialogue, see John A. Saliba, "Dialogue with the New Religious Movements," *Journal of Ecumenical Studies* 30 (1993): 51–80.

68. The following are some of the better-known seminal documents of the World Council of Churches: "Dialogue Between Men of Other Faiths," *Study Encounter* 2 (1970): 15–32; "Christians in Dialogue with Men of Other Faiths," *International Review of Mission* 59 (1970): 382–91; "The World Council of Churches and Dialogue between People of Living Faiths and Ideologies," *Ecumenical Review* 23 (1971): 190–98. These documents can also be found in *Living Faiths and the Ecumenical Movement*, ed. S. J. Samartha (Geneva: World Council of Churches, 1971). Other documents include: "Dialogue in Community," *Ecumenical Review* 29 (1977): 354–62; and "Guidelines on Dialogue," in *Mission Trends, No. 5*, ed. Gerald A. Anderson and Thomas F. Stransky (New York: Paulist Press, 1981), pp. 133–55. For a study guide on dialogue see *My Neighbour's Faith and Mine* (Geneva: WCC Publications, 1986). The WCC biannual publication, *Current Dialogue,* contains information about the many meetings between representatives of different faiths. The World Council of Churches' Web page, http://www.wcc-coe.org, contains information about general and practical resources, consultation reports, and other sources of information. The *Journal of Ecumenical Studies* contains main articles on interreligious dialogue as well as reports of meetings between people of different faiths.

69. See, for example, "Guidelines on Dialogue," in *Mission Trends, No. 5*, pp. 146–48.

70. "Summary Statement and Recommendation," in *New Religious Movements and the Churches*, pp. 171–79.

71. "Summary Statement and Recommendation," in *New Religious Movements and the Churches*, p. 172.

72. "Sects or New Religious Movements: Pastoral Challenge," *Origins* 16 (May 22, 1986): 8

73. Paul Garden, "Confronting Cults on World Mission Fields," *Evangelical Missions Quarterly* 32 (2000): 197.

74. J. Gordon Melton, "Emerging Religious Movements in North America: Some Missiological Reflections," *Missiology: An International Review* 27 (2000): 96.

75. An exception to this is the Raëlian movement, a UFO group that originated in French-speaking Canada and is headquartered in the Montreal area. For a brief profile of this movement see Faye Whittenmore, "Raëlians" (1998), available at Jeffrey K. Hadden's Web page, http://religiousmovements.lib.virginia.edu/nrms (accessed January 4, 2003). Recently the Raëlians were in the headlines for claiming that they had cloned two individuals. See, for example, Noam Cohen, "The Raëlian Agenda," *New York Times* (January 5, 2003): WK7.

76. "A Scientology Catechism," in *What Is Scientology*, p. 545. One must admit, however, that it is difficult to see how anyone can become a member of the Church of Scientology and remain committed to the Christian faith. Scientology offers a belief system that in many areas, such as the nature of God and the place of Christ, is incompatible with Christianity. Besides, Scientology provides religious services, such as christening, marriage, and funeral rites, which make it practically impossible and meaningless for its members to participate in the same services offered by other faiths.

77. For various discussions of the nature of religious conversion, consult Walter Conn, *Christian Conversion: A Developmental Interpretation of Autonomy and Surrender* (New York: Paulist Press, 1986).

78. Giuseppe Casale, *Nuova Religiositá e Nuova Evangelizzazione* (Turin: Piemme, 1993), p. 82.

79. J. Gordon Melton and Robert L. Moore, *The Cult Experience: Responding to the New Religious Pluralism* (New York; Pilgrim Press, 1982), p. 123.

80. "Pastoral Constitution on the Church in the Modern World," *The Documents of Vatican II*, pp. 201–2.

81. Ernesto Corripio Ahumada, *Catholic International* 2 (July 1–14, 1991): 618. See also John A. Saliba, *Signs of the Times: The New Religious Movements in Theological Perspective* (Sherbrooke, Canada: Médiaspaul, 1996).

CHAPTER SEVEN
COUNSELING AND THE NEW RELIGIOUS MOVEMENTS

The foregoing psychological, sociological, legal, and theological reflections on the new religious movements provide a deeper understanding of the current religious ferment. However, by themselves, they do not automatically suggest practical ways for handling all the personal problems brought into being by their presence. Counselors and psychologists, who are called upon to help both parents and their children in their personal anguish and emotional states, face a formidable task. How do they prepare themselves to treat the psychological and mental difficulties that may precede or result from membership in a new religious movement? What does one say to those young adults who have already become members of a new religion and to their distraught parents? What advice can be given to those who are searching for a deeper meaning of life or for a religiously oriented, communal lifestyle outside the religion of their upbringing? Can, and should, any preventive measures be applied that would redirect people to seek spiritual nourishment within the traditional churches? And how should one address the religious and social issues that have reemerged in the wake of the new religions?

In chapter 6, some of these questions were examined from a theological point of view. This chapter will first consider the major problems that psychologists and psychiatrists encounter in counseling and treating those individuals who have been affected by the new religions. Then, it will look at several fundamental counseling principles and guidelines that need to be applied when dealing with parents and members of the new religions. Finally, it will propose some procedures that might prevent people from joining new religions, offer advice to members of new religions and their parents, and suggest how one might respond to the evangelizing techniques of new movements.

Major Problems in Counseling and Therapy

It is a common assumption in the counseling profession that the new religious movements are not just innocuous groups that are, at worst, social nuisances; they are rather dangerous institutions that inflict mental and psychological harm on their members.[1] Counseling, therefore, tends to be a device for attacking their activities and drawing attention to their negative features. It can easily become a strategy session about ways their members can be persuaded to give up their membership and return to a "normal" lifestyle. Such an approach is marred by a narrow, limited, and superficial perspective that actually makes counseling largely ineffective in dealing with the real issues behind the new religions. It starts with the debatable presupposition that new religions are evil entities that ensnare young adults and use them to conduct their nefarious or illegal activities. It does not seriously take into consideration that involvement in a new religion may not only be the cause of personal, psychological problems, but also an indication of deeply rooted social, religious, and family-related difficulties. And it leaves out completely the possibility that some young adults are religious seekers who join new religions willingly, even if their knowledge about them is still rudimentary. Several wider considerations are necessary if counselors and therapists are to treat effectively cult-related cases.

Another common assumption is that involvement in a new religion is a form of religious psychopathology.[2] This conforms with the psychiatric opinion that any deep religious involvement or commitment is detrimental to mental health.[3] Even those who do not agree with such a general statement admit that there might be some link between cult members and mental or psychological illness. Joni Aronoff, Steven Jay Lynn, and Peter Malinowski, for example, admit that those who join new religions do not usually suffer from psychopathology and that most members are well adjusted. Yet they state that "pathology may be masked by conformity pressures and demand characteristics associated with cultic involvement."[4]

Religious problems that need professional advice or treatment are not new to the mental-health professions. Traditional therapists and pastoral counselors disagree on the nature of religion and on its effects on human beings.[5] All maintain, however, that there is a relationship between some religious expressions and personality disorders. Scrupulosity is a classical example of an extreme form of religious behavior that is directly linked with psychopathology,[6] although it is certainly not the only one. Religious feelings and behavior are frequently associated with anxiety, obsessive-compulsive disorder, depression, guilt and suicide, psychosis and delinquency, criminality, and drug abuse.

The presence and activities of the new religions have both created and brought to the fore several difficulties that therapists must face in dealing with cult-related problems. Four principal questions can be identified: (1) How does one get information about a specific new religious movement? (2) To what extent is cult involvement a psychological and not a sociological matter? (3) Is conversion to a fringe religious group a sign of unhealthy development in one's personality? (4) How can one come to terms with the expanding religious pluralism of the past forty years?

Information about the New Religions

Counselors or therapists who are called on to assist people involved in, or affected by, one of the new religious movements may feel perplexed and inadequate to handle the case. Contemporary psychologists and psychiatrists do not usually receive any training in religious subjects, thus making them incompetent to counsel people in spiritual matters. They have little knowledge about the new movements and the various Eastern religious and philosophical systems from which many of them stem. Some therapists, such as Brian J. Zinnbauer and Kenneth I. Pargament, are fully aware of the inadequacies of counselors in this matter. They write:

> Those counselors who intend to work with religious and spiritual clients should acquire adequate training, experience, and information about different religious and spiritual traditions and beliefs. This may include gathering information from clients themselves or learning about specific religious or spiritual beliefs through study of religious texts and other material. Gaining adequate experience with specific groups of religious and spiritual clients may require extensive exposure to such groups and proper supervision from those familiar with such therapy.[7]

The counseling of both cult and ex-cult members and their parents is a heavy undertaking. How does one give advice or treatment in a situation where religious factors are prominent? Further, psychological training in the West has, until recently, been rather culture bound, with relatively fewer explorations in cross-cultural psychology and psychiatry.[8] While this is obviously changing, "it requires a different kind of research than is usual in the psychology of religion."[9]

The initial question pertinent to counseling concerns the background and training that therapists must have to provide adequate advice. Psychologists and psychiatrists need to know about the particular religious movement before they can diagnose the problem, give reliable advice, and/or administer the proper therapy. Similarly, parents of cult members expect and need accurate information about the new religions, information that can itself be part of the therapy or recommendations they receive. This information that counselors and therapists distribute to their clients is consequently an important adjunct to the therapeutic process itself.

The first source of information about the new religions is found in social-scientific literature.[10] Accurate descriptions of the major new religions and the social conditions in which they flourish are found largely in sociological literature. So also are different models of understanding them in a broader religious or cultural setting. Unfortunately, those who are called upon to advise ex-cult members and their families usually ignore this literature.[11] The 1992 report of the American Psychiatric Association states:

> Information about the beliefs, rites, and organizations of the "new religions" is difficult to obtain. These groups are isolated from the surrounding community. . . . Their recent origin prohibits accumulation of reliable history or knowledge about their aims and ways.[12]

Anyone familiar with the sociological literature on new religions, however, is fully aware of the many monographs and research papers on new religions, especially on the more controversial ones. Besides, sociology has provided a method for getting reliable information on the practices and ideologies of these movements. Moreover, studies on Eastern religions, from which many of the new movements stem, have been available for a long time. The 1992 statement of the American Psychiatric Association was inaccurate and misleading even when it was published eleven years ago. Since then information on the new religions is even more abundant, not only through many publications but also through the Internet. Counselors and therapists would be well advised to consult this literature and let it influence the proposals they make to their clients.

A second source of information comes from many anti-cult groups that have been active since the 1970s. Led mainly by parents of cult and ex-cult members and spurred by several psychologists and psychiatrists who seem to have embarked on a crusade against the new religions, anti-cult organizations have been active in disseminating information about the new religions and in publicizing their negative features. Several ex-cult members who have been forcibly deprogrammed have contributed to the anti-cult campaigns. They are the major source of the horror stories about the practices of new religions that circulate both in anti-cult conferences and in newspaper and magazine articles.[13] While information gathered from parents and former friends of members of new religions, as well as from those who have left, is necessary, there still seems to be an inherent flaw in an approach that relies largely or solely on belligerent and disgruntled apostates or distraught parents for information. One should have reservations about a counseling method that assumes that members of new religions are insincere and do not have a right to be heard, or that takes atrocity stories by ex-members as invariably factual and objective records of what happens in all new religions.

The first responsibility of counselors is to sift through the information on new religious movements and to present their clients with a balanced picture of the beliefs, ritual practices, and lifestyle of the particular group under consideration. They should be prepared to alert their clients to potentially dangerous situations without exaggerating or sensationalizing those relatively few occurrences that are a cause for concern.[14] Presenting the mistakes of a few members of one religious group as normative of all members and of all movements will not assist parents and relatives to assess the situation at hand and much less to cope with a very unpleasant situation.

The Sociological Question

It has been an implicit assumption in much anti-cult literature that those who join new religions are young adults who are going through a major crisis in their lives and are thus rendered vulnerable or susceptible to the influence of heavy propaganda.[15] Members of new religions step in at the right time and lure the unsuspecting and weak individuals from their traditional lifestyle with grandiose promises of peace, happiness, and self-fulfillment. Whether a person joins a new religion or not is thus largely a matter of an individual's weak psychological state coupled with the cunning and deceptive tactics of zealous cult members.

While one cannot rule out the individual's psychological state as a predisposition for entering a new religious movement, nor neglect the effects of good propaganda or evangelizing methods, one has to bear in mind that responding positively to the missionary efforts of new religions is a much more complex phenomenon. Many young adults suffering from adolescent problems have been accosted by members of new religions and never even considered joining them. As has already been pointed out in chapter 3 there is no simple and exact formula that specifies what type of personality makes one respond positively to the missionary endeavors of any particular group.

There are broader sociological reasons that must be taken into consideration in order to explain why new religions have come into being in a certain historical period and why some people become interested in dedicating themselves to their goals and activities. The conflicts between members of new religions and their parents cannot be viewed solely as clashes instigated by the new religions themselves. Family relationships prior to joining a new religion are important factors that cannot be disregarded in the counseling of members of new religions and their families.[16] More specifically, it has been theorized that there are cult-vulnerable families. Children who receive double messages from their parents, who have a poor father-child relationship, who are beset with sexual pressures and the demands of adulthood, and who have strong dependency needs (which are sometimes satisfied by drugs) are probably more likely candidates for membership in a marginal religious group. A consideration of the changing social and family situations in contemporary Western culture[17] would probably shed more light on the emergence and success of new religions than an articulate description of a young adult's personality profile or a vivid exposition of the techniques of evangelization employed by new religious groups.

The question raised here is whether the cult problem is more a sociological than a psychological one. If it is, then treating the individual may alleviate his or her ailments, but it will not solve the deeper issues. Again, if the roots of involvement in a new religion lie in the conditions of Western culture, then no attacks against the recruitment efforts of the cults will stem the conversions to their ranks. If the rise of new religions is part and parcel of the restructuring of religion that is taking place in Western society, then vivid attacks against cult leaders may persuade some members of these religious movements to abandon their newly found commitments. But they will not stop new religious movements from coming into being, nor young adults from joining them. Although the individual problems of clients should neither be minimized nor tacitly ignored, they certainly cannot be dealt with by virulent denunciations of the cults' ideologies and lifestyles.

The Issue of Conversion

At the center of the controversy about new religions is the claim by their members that they have gone through a religious experience that has radically changed their attitudes, beliefs, and actions. Members of new religious movements see themselves as converts, even though the theological or spiritual validity of this change of heart may be open to question. There are no universally accepted criteria to evaluate a deep experience and new awareness that has resulted in a radical change in a person's life. Determining the authenticity of a spiritual conversion is even more problematic.

The history of the psychological disciplines attests to the inability of psychologists and psychiatrists to understand and deal with religious conversions. One of the more common interpretations of these conversions is that they are simply an expression of adolescence.[18] The tendency in psychological literature has been to focus attention on sudden conversions that have been consistently judged to be signs of pathology. Great Christian saints, such as St. Paul[19] and St. Augustine,[20] have been subjected to intensive scrutiny and sometimes declared to have been disturbed individuals, if not psychopaths. To treat conversions to new religions in this fashion will not enhance the understanding of what happens when an individual abandons one's traditional lifestyle to join a marginal religious group or commune.

Most counseling centers that treat cult-related issues usually adopt the position that conversion to a new religion is usually a sudden one[21] forced on individuals by outside pressure.[22] They do not take into consideration the possibility that some measure of free will might be present. Consequently, they are unable to see the useful and beneficial aspects that might flow from religious commitment. With this frame of mind counselors cannot help parents understand the process that leads their sons and daughters to join new religions nor can they initiate or promote a dialogue between cult members and their distraught parents.

The Nature of Pluralistic Society

Contemporary religious movements and the societal reactions to them are an indication of an increase in, and a growing awareness of, religious pluralism in democratic countries.[23] The religious seeker is faced with a large variety of religious beliefs and practices unsurpassed in the history of the human race. Pluralism is the cause of several distinct, though interrelated issues, that must be addressed whenever one counsels those who have been affected by the new religions. People have psychological, sociological, and theological problems accepting or tolerating a variety of religious options, especially when such options exist within the close family circle. One of the main challenges to counselors is to suggest to parents of cult members ways of coping with religious pluralism.

Pluralism as a Psychological Problem

From a psychological point of view, religions offer different and irreconcilable worldviews and lifestyles. Families that are split by contradictory beliefs about the nature of ultimate reality and the afterlife and by diametrically opposed ethical norms understandably have to endure mental and emotional strains. The human mind aims at resolving contradictions and naturally suffers when confronted with insoluble dilemmas that are not subject to empirical verification or to a final, universally accepted, authority. Religious organizations request that their adherents make a choice or commitment[24] that is always accompanied by some personal risk. People who come in contact with many diverse belief systems for the first time, and parents who may learn what dedication to a religious ideology and full commitment to a missionary religious group entail when their children join a new religion, are bound to encounter emotional and intellectual problems.

Religious pluralism creates barriers among people. The unequivocal truths and normative ethical standards that religions promote discourage dialogue and compromise. One of the common reactions of parents whose children have joined a new religion is disbelief followed by confusion. Communication, especially if they are already strained, frequently breaks down completely. It is next to impossible for families of converts to carry on a close relationship with relatives who might have adopted non-Western-style clothing, a vegetarian diet, and out-of-the-ordinary behavioral patterns. At times, members of new religions become a source of annoyance and aggravation, rendering communication even more impossible and undesirable.

Pluralism as a Sociological Problem

Since cults and sects form new communities and/or subcultures, coming in touch with them is also taxing from a sociological point of view. One of the attractive features of the new religions has been to bring together people who want to share a lifestyle that includes a common ideology, a set of agreed-upon utopian goals, and a system of shared religious practices. Close-knit communities erect obstacles between themselves and the rest of society, which is portrayed as an evil world headed for destruction. Marginal religious groups build walls of separation between themselves and the larger society in which they thrive.

Many new religions contend that they represent the perfect solution to all human problems. Their adherents insist that membership has improved dramatically their spiritual and emotional lives. They directly or indirectly criticize or condemn the religion in which they were raised. Such attitudes are not found only among members of fringe religions and are not limited to religious topics. Many people think that their countries offer the best cultural and political alternatives and that their respective religious adherence teaches the only truth and proposes the one exemplary path to God or to the holy. Ethnocentrism,[25] the tendency to use norms and values of one's culture or subculture as a basis for judging others, is an almost universal characteristic found among people of different technological developments throughout human history. All human beings are raised in one particular culture that becomes standard and is taken for granted. All other cultures appear strange and are judged to be inferior.

Applied to religion, ethnocentrism means that a person holds that other people's belief systems are bizarre and totally false. The negative reaction of many to the belief in reincarnation and/or to the practice of vegetarianism for religious reasons is a typical example of ethnocentrism. People fail to realize that their own religious beliefs, like that of the resurrection of the dead on the last day, a belief that they never question, may appear to be far fetched to those who believe in reincarnation. They never reflect on the fact that some of their religious practices, such as that of not eating pork, which they may have practiced all their lives, probably appear bizarre to those whose religions have no dietary restrictions.

Social scientists have pointed out that ethnocentrism serves the functions of cementing group solidarity, legitimizing one's culture, and discouraging assimilation into other groups. The sense of belonging to a specific group, society, or religion implies some degree of ethnocentrism. When people react negatively to new religious ideals and practices that have been adopted by their relatives or friends, they are expressing an ethnocentric view of their own beliefs and values. In like manner, when members of the new religions proselytize in aggressive and sometimes annoying ways, they are stating that their newly acquired philosophical outlooks and codes of behavior are better than the ones they have abandoned. They too are being ethnocentric. Converts have to justify their new commitments. Criticizing their parents and attacking mainline churches are ways of doing so. Many family conflicts and debates that come to the surface when a young adult joins a new religion are excellent examples of clashes between two ethnocentric points of view.

Pluralism as a Theological Problem

The new religious movements have intensified the theological problem of religious pluralism.[26] While it is possible to come to terms with different languages and cultures by applying a relativistic perspective, the very nature of theological discourse does not allow for such an easy solution. Religion proposes unquestionable doctrines and divine injunctions that cannot be taken lightly. The apparently irrevocable decision to abandon one's faith for another can easily be seen as a negative judgment on one's parental religious tradition. This might explain why parents are generally less concerned when their children cease to practice their religion on a regular basis or abandon it altogether than when they join another religious organization. That parents are confused, upset, and frightened when their sons or daughters join new religions should not come as a surprise.

In Western societies several ways of handling religious diversity have been developed. One way is to stress religious freedom and toleration, both of which can be buttressed by appealing to religious and secular ideologies. Another approach is to divorce religion from public life, a process known as secularization. Still another way is to make religion a private matter, reducing to a bare minimum religious exchanges or interactions between people of different faiths. In many respects people still live in religious isolation. They converse on religious topics only with people of their faith, and their knowledge of other religions is severely limited or nonexistent. Religious conflict is thus reduced or avoided.

Although pluralism is not an issue peculiar to this recent period of history, the current wave of new religious movements has brought with it several new features, the most important of which is the importation of Eastern religious traditions on a relatively large scale. A convert to evangelical Christianity or to an established Christian sect is still considered to be within the Christian fold. A convert to a Buddhist or Hindu religious group appears, however, to have completely severed the ties with one's religious heritage. To the average person brought up in Western culture it is the people in the East who need Christian missionaries to save them from their pagan ways. To have Zen monks and Hindu gurus travel across Europe and North America preaching to and converting young adults to Eastern religious beliefs and practices is a reversal of commonly recognized roles. Accepting or tolerating religious pluralism is one thing; relating to, and communicating with, close relatives who have abandoned one's church to join an Eastern religion and are actively looking for converts is quite another.

Counseling and the New Religions

Many people who have come in touch with the new religions have sought psychological counseling or therapy. In psychology, counseling is used as a generic term to include several processes of interviewing, testing, guiding, and advising individuals in, for example, marital difficulties, drug abuse, vocational selection, and community work. Therapy, on the other hand, refers to the treatment of psychological disease or disorder. Although counseling and therapy are related, the latter refers more technically to the cure of mental illness. While counseling is usually done by choice, therapy can, in certain situations, be prescribed and carried out without the patient's explicit consent.

Types of People Who Might Need Counseling

The parents of members of new religions usually take the first step and approach psychologists and psychiatrists seeking help for their children. They are, however, not the only ones who need advice or treatment. Four main groups of people who have had direct or indirect contact with the new religions may need professional assistance. It is important to distinguish between these individuals because their relationships with a marginal religion differ. Since they approach the counseling sessions with different attitudes, reactions, questions, and aspirations, they may need different counseling procedures.

The first group consists of the parents of cult members who have to face a "loss" in the family and learn how to react to and, if necessary, come to terms with, the decision of their children. A second group is made up of ex-cult members. While the evidence indicates that the majority of those who leave a new religious movement do so voluntarily with little deleterious effect on their well-being, some, especially those who have been removed forcibly, have found it difficult to readjust themselves to their pre-cult worldviews and lifestyles. Those who have spent several months or years in a new religion may have discovered that intense commitment to a strict religious institution can be more demanding on their general well-being than they had originally thought. The third group includes those young adults who are actually interested in alternative lifestyles and religions but haven't yet made up their minds. They can be labeled "religious seekers." Because they ultimately have to make a momentous decision that may adversely affect not only themselves but also their relatives, many of them might benefit from professional advice during which more pressing religious issues and other problems might surface. Lastly, there are the members of new religions who are reconsidering their commitments and would benefit from outside, professional counseling that directs them to make a free, independent decision.

In practice the vast majority of people who have actually received counseling are parents and ex-cult members, most of the latter having been forced or persuaded to do so by their parents or exit counselors. Most parents, surprised by the departure of their sons or daughters, have one basic concern and goal, namely, the return of their children to their previous state. Parents feel desperately in need of emotional support and practical assistance in this new, unexpected crisis in their lives. They have no idea how to relate to their children who have abandoned their cultural and religious moorings to join a marginal religious institution. Their efforts to persuade them to abandon their new commitments have failed and instead seem to have aggravated the already tenuous family relationships. Unable to cope with the matter, they have little choice but to have recourse to a counselor or therapist.

Ex-members might also require therapy. They may have been brought to the therapist's office in a state of doubt, shock, or confusion. Since they have joined a subculture that usually rejects traditional therapy, they might exhibit antagonism toward their counselors and resist any treatment. Psychologists and psychiatrists may have difficulty initiating and maintaining rapport with them. To be of assistance to parents and cult members alike, counselors have to apply their professional attitudes, principles, and skills to cult-related cases.

General Counseling Principles and Guidelines

It should be borne in mind that one of the counselor's goals is to help those individuals who seek advice. Counselors should not adopt the parents' major objective, namely, to retrieve their child from the new religion. The person who seeks advice is a worried parent who is experiencing emotions of regret, confusion, fear, and guilt, and it is precisely these feelings that have to be treated. In like manner, when a member of a new religious movement is brought in for counseling, the main goal of the counselor is to direct the client tactfully into making a responsible and free decision, even if this ends up to be one the parents find hard to accept.

Neutrality

The counselor's attitude of neutrality is an essential factor in dealing with issues brought about by involvement in new religious movements. To start with the assumption that the religious group under question is a "destructive cult" that practices mind control limits the kind of advice that can be given to both parents and members of new religions. Arthur Reber provides a model for psychological counseling by adopting a neutral, less judgmental, and more realistic, though obviously incomplete, view of a cult that he describes as

> A loosely constructed type of religious organization with an amorphous set of beliefs and rituals. A distinguishing feature of a cult is the adherence to a particular individual who is seen as the guiding spirit behind these beliefs and rituals.[27]

Counselors should work with a comparable dispassionate view of a new religion because it facilitates counseling and therapy. It more easily elicits the cooperation of the person being counseled. It also has the advantage of allaying the fears that are associated with the word "cult."

Counselors and therapists are not the judges of the lifestyles and religions of their clients. Their objective is certainly not to try to "deconvert" or dissuade individuals from their commitments. Judgments about belief systems are never appropriate in a counseling context. Counselors who dwell on the fantastic and irrational nature of cult beliefs, who ridicule the rituals that cult members practice, and who cite select examples of weird or criminal behavior as evidence against new religions in general are not offering counseling services. They are rather expressing their own personal ideological positions and ethnocentric viewpoints or, worse still, passing condemnatory judgment on religion as a whole.

It is useful in this context to remember that all religious beliefs are beyond the kind of empirical testing one comes across in scientific investigations. Many religious doctrines, such as the beliefs in the Trinity and in many gods and goddesses, are empirically unprovable tenets that one accepts on scriptural evidence and/or faith. The same can be said about the many religious customs and rituals of the new religious movements. No counseling session should, therefore, be turned into an all-out attack on their leaders, beliefs, goals, and ritual practices. If these seem to require criticism or questioning as, in fact, sometimes they do, the counselor should skillfully steer his or her patients to reflection. Thus, for instance, members of new religions could be helped to assess their faith commitments without fear of being threatened, and ex-cult members encouraged to reach insightful and profitable appraisals of their past experiences. Ex-cult members will not be helped if the counselor joins them in dwelling on their foolish mistakes and in engaging in angry tirades against their former spiritual guides or gurus. Moreover, counselors should not participate in, much less initiate, attacks, verbal or otherwise, against fringe religions, no matter how reprehensible their behavior might appear to be.

One example will illustrate the kind of counseling being proposed. A common criticism against new religions has been directed toward their leaders who are represented, sometimes rightfully so, as psychopaths or as tyrants whose morality is questionable and intentions dubious. These accusations, more often than not, make little or no impact on convinced devotees who can interpret them as fabrications and forms of persecutions that all true prophets in the past had to endure. Cult or ex-cult members, who are faced with assaults against the religious leaders they revere or once revered, might have their self-confidences devastated by the disclosure of the alleged misconduct of their gurus or by the challenging insinuation that they have dedicated their lives to false prophets. In each case, the counseling or treatment that has centered on attacking the guru may produce more harm than good. Nothing can be gained by increasing the anxiety of the counselees, by amplifying their doubts, and by instilling guilt feelings in their already troubled consciences. Cult and ex-cult members can, however, first be asked to reflect on the spiritual principles of conduct that are inculcated in the new religions themselves. Then they can be tactfully led to reflect on how, or whether, their leaders live up to their own teachings and moral injunctions. In this way they will be able to draw their own conclusions on their respective gurus or religious guides. The outcome of such considerations should be more beneficial, less traumatic, and more lasting.

The view maintained here is that a balanced presentation of the nature of a new religion is the best way of helping both the counselees and their parents. Counseling sessions that are in essence diatribes against the new religions increase the distress, fear, and belligerency of parents. Parents who were upset, but not frightened, by their children's decision to join a new religion have attended counseling sessions or cult conferences and emerged more worried and scared than ever. The lectures they heard and the advice they received led them to believe that the only way of saving their children from serious mental and physical harm is to extricate them, by force if need be, from the new religion. Parents may end up having more problems than they had originally started with. Failed attempts to remove members of marginal religions from their new environments can alienate them even further, create new difficulties for the parents and their children, and aggravate the psychological and physical misfortunes both were endeavoring to assuage.

Understanding

One of the main tasks of counselors and therapists is to help their clients understand the situation and their own reactions to it. Parents frequently fail to realize that many factors have contributed to their sons' or daughters' behavior, factors over which they or their children had little, if any, control. While allowing and/or encouraging ex-cult members and their parents to express their frustration and anger is a legitimate therapeutic method, counselors should facilitate their clients' transition from the angry stage to a more productive one. Irate parents, ready to embark on the warpath against a new religious movement, are not ready to engage in dialogue with their sons and daughters. Once they have passed through this phase of anger they may be prepared to put aside their disagreements with their sons and daughters and begin the process of understanding the conscious and unconscious motivations that might have led to their involvement in new religions. Parents should be encouraged to examine their religious and cultural reactions in the light of the facts (not rumors) and of broader principles that might be at stake.

Understanding must be preceded by accurate information about the new religions, accurate knowledge about which should be part of the counseling process. The following suggestions are meant to help guide counseling centers in the information they disseminate.

First, sensational literature is certainly not the best material that can be placed in the hands of family members of those who have joined the new religions. Increasing the anxiety of clients has never been one of the goals of counseling and therapy.

Second, information on new religions should be drawn from reliable, professional sources. Reports on new religions written after one short visit to their training camps or centers are not accurate, complete, or penetrating. Newspaper articles that highlight the negative and "weird" elements of cults are a hindrance rather than an aid to the therapeutic process. Most anti-cult literature distributed at counseling centers is untrustworthy because it presents only one particular point of view, namely, that the new religious movements are evil and destructive institutions that must be curtailed, if not completely suppressed.

Third, the literature by ex-cult members who have embarked on an anti-cult campaign presents a one-sided picture of enraged individuals who have rejected the teachings and lifestyles of the new religions. It habitually presents an inaccurate, lopsided, and rather frightening caricature of cult life, a caricature that cannot make a positive contribution to the psychological well-being of those who seek help.

Fourth, literature that explores the social and religious causes of why people might join new religions could help parents understand the behavior of their children without blaming themselves or the new religions. It is essential that parents acquire this understanding before they respond to their children's new commitment and before they start the process of dialogue.

The need to understand parents who have religious concerns should be emphasized. Counselors who do not feel competent to handle religious issues should direct their clients to those who are trained to deal with such situations. In fact, some psychotherapists[28] have argued that mental health professionals must be cognizant about the belief system of their patients, since this may influence not only the way their patients' conceive of their problems, but also the therapy applied. Because of the variety of religions, the advice and treatment given may depend on the patient's belief system.[29] Those parents with a Christian fundamentalist background who are worried about the spiritual welfare of their children, and Orthodox Jewish parents whose main frustration centers around the fact that their children have abandoned and betrayed their tradition, may require different advice.[30] Those counselors who share similar religious worldviews with their clients, or who have knowledge of and empathetic understanding of their faith, could play a central role in the healing process.

The addition of a section on religious or spiritual problems in DSM-IV has some important ramifications. It challenges counselors and therapists to develop conceptual frameworks both to understand and to deal with these problems. Zinnbauer and Pargament have pointed out that there are four current orientations in counseling patients with religious issues. The first is "rejectionism," which starts with the denial of the supernatural and the beliefs that flow from it, such as belief in God and in an afterlife. The second is "exclusivism" (also called the "orthodox position"), which assumes that there is only one true religion and hence only one way to salvation. This approach also holds that the counselor, to be effective, must belong to the faith perspective of the client. The third is "constructivism," which does not start from any particular believer's standpoint, but "recognizes the ability of individuals to construct their own personal meanings and realities." And finally, "pluralism," which, while recognizing the existence of a spiritual reality, acknowledges that there are different paths to it and is thus able to empathize with the religious patient. Zinnbauer and Pargament propose that the constructivist and pluralist approaches are the best ways to deal with religious and spiritual problems in counseling. These approaches, with some qualifications, can be modified and applied also to members of new religious movements and their parents, even though Zinnbauer and Pargament do not do so.

Using religion and spirituality in the counseling sessions may not be easy and may require additional ethical guidelines. Both the American Psychological Association[31] and the American Counseling Association[32] include in their ethical principles the need for counselors who treat religious patients to have the training, experience, and information that includes knowledge and understanding of the clients' respective religion. This should apply also to the treatment of members of new religions. The counselor's knowledge of these religions is thus an important part of the counseling and therapeutic processes.[33] Further, the therapists may opt to use spirituality as an integral part of their treatment. P. Scott Richards and Allen E. Bergin have pointed out that those "who use a theistic, spiritual strategy are faced with a number of potentially difficult ethical questions and challenges."[34] They have, therefore, proposed some ethical guidelines and recommendations to help therapists in their work.

Generally speaking, counselors should not dictate to their clients a specific course of action, but rather assist them in assessing the situation and reaching a decision. While, in some extraordinary cases, directive counseling or therapy might be called for, the decision for any course of action must usually rest with parents or the members or ex-members of a new religion, as the case may be.

Religious Pluralism

Guidelines to help individuals understand and live with theological diversity, especially when this is close to one's home, are not easy to come by. The sense of loss, the feeling of guilt, and the fear that a loved one is on the wrong spiritual path are emotions that do not have a simple antidote. The task of counselors to help people cope with religious pluralism is rendered more arduous by the fact that they too see the new religions ethnocentrically and are, therefore, more apt to pass a negative judgment on their beliefs and activities.

The person who wishes to live and participate in a religiously pluralistic society must, first of all, start by confronting his or her own ethnocentricity. Though one is definitely not to be urged to give up one's sense of belonging to a particular religious or ethnic group, one should be reminded that too much insistence on the uniqueness and righteousness of one's religious and cultural identity may have negative consequences. Ethnocentrism may contribute to irrational prejudice, cause conflict and hostility between people, and generate contempt toward outsiders. Both parents and cult and ex-cult members should be made aware that relating to one another ethnocentrically acerbates rather than solves problems and leads to the denial of some of the deepest religious aspirations that both sides affirm. Thus, to give but a couple of specific examples, from a Christian point of view, ethnocentrism cannot be reconciled with the injunction to love one's neighbor and one's enemy. While, from a Hindu standpoint, it runs counter to the tolerance that Hinduism in its long history has exhibited toward other beliefs and worldviews.

Second, one needs to understand that the nature of spiritual and moral truth is such that no rational solution is possible to the conflicting views that different religions promote. Stressing the differences between different religions is not conducive to harmony and the resolution of conflicts. Exploring the similarities and common links between the various beliefs and ritual practices may lessen the sense of strangeness and promote intellectual and emotional bridges, thus avoiding the creation or intensification of the impregnable walls of mental confusion and emotional distance. Ultimately, one has to accept the fact that religious belief and commitment are matters of personal choice. One, consequently, has to respect a person who has made an alternative decision, even if he or she happens to be a close relative.

Third, the theological attitude that condemns all conflicting religious views must be scrutinized and carefully reconsidered. People can still view their own religion as the embodiment of truth, while at the same time developing a healthier and more positive approach to others' religions. In this context both parents and cult members should be encouraged to explore the ways in which their religious traditions have answered such a complex question. As was pointed out in chapter 6, many churches and denominations have contributed to the great strides that have been made in building a relationship of reciprocal understanding and cooperation between people of many faiths without compromising their respective theological stance.

Fourth, it is possible that a deeper understanding of Eastern religions and an appreciation of their worth could help reduce the fear and bewilderment of those who come in touch, directly or indirectly, with many of the new movements. Seeing the positive aspects of different religious traditions might also lessen the sense of alienation and abandonment parents might feel when they realize that their sons or daughters have joined an Eastern religion.

Fifth, counselors and pastors could guide their clients to reflect on their own faith commitments. A realization that faith is not something parents or educators simply pass on, respectively, to their children or students is a necessary step if one is to begin to fathom the conversion process or change that a person who joins a new religion goes through.

Empathy

Another objective in the counselor's profession is to establish a trusting, working relationship with clients. This is usually achieved by empathy, which refers to the "capacity to participate in another's feelings and expressions and to understand them."[35] The ability to empathize with one's patients is considered to be one of the qualities of a good counselor. Though there might be dangers in overidentifying oneself with one's clients or patients, some measure of empathy is a requirement if the counseling process is to make headway. Seeing one's client's point of view and relating to his or her individual intellectual and emotional states are necessary prerequisites for any successful psychological treatment.

Empathy is a must, irrespective of whether the client is an irate parent of a member of a new religion, a cult member who has been persuaded or forced to talk to a counselor, or an ex-cult member who is having difficulties readapting to the larger sociocultural background that had been previously abandoned. Counselors who attack the belief systems of members of new religions, who refuse to listen to their points of view, and who make no effort to understand the various factors that attracted them to the new religions are simply disregarding the empathetic approach. Counselors, understandably, may find it difficult to empathize with clients who have adopted different religious values and cultural lifestyles. Studies on clinical empathy with clients from different ethnic backgrounds[36] might be useful tools in the hands of those counselors who treat and advise members and ex-members of new religious movements.

Application of Other Therapeutic Treatments to the New Religions

Above all, counselors should be ready to apply and adapt their knowledge and experience to the new situation that membership in new religions has brought into being. They might, for instance, gain therapeutic insight regarding cult-related cases if they reflect on the psychological studies of the way people react to death. Elizabeth Kubler-Ross made a seminal analysis of the feelings dying patients have about their impending death. She pointed out that there are five stages they pass through at this important juncture of their lives: (1) denial and isolation; (2) anger; (3) bargaining; (4) depression; and (5) acceptance.[37] It is possible that, with modifications, these stages can also be applied to those parents whose sons and daughters have been members of a new religious movement for some time and are expected to remain so for the foreseeable future. In such cases counselors should help them overcome their strong emotions of disbelief, grief, guilt, and anger. Learning to make sense of and accepting with resignation their children's choice of another religion and lifestyle may be a necessary, even though regrettable, option.

Ex-cult members might also share in the parents' feelings about the religious movements to which they had previously given their allegiances. Resentment and antagonism dominate their moods as they embark on lecture tours denouncing the beliefs and practices of the groups to which they once belonged. They may expresses their negative feelings by involvement in the anti-cult movement. Continued feelings of guilt and animosity are, however, not signs of psychological strength and balance. The counselors' careful handling of their clients should encourage antagonistic ex-cult members to embark on more rewarding and satisfying careers than speaking at anti-cult conferences and running exit-counseling programs aimed at persuading cult members to abandon their commitments. Ex-cult members at times end up stuck in the psychologically unhealthy state of anger against the new religions.

Some counselors have adopted the deprivation theory of cult formation. Hence, they argue, people join and stay in cults because their needs are being met. Beth Robinson, Ellen M. Frye, and Loretta J. Bradley include the following with their recommendations to help counselors who are consulted by cult members and their families.

> Clients are attracted to cults because of legitimate needs, and they [the counselors] would do well to identify what those needs are (affirmation, belonging, security, lack of ambiguity, life purpose involving commitment and service, etc.). Once they have identified those needs, clients have the right to autonomously decide how to meet them. The information provided by the counselor who is knowledgeable about cults in general (and the cult in question, in particular) can be used to assess how well the cult is likely to meet the client's needs in the future. Clients may consider alternative ways to meet their needs and evaluate the relative promise of long-term satisfaction.[38]

Prevention

The question that is constantly raised when one discusses the new religions and their impact on traditional institutions, like religion and the family, is whether people can be prevented from joining cults and what kind of preventive measures can be used.

Many new religions might be deviant expressions of deep-rooted social and psychological problems or they might be simply providing religious and cultural alternatives. In either case, any quick solution to the difficulties brought about by involvement in them is hardly possible. One should, therefore, be aware that counseling may be a long process and that, by itself, it may not address, much less solve, all the difficulties that the new religions have brought in their wake. Serious psychological weaknesses and family conflicts usually have a long history and are not subject to immediate remedies and cannot be resolved by magical or miraculous formulas. Rather, they require a prolonged program of psychological advice and social reform. One must bear in mind that religious issues raised by members of new religious movements are not subject to solutions that can be put into effect at once. Although a long-range agenda might not be very appealing to those parents whose children have become members of one of the new religious movements, careful reflection points to the conclusion that stopgap measures are unsatisfactory. In cult-related issues prevention is certainly better than cure.

Deterrents to Involvement in New Religions

Surely, there are preventive measures that can be used to deter people from abandoning their religious heritage and joining a new religion. But to do so one must understand the roots of the problems that make involvement in a new religious movement an alternative proposition.

To a large degree, new religions appeal to those individuals who are not well grounded in any particular faith. Young adults who are spiritually, emotionally, and intellectually on the move form a large percentage of those who become cult members. Those who are disenchanted or disillusioned with the churches of their upbringing are also susceptible to respond positively to the evangelizing efforts of the new religions. Young school and/or college students who feel that the Christian faith has been forced upon them, adult members of Christian Churches whose participation in church life is limited to an occasional, half-reluctant presence at the Sunday service, and faithful believers whose knowledge of their own faith is inadequate might all be suffering from a severe case of spiritual malnutrition. The spiritual growth and strength of adults of all age groups must, consequently, be the constant concern of religious educators.

Cults offer religious experiences, propose different theological ideas, and demand the unflinching commitments of their members. They call people to greater involvement that is presented as an attractive engagement with practical, beneficial results. They do not tolerate halfhearted measures. Religious education programs that the mainline churches offer must compete with this idealistic approach of the new religions. They have to be so structured in content and format so as to draw a spontaneous, wholehearted response from those Christians to whom they are addressed. It is just not enough to run anti-cult programs and seminars that dwell on the evils of "destructive cultism" and propose means of resisting mind control.[39]

Educators might get a fairly good idea of where the problem lies if they took time to visit some of the centers of new religions and talk with their members and listen carefully to what they have to say. They might also profitably dedicate a few hours attending a psychic fair where they will encounter people who are searching for spiritual and religious knowledge and experience on their own initiative. A conversation with an individual who is interested in astrology might reveal that he or she has been reading and studying books on the subject for years and consulting an astrologer on a regular basis. Not only is such a person religiously committed to the worldview of astrology, but he or she also dedicates sufficient time to exploring the subject and growing in the knowledge of the field and then to applying it to practical problems. Religion, to such an individual, has ceased to be a formal, customary way of believing and behaving, accepted without question and taken for granted. It has become a living reality, something to be pursued because it is worthwhile and because it provides guidance in one's life.

A Long-Term Agenda

The success of the new religions points to the need to reevaluate the efficacy of the religious programs of many Christian Churches. These programs should start with the assumption that religious education is a continuous process that challenges the believer to seek genuine religious experiences and growth in the knowledge of one's faith. A religious education is deficient if, by the time students have finished their secondary education or graduated from college, they have no idea of what religious experience is all about and think that no further knowledge in their faith is really needed. The Vatican report on the new religions is right on target when it dedicates a section to "Formation and Ongoing Formation."[40] Compared to members of many cults and sects, the adherents of the mainline religions dedicate little of their time and energy to grow in the knowledge of, and to mature in, their faiths.

It must be emphasized that there is no swift solution to the problems raised by the new religions. The social, cultural, and religious factors that foster cult involvement must be dealt with over a relatively long period of time. The stress of prevention does not mean that little can be done to help those parents who have already suffered from their children's involvement in the new movements. The practical suggestions that follow are not applicable to all cases and hence must be adapted to the immediate needs of those who seek counseling.

Some Practical Recommendations

Advice to Parents

The parents of cult members are probably the most difficult group to counsel. The decision of their sons or daughters to join new religions, a decision they frequently learn of after it has been executed, is a great shock to them. They are afraid that the physical, mental, and/or spiritual welfare of their children is in real danger. Heightened by numerous reports on the dangers of joining new religions and by the thundering denunciations of ex-cult members and self-made deprogrammers at anti-cult conferences, this fear could reach irrational proportions. Parents are further plagued by the apprehension that they might be partly to blame for what has happened. They are deeply concerned and expect instantaneous results from counselors (or clergymen), whom they at first imbue with extraordinary powers that can immediately persuade their children to abandon their new commitments.[41]

Counselors must take into serious consideration the fact that the presence of the parents in their office is indicative of two related problems. The first is the reason why the parents have made an appointment, namely, to discuss involvement of their child in a new religious movement. The second, not always recognized by the parents, is their own emotional condition and intellectual state of mind that make the crisis situation unbearable. The perceived disaster has had a traumatic effect on their lives. Counselors cannot always deal immediately with the former issue; but they can certainly begin by tackling the latter.

When faced with a crisis situation the best help that a counselor can give her or his clients is, first of all, to calm them down and to guide them from an irrational and highly emotional state of panic to a more quiet condition that is conducive to reflection. Counselors who participate in the parents' emotional outbursts against the new religions and who join in anti-cult tirades do not contribute to the parents' understanding of their child's problems; they are much less able to assist them to cope and, if need be, live with their child's new commitments. Counselors should tactfully redirect the parents' considerations to the major problem, namely, their own psychological condition. In some cases it might be clear that the family situation is one of the main underlying causes behind their child's involvement in a new religion. Counselors are again faced with the unenviable duty of directing the parents to deal first with their own personal problems.

Second, the counselor's tranquil and unruffled manner is necessary if parents are to be led to face the situation squarely and make the right decisions. The counselor's attitude and handling of the parents must convey a message of empathy, balanced by knowledge and understanding of the phenomenon of new religions. It might take several sessions before a counselor can succeed in calming down the irate parents to a relatively serene state of mind. The time spent is well worth it. Parents become conscious participants in the counselor's second step, namely, to unearth the facts about their child's membership in the new religion and to propose various ways of dealing with the situation. The counseling session can be considered to have been successful only if the counselor has succeeded in easing the parent's concerns to such a degree that they are able to reflect intelligently on the issue.

The counselor is responsible for assisting the parents in discerning why their child decided to join the new religion in the first place. Becoming a member of a new religious movement might appear at first sight to be an irrational act, performed under duress or tension. But careful consideration could reveal that sociological and psychological pressures, over which neither the parents nor their child have complete control, play a considerable, if not overriding, role. Such insight should go a long way in relieving the guilt feelings of the parents who cannot be held accountable for all the decisions that their adult child makes.

It might be the case that when parents approach a counselor for advice, the relationship between them and their child has all but broken down. The counselor might find him- or herself playing the part of a mediator. Communication between the parents and their child who is a member of a new religion should be encouraged, even though it might call for a lot of patience on both sides.[42] The contacts that parents maintain with their child could be the major, if not the only, link cult members maintain with the outside world. Parents would be well advised to avoid being drawn into arguments about the merits of the new religion in question and to ignore their child's attempts to criticize traditional religious beliefs and activities. One of the goals of counseling should be to establish and improve communications that could bring about mutual understanding, in spite of irreconcilable disagreements, between parents and their adult children. A good relationship between parents and members of new religions will make it easier for the latter to reflect on and discuss their new religious involvement without fear of being threatened.

Arnold Markovitz has suggested some excellent advice to parents.[43] He writes that family members should be good listeners. They need to be patient, since former members may not be responding well to the parents' and counselors' initiatives. They should avoid being overprotective. He concludes:

> Create an environment that is low in tension, conflict, and overstimulation. Intense affect and tension in the family can precipitate internal stress for the former cult member. Conflict, intense group discussions, verbal interruptions, and argument can be difficult to manage. Decrease stress by reducing the emotionality and intensity of family life.[44]

Advice to Members of New Religions

It is unfortunate that many members of marginal religious groups do not realize that they too need suggestions as to how to inform their parents about their decisions to join new religions and to relate to them from their new faith perspective. Becoming a member of a new religious movement bears some resemblance to entering a traditional monastic or religious order. Family ties and relationships are radically altered and both parents and their children must make the necessary adjustments.

One of the most disturbing elements that one comes across in cult-related counseling is the fact that many young adults apparently join a new religious movement without a word to their parents who are caught by surprise when the news reaches them, sometimes indirectly. One normally talks with relatives and friends about career decisions. Such reticence could mean that there are psychological issues within the family that are hidden or that have not been resolved. Even if such problems do not exist, it is understandable that young adults may not find it easy to confide to their parents their unhappiness with traditional religion and lifestyle. Joining a new religious movement will always appear to be a rejection of the religion of one's parents. But cult members and those thinking of joining one can save themselves a lot of vexation, and their parents much useless agony and anxiety, if they spoke openly about their concerns and search for a different lifestyle. Members of new religions should be encouraged to make efforts to keep the lines of communication with their parents open, even if, at times, some risks have to be taken.

A regular concern of parents of cult members is that their children seem mentally unable to conduct a prolonged conversation unless it relates to their new beliefs and practices. This is probably at the root of the accusation that cult members behave as if they have been brainwashed. Parents could also feel that their own children are proselytizing them. Such enthusiasm from converts to a new religion is not unique, but it is certainly very annoying and definitely not conducive to harmonious family relationships. Members of new religious movements should reduce to a minimum their conversion tactics on their parents. They must realize that heavy religious propaganda between relatives and friends has one major effect, namely, to create friction or worsen the already existing tensions.

Advice to Ex-Cult Members

Given the generally accepted fact that the turnover rate of cult membership is rather high, there must be many ex-cult members who have abandoned their commitment without any regrets or ill feelings. Many of these may not need counseling at all. Membership in a new religion has been a stage in their growing up. The best elements of their experiences may have been incorporated in their lives without any deleterious mental or psychological consequences.

Some therapists[45] have drawn up lists of post-recovery issues, such as depression, a sense of purposelessness, and guilt feelings. Those ex-members who are encountering such difficulties should certainly seek treatment, even though the problems they experience are not peculiar to their previous religious involvement but are common to many people who make radical career changes.

Ex-members of new religions, particularly if they have been deprogrammed, might feel resentment, anger, and antagonism against their former affiliations. Once again, one has to advocate the approach of empathy and understanding in treating those individuals who, in retrospect, consider their past involvement to have been a waste of time and an impediment to their future plans. Both deprogramming and exit counseling programs seem to be designed to instill or heighten such feelings and to turn ex-members into anti-cult crusaders.[46] While it is both legitimate and necessary for such emotions to be expressed, the goal of counselors should be to help their clients accept the fact that cult involvement is part of their history and to direct their energies to more creative and wholesome activities. Consequently, advising ex-members of new religions, as is often done,[47] to get involved in anti-cult groups and to consider filing legal charges against their former leaders should not, as a rule, be recommended. Such advice is self-destructive and could prolong their reincorporation into mainline religion and culture. It is also difficult to see what some of the techniques for coping, which previous members are encouraged to pursue, can achieve. Madeleine Tobias, for instance, counsels ex-cult members, among other things, to: (1) "Turn the car radio on loud and scream in the car, but not while driving," and (2) "Fantasize taking revenge—it's okay to imagine it."[48] The first suggestion is rather ridiculous; the second is conducive to violence. Neither will diminish tension and anxiety or lead to peace of mind.

It should be emphasized that continued involvement in anti-cult activities and commitment to a new religion have much in common. The intense emotional level and propaganda efforts and methods are almost identical. Just as membership in a new religion could point to unresolved problems, so could prolonged participation in the anti-cult movement. Counselors should help their clients evaluate their experiences and, whenever possible, incorporate into their lives the positive aspects of their past membership. Carol Giambalvo, in spite of her totally negative approach to the new religions, states that "integral to the recovery process is developing an attitude that there are some positives to be gained from the cultic experience."[49] Lorna Goldberg, even though she tends to dwell on the destructive features of the new religions, asserts:

> Not all cult-induced behaviors are negative. Some former cultists express
> that they can be proud of having pushed themselves to the limit of their

goals. Others state that they became more outgoing and self-confident as a result of the proselytizing demanded by the group. Many learned valuable skills, which can be used in post-cult life.[50]

In cult-related counseling it must be remembered that there are a large variety of problems that come to the surface and that the above suggestions may not always be applicable. Particularly when serious family or individual problems antedate cult involvement, the counselor might wish to refer his or her clients to a trained family therapist or psychotherapist. When there is serious mental dysfunction, the services of a psychiatrist might be required.

Advice to Would-Be Cult Members

Young adults who feel attracted to an alternative religion do not normally seek advice on the matter. Though cult members might have been on a religious quest for some time before they finally decided to join a particular movement, there is little evidence that they have sought professional advice. It is a general view in the social sciences that the advent of a crisis is a precipitating factor that contributes to the final decision to join. Membership in a new religious movement, however, does not automatically resolve a crisis situation; it might avoid it or camouflage it. Consequently, those who are considering commitment in a new religious movement (or a monastic order) will profit by seeking religious and psychological advice. The high rate of defections from new religions indicates, if nothing else, that the decisions many individuals have taken to join them were in fact mistaken. The source of the reluctance to look for guidance in making a choice that affects one's entire life is not hard to locate. Parents are bound to react negatively to any hint that their children are thinking of becoming members of a new religion. Religious teachers and ministers are more apt to interpret the questioning of young adults as a temptation to abandon one's traditional upbringing or as a sign that the individual is losing one's faith. Counselors and psychologists could interpret the desire to join a new religion that endorses ascetical practices as a sign of pathology. Young adults in search of spiritual fulfillment are very much alone, unless they make contact with people who are already committed to an alternative religious system or who have also embarked on a religious pilgrimage.

Most of the cult-prevention programs focus on the evils of destructive cultism. These programs sometimes start with a lecture on the Jonestown tragedy as a paradigm of a cult. They aim at depicting membership in a marginal religious group in a negative light, hoping to instill fear in young adults. The effectiveness of this technique remains to be tested. There are several positive steps that counselors and pastors can take; steps that concentrate not on the new religions as such, but on the intellectual and spiritual states of young people themselves.

Counselors who have some knowledge of world religions can provide sound, neutral advice to young adults who have decided to go on a religious quest. They can counsel these seekers to make intelligent and less drastic alternatives without promoting a specific faith commitment. When consulted about spiritual matters, religious counselors could provide the necessary information and insight that will enable the religious seeker to reach a mature decision only after serious reflection. Counseling sessions should not be used for evangelizing or promoting the counselor's own religious convictions or for indulging in anti-cult rhetoric.

Those persons who are interested in exploring different spiritualities and are obviously seeking a richer religious fulfillment should be advised to start their journeys by looking into different religious options, including those in which they have been raised. Many people have committed themselves to an Eastern religion with little thought about the seriousness of the steps they were contemplating, with even less evaluation of the beliefs and practices of the new religion, and with practically no attempt to examine the possible outcomes of their decisions. Others have ruled out the religion in which they were raised without making a conscientious effort to find out what it has to offer. The Christian, for example, who is seeking a more intense religious commitment, does not necessarily have to enter a Zen Buddhist monastery or a Hindu ashram. The variety of Christian monastic and religious institutions can probably satisfy his or her spiritual aspirations and should, at least, be included in the deliberations.

The religious seeker must also be alerted to the demanding nature of religious commitment. Quick, sudden decisions should be discouraged. Before abandoning college, giving up a career, or donating one's savings to a new religion, the individual should wisely seek counseling assistance and advice. In this way one's personal motives can be examined and any underlying problems unearthed. Testing the genuineness of one's religious calling is a wise procedure that should be strongly recommended.

The basis for such caution is not difficult to understand. The person who makes a commitment to join a new religious movement may find it difficult and painful to change one's decision. There is a grain of truth underlying the popular accusation that new religions enslave or entrap their members and put a number of physical and/or psychological restraints on them to maintain their allegiances. The truth does not lie in the common view that the cults brainwash or hypnotize their members and physically restrain them from returning home; nor in the widespread belief that members cannot leave the cult environment without some outside intervention. The truth is rather much more complex. The person who becomes a member of a new religious movement usually changes or severs all his or her relationships with relatives and friends, adopts a different worldview and lifestyle, and becomes a member of a subculture. After a while all one's emotional, intellectual, and social ties are with the members of the group. Psychological, economic, and communal pressures come into being, making the decision to leave rather difficult. Members of Christian religious orders or monasteries have experienced similar obstacles when they abandoned their lifestyle only after years of painful deliberation and soul searching.

From the religious seeker's point of view, the demands of a new religious movement might not appear encompassing and restricting. Idealistic, enthusiastic young adults are willing to take in stride a major change in their faith commitments and lifestyles, no matter how difficult and arduous these might appear to be. This does not alter the fact, however, that such a change can be traumatic and cause upheaval in one's individual and family lives. It could be a sign of faddishness as well as an indication of serious psychological and/or social unbalance. Counselors have the task of making people aware of these problems. If they succeed in engaging their clients in self-reflection, many of the difficulties associated with joining a new religion might be assuaged, if not altogether avoided. Such a counseling procedure should bear more positive results than anti-cult tirades and/or the indiscriminate listing of the evil intentions and pathological characteristics of the leaders of the new religions.

How to Deal with Present-Day Evangelizers

The Western world has been accustomed to the idea of sending Christian missionaries to foreign lands. Hence, its experience of Eastern missionaries on its own turf, so to speak, is a disconcerting novelty. How can one respond to evangelizers who persistently knock on people's doors or who aggressively accost them on the streets?

The Mission of the New Religions

Several of the new religious movements have been criticized for their recruitment practices, the most common accusation being that their methods of drawing new members are largely deceptive. Although there are grounds for believing that in some cases this allegation is valid, the majority of those new religions that practice heavy evangelization and proselytization methods are using techniques that are hardly unknown in Western culture and that have been, and still are, used by Christian evangelical sects.

Two major world religions, Christianity and Islam, would never have become so widespread without extensive and at times forceful, missionary endeavors. More recently, nineteenth-century sects, like the Church of Jesus Christ of Latter-day Saints (Mormonism) and the Church of Christ, Scientist (Christian Science), became established through organized propaganda. Several contemporary traditional Christian groups make continuous efforts to spread their respective versions of Christianity by literature, radio talk shows, and television programs. It is not only the activities of the members of the Unification Church and of the devotees of the Hare Krishna movement that urge us to consider ways of reacting to proselytizers who can be both a public nuisance and a source of individual annoyance.

The mainline Christian Churches have not abandoned their missionary goals to convert the world. They have, however, developed a need for dialogue and for improving relationships that lead to fewer conflicts. They have also become sensitive to religious freedom and less aggressive in their evangelization methods. And they are more aware of the need to minister to their respective adherents and have tended to limit their overt conversion programs to the traditional mission lands of Asia and Africa. Like some of the new religions, mainline churches have, at times, expressed a desire and proposed a program for the bettering of social conditions.[51] Unlike some of the new religious movements, however, these proposals are not made in the context of a coming millennium or of an imminent apocalyptic end.

Persecution and the New Religions

There are several things that must be avoided when responding to evangelizers. The first is not to persecute them or even give them the slightest reason to suspect that they are being oppressed. New religious movements thrive on persecution, real or putative. It is a sociological axiom that one of the optimal conditions under which new movements grow and prosper is persecution. Public antagonism against a group actually consolidates it. It makes martyrs of those who endure insults, animosity, and attacks because of their beliefs. Paradoxically, the anti-cult movement has strengthened the new religions by providing their members with an ideal opportunity to suffer together for what they perceive to be a noble and divine cause. Moreover, it has given the new religions greater importance than they actually deserve and has furnished them with free, widespread publicity.

One should also avoid a response characterized by fear and panic. Those who react as if the new movements were just about to overrun the traditional social and religious institutions of Western culture are behaving as losers. The new religions are minor competitors in the religious field. They are attracting fewer people than the current revivals within the mainline and Evangelical Churches. Those convinced that their churches are still viable and vibrant and, therefore, quite able to satisfy their members' spiritual aspirations and needs, are not at all disconcerted or scared by the modest success stories of the new religions.

In responding to the new movements, one should also avoid making criticisms and accusations that might be applicable to the major churches themselves. One common complaint against the new religions is that their members are overworked and used as cheap laborers. The same can be said about priests and nuns in the Catholic Church and volunteers in humanitarian programs run by many Christian denominations and charitable organizations. Dedicated believers tend to work longer hours and to expect less in material rewards. Similarly, restricting the religious freedom of the new religions may have unforeseen repercussions on the religious freedom of other religious groups. This is not to deny that religious freedom can be, and sometimes is, abused. One cannot, however, grant religious freedom to all without opening up the possibility of its being misused. Blanket restrictions should not be advocated just because a small minority tends to take advantage of the situation.

Conclusion: A Counseling Response to New Religions

To those parents whose children have joined a new religion and to ex-cult members themselves many of the above proposals are rather late. Many parents feel that the only solution to their urgent problem is to remove their children from their new environment and rehabilitate them, an expensive solution achieved by the method of "deprogramming."[52] Or, as an alternative, they adopt an equally expensive method of "exit-counseling," which attempts to persuade cult members to abandon their commitment.[53] Such drastic actions, however, create pressing moral, social, legal, or religious questions and may bring with them more problems than they were originally intended to solve.

Most of the studies of disaffiliation from both new and traditional religions have been carried out by sociologists.[54] It is possible that several of those who have been forced to leave a new religion have simply joined alternative groups that are more acceptable to their parents. There are a few studies of deprogramming attempts that either failed or worsened the condition of those forced or persuaded to defect.[55] But since most members leave voluntarily, it would probably be wiser to encourage families to maintain an open dialogue with their children and to be patient.

The many cult-counseling centers that have flourished in the West have relied on the theory of brainwashing or mind control to explain the rise and success of the new religions. This theory has left an indelible mark on most of the advice given to those who have been affected by the new religious movements. Carol Giambalvo states that "the most helpful tool for recovering ex-cultists is learning what mind control is and how it was used in their specific cult."[56] Such a perspective, however, ignores the rate of defection from the new religions. Since many cult members leave without any outside intervention, the indoctrination programs cannot be very strong. Further, the mind control theory applied to counseling does not take into account two important factors—the religious aspirations of young adults and the cultural conditions in which the new religions thrive. These factors should play a key role in a theory of new religions and in educational and counseling programs aimed at benefiting both members and ex-members of the new religions and their parents.

Those who counsel people affected by the new religions must start by being realistic and admitting that the new religions are here to stay and that their attractiveness to most young adults is, more often than not, temporary. One can then sit down in meaningful exchange and dialogue, thus opening the doors for a better understanding of what is happening in Western culture and for coping with the problems Western society has been experiencing for the past thirty or forty years. Keeping the lines of communication with the new religions open will provide the necessary information for differentiating between genuine religious movements and problematic ones.[57] It will also help distinguish between the factual and the fictional stories about the new religions. Only then can appropriate counseling strategies be devised to help those individuals whose lives have been adversely affected by the impact of the new religions in the West.

Notes

1. See, for example, Rachael Andres and James R. Lane, eds., *Cult and Consequences: The Definitive Handbook* (Los Angeles: Jewish Federation Council of Greater Los Angeles, 1989); and Madeleine Landau Tobias and Janja Lalich, *Captive Hearts, Captive Minds: Freedom and Recovery from Cults and Abusive Relationships* (Alameda, CA: Hunter House, 1994).

2. For discussions on the relationship between religion and mental health, consult John F. Schumaker, ed., *Religion and Mental Health* (New York: Oxford University Press, 1992).

3. See, for example, Wendell W. Watters, "Christianity and Mental Health," *Humanist* 47, no. 6 (1987): 5. The author argues that Christian doctrine "is incompatible with the principles of mental health and contributes more to the genesis of human suffering than to its alleviation." For a reply to Watters, see Peter R. Breggin, "Mental Health versus Religion," *Humanist* 47, no. 6 (1987): 13–14.

4. Joni Aronoff, Steven Jay Lynn, and Peter Malinowski, "Are Cultic Environments Psychological Harmful?" *Clinical Psychology Review* 20 (2000): 91.

5. John Gartner, Dave B. Larson, and George D. Allen, "Religious Commitment and Mental Health: A Review of the Empirical Literature," *Journal of Psychology and Theology* 19 (1991): 6–26.

6. Bernard Spilka, Ralph W. Wood, and Richard Gorsuch, *The Psychology of Religion* (Englewood Cliffs, NJ: Prentice-Hall, 1985), pp. 293–94.

7. Brian J. Zinnbauer and Kenneth I. Parament, "Working with the Sacred: Four Approaches to Religious and Spiritual Issues in Counseling," *Journal of Counseling and Development* 78 (2000): 167.

8. Guy L. Claxton, ed., *Beyond Therapy: The Impact of Eastern Religions on Psychological Theory and Practice* (London: Wisdom Publications, 1986); see also John A. Saliba, *Psychiatry and the Cults: An Annotated Bibliography* (New York: Garland, 1985), p. 185ff.

9. Jacob A. Belzen, "The Future of Psychology of Religion," *Pastoral Psychology* 49 (2000): 3.

10. A good guide to information sources is provided by Jonathan B. Jeffrey and Patricia W. Jeffrey in their essay, "Information Search Strategies: Cults and the Family," in *Cults and the Family*, ed. Florence Kaslow and Marvin B. Sussman (New York: Haworth Press, 1982), pp. 175–85.

11. Kevin Garvey, "The Importance of Information in Preparing for Exit Counseling: A Case Study," in *Recovery from Cults: Help for Victims of Psychological and Spiritual Abuse*, ed. Michael D. Langone (New York: W. W. Norton, 1993), pp. 181–200. The author refers to various sources but omits any reference to sociological studies of new religions.

12. Committee on Psychiatry and Religion, *Leaders and Followers: A Psychiatric Perspective on Religious Cults* (Washington, DC: American Psychiatric Press, 1992), p. viii.

13. Anson D. Shupe and David G. Bromley, "Apostates and Atrocity Stories: Some Parameters in the Dynamics of Deprogramming," *The Social Impact of New Religious Movements*, ed. Bryan Wilson (New York: Rose of Sharon Press, 1981), pp. 179–215.

14. Eileen Barker, *New Religious Movements: A Practical Introduction* (London: Her Majesty's Stationary Office, 1989), p. 137.

15. Lita Linzer Schwartz, "Cults and Family Therapists," *Interaction* 2 (1979): 145–54; David A. Halperin, "Group Processes in Cult Affiliation and Recruitment," *Group* 6, no. 2 (1982): 13–24; and Michael D. Langone, *Cults: Questions and Answers* (Weston, MA: American Family Foundation, 1988), p. 5.

16. Arnold Markowitz, "The Role of Family Therapy in the Treatment of Symptoms Associated with Cult Affiliation," in *Psychodynamic Perspectives on Religion, Sect and Cult*, ed. David A. Halperin (Boston: John Wright, 1983), p. 323ff.

17. For discussions on the issues facing contemporary families, see Patrick C. McHenry, ed., *Families and Change: Coping with Stressful Events* (Thousand Oaks, CA: Sage Publications, 1994).

18. There are some exceptions to this, however. See, for example, Robert O. Fern, *The Psychology of Christian Conversion* (Westwood, NJ: Fleming H. Revell, 1959), who argues that the conversions of historical figures such as St. Paul, Martin Luther, and John Wesley cannot be interpreted as adolescent phases in their lives.

19. Felix A. Anderson, "Psychopathological Glimpses at the Behavior of Some Biblical Characters," *Psychoanalytic Review* 14 (1927): 56–70.

20. Charles Klingerman, "A Psychoanalytic Study of the Confessions of St. Augustine," *Journal of the American Psychoanalytic Association* 5 (1957): 469–84. Augustine's conversion has been the subject of many studies; see, for instance, "Symposium on Augustine's Confessions," *Journal for the Scientific Study of Religion* 25 (1986): 56–115.

21. For references to early studies on sudden conversions, see Saliba, *Psychiatry and the Cults*, p. 40ff.

22. This view, still widely accepted today, was first articulated at some length in Flo Conway and Jim Siegelman's book, *Snapping: America's Epidemic of Sudden Personality Change* (Philadelphia: J. P. Lippincott, 1978).

23. See, for example, S. J. D. Green, "Religion and the Limits of Pluralism in Contemporary Britain," *Antioch Review* 49 (1991): 571–86; and Wade Clark Roof and William McKinney, "Denominational America and the New Religious Pluralism," *Annals of the American Academy of Political and Social Science* 408 (July 1985): 24–38.

24. "Post-Cult Problems: An Exit Counselor Perspective," in *Recovery from Cults*, p. 150.

25. Compare K. J. Gergen and M. M. Gergen, "Ethnocentrism," in *Encyclopedia of Psychology*, ed. Raymond J. Corsini (New York: John Wiley and Sons, 1994), vol. 1, pp. 515–16.

26. For discussions on religious pluralism, one can consult Ted Peters, "Pluralism as a Theological Problem," *Christian Century* 100 (September 5, 1983): 843–45; John Hick, *Problems of Religious Pluralism* (Houndmills, U.K.: Macmillan, 1985); Leroy S. Rouner, ed., *Religious Pluralism* (Notre Dame, IN: University of Notre Dame Press, 1984); and Paul J. Griffiths, *Problems of Religious Diversity* (Malden, MA: Blackwell, 2001).

27. Arthur Reber, *Dictionary of Psychology* (New York: Penguin, 1985), p. 169.

28. P. Scott Richards and Allen E. Bergin, "Towards Religious and Spiritual Competency for Mental Health Professionals," in *Handbook of Psychotherapy and Religious Diversity*, ed. P. Scott Richards and Allen E. Bergin (Washington, DC: American Psychological Association, 2000), pp. 3–26.

29. See, for example, the P. Scott Richards and Allen E. Bergin, eds., *Handbook of Psychotherapy and Religious Diversity*, where psychotherapy with patients from diverse religious backgrounds is discussed. Though none of the new religions are treated, this book includes chapters that deal with psychotherapy with fundamentalist Christians, Latter-day Saints, and Seventh-Day Adventists, all of which have at times been given the label of "sects" or "cults."

30. Confer, for example, Nancy Stiehler Thurston, "Psychotherapy with Evangelical and Fundamentalist Protestants," and Aaron Rabinowitz, "Psychotherapy with Orthodox Jews," in the *Handbook of Psychotherapy and Religious Diversity*, pp. 131–53 and 237–258, respectively.

31. *Ethical Principles of Psychologists and Code of Conduct* (Washington, DC: American Psychological Association, 1992); and *Guidelines for Providers of Psychological Services to Ethnic, Linguistic, and Culturally Diverse Populations* (Washington, DC: American Psychological Association, 1993).

32. *Code of Ethics and Standards of Practice* (Alexandria, VA: American Counseling Association, 1993).

33. Confer P. Scott Richards and Allen E. Bergin, *A Spiritual Strategy for Counseling and Psychotherapy* (Washington, DC: American Psychological Association, 1997). Although the authors do not include new religious movements in their considerations, many of their suggestions are applicable to new religions.

34. Richards and Bergin, *A Spiritual Strategy for Counseling and Psychotherapy*, p. 143.

35. Stuart Sutherland, "Empathy," *The International Dictionary of Psychology* (New York: Continuum, 1989), p. 137. For a short discussion of different approaches to empathy, consult E. Stotland, "Empathy," *Encyclopedia of Psychology*, vol. 1, pp. 479–80.

36. See, for example, Erwin R. Parsons, "Ethnotherapeutic Empathy, I: Definition, Theory, Process," *Journal of Contemporary Psychotherapy* 23, no. 1 (1993): 5–18.

37. Elizabeth Kubler-Ross's book, *Death and Dying* (New York: Macmillan, 1969), is one of the basic and earliest works on the subject.

38. Beth Robinson, Ellen M. Frye, and Loretta J. Bradley, "Cult Affiliation and Disaffiliation: Implications for Counseling," *Counseling and Values* 41 (1997): 172.

39. This is precisely what the International Cult Education Program in the United States does. See its publication *Too Good to Be True: Resisting Cults and Psychological Manipulation* (New York: International Cult Education Program, 1992).

40. See par. 3.2 of the document in "Sects and New Religious Movements: Pastoral Challenge," *Origins* 16 (May 22, 1986): 7.

41. David A. Halperin, "Families of Cult Members: Consultation and Treatment," in *Cults and New Religious Movements: A Report of the American Psychiatric Association*, ed. Marc Galanter (Washington, DC: American Psychological Association, 1989), p. 117.

42. Barker, *New Religious Movements*, pp. 111–13.

43. Arnold Markovitz, "Guidelines for Families," in *Recovery from Cults*, pp. 293–94.

44. Markovitz, "Guidelines for Families," pp. 294–95.

45. Carol Giambalvo, "Post-Cult Problems: An Exit Counselor's Perspective," in *Recovery from Cults*, pp. 151–52.

46. One of the major differences between deprogramming and exit counseling is that the former requires the temporary physical restraint of those being treated, while the latter is a voluntary process. See David Clark, Carol Giambalvo, Noel Giambalvo, Kevin Yarvey, and Michael D. Langone, "Exit Counseling: A Practical Overview," in *Recovery from Cults*, p. 156. For a description of exit counseling see Steven Hassan, "Exit Counseling: Working to Undo the Shackles of Mind Control," in *Counseling Cultists and Their Families*, ed. R. E. Schecter (Weston, MA: American Family Foundation, n.d.), pp. 25–33.

47. Tobias and Lalich, *Captive Hearts, Captive Minds*, p. 136; Madeleine Landau Tobias, "Guidelines for Ex-Members," in *Recovery from Cults*, pp. 313–14.

48. Tobias, "Guidelines for Ex-Members," in *Recovery from Cults*, p. 313.

49. Giambalvo, "Post-Cult Problems," in *Recovery from Cults*, p. 150.

50. Lorna Goldberg, "Guidelines for Therapists," in *Recovery from Cults*, pp. 247–48.

51. See, for example, Pope John Paul II's encyclical letter on social concerns, "Sollecitudo Rei Socialis," *The Pope Speaks: The Church Documentary Quarterly* 33 (1988): 122–215.

52. There is evidence that deprogramming has become a much less frequent phenomenon. Confer Stephen A. Kent and Joseph A. Szimhart, "Exit Counseling and the Decline of Deprogramming," *Cultic Studies Review* 1 (2002): 241–91

53. Michael Langone predicts that "deprogramming will become increasingly uncommon and will fade into practical insignificance." Confer his essay "Helping Cult Members: Historical Background," in *Recovery from Cults*, p. 43.

54. For a study of defections from new religions, confer Stuart A. Wright's *Leaving the Cults: The Dynamics of Defection* (Washington, DC: Society for the Scientific Study of Religions, 1987). See also David G. Bromley, ed., *Falling from the Faith: Causes and Consequences of Religious Apostasy* (Newbury Park, CA: Sage, 1988). Bromley's book is partly dedicated to studies of defections from the mainline churches. For a review article see David G. Bromley, "Unraveling Religious Disaffiliation: The Meaning and Significance of Falling from the Faith in Contemporary Society," *Counseling and Values* 35 (1991): 164–85.

55. See David G. Bromley, "Deprogramming as a Mode of Exit from New Religious Movements: The Case of the Unificationist Movement," in *Falling from the Faith*, pp. 185–204. Bromley reports "that the success rates of deprogramming from the UM has approached two-thirds," p. 199.

56. Giambalvo, "Post-Cult Problems," in *Recovery from Cults*, p. 150.

57. Kay Marie Porterfield, in her book, *Blind Faith: Recognizing and Recovering from Dysfunctional Religious Group* (Minneapolis, MN: CompCare Publishers, 1993), provides some helpful hints for identifying genuine and trustworthy spiritual leaders or gurus (p. 113) and for distinguishing a healthy from an unhealthy relationship with such leaders (p. 117). See also Dick Anthony and Bruce Ecker, "The Anthony Typology: A Framework for Assessing Spiritual and Consciousness Groups," in *Spiritual Choices: The Problem of Recognizing Authentic Paths to Inner Transformation*, ed. Dick Anthony, Bruce Ecker, and Ken Wilber (New York: Paragon, 1987), p. 57ff; and LaVonne Neff, "Evaluating Cults and New Religions," in *A Guide to Cults and New Religions*, ed. Ronald Enroth and Others (Downers Grove, IL: InterVarsity Press, 1983), p. 197.

INDEX

ABOUT THE AUTHOR

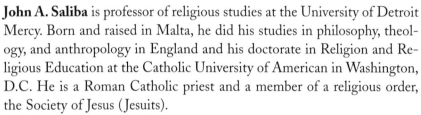

John A. Saliba is professor of religious studies at the University of Detroit Mercy. Born and raised in Malta, he did his studies in philosophy, theology, and anthropology in England and his doctorate in Religion and Religious Education at the Catholic University of American in Washington, D.C. He is a Roman Catholic priest and a member of a religious order, the Society of Jesus (Jesuits).

His main area of teaching has been comparative religion and most of his published research deals with the new religions. He has been consulted on cultic issues by several organizations and has often appeared on radio and TV to discuss the impact of new religions on modern society.

Among other works, Professor Saliba is the author of two major bibliographies on new religions, *Psychiatry and the Cults: An Annotated Bibliography* and *Sociology and the Cuts: An Annotated Bibliography*, a study on the New Age Movement, *Christian Responses to the New Age Movement*, and numerous articles and book chapters on new religions.